The Princeton Review®

LSAT®
DECODED
For PrepTests 72–76

The Staff of The Princeton Review

PrincetonReview.com

D0813558

Penguin Random House

The Princeton Review
24 Prime Parkway, Suite 201
Natick, MA 01760
E-mail: editorialsupport@review.com

Published in the United States by Penguin Random House LLC, New York, and in Canada by Random House of Canada, a division of Penguin Random House Ltd., Toronto.

Terms of Service: The Princeton Review Online Companion Tools ("Student Tools") for retail books are available for only the two most recent editions of that book. Student Tools may be activated only twice per eligible book purchased for two consecutive 12-month periods, for a total of 24 months of access. Activation of Student Tools more than twice per book is in direct violation of these Terms of Service and may result in discontinuation of access to Student Tools Services.

ISBN: 978-1-101-91975-0
eBook ISBN: 978-1-101-91976-7
ISSN: 2470-0509

LSAT and Official LSAT PrepTest are registered trademarks of the Law School Admissions Council, which is not affiliated with The Princeton Review.

The Princeton Review is not affiliated with Princeton University.

Editor: Meave Shelton
Production Editors: Liz Rutzel and Kathy G. Carter
Production Artist: Deborah A. Silvestrini

Printed in the United States of America on partially recycled paper.

10 9 8 7 6 5 4 3 2 1

Editorial
Rob Franek, Senior VP, Publisher
Casey Cornelius, VP Content Development
Mary Beth Garrick, Director of Production
Selena Coppock, Managing Editor
Meave Shelton, Senior Editor
Colleen Day, Editor
Sarah Litt, Editor
Aaron Riccio, Editor
Orion McBean, Editorial Assistant

Random House Publishing Team
Tom Russell, Publisher
Alison Stoltzfus, Publishing Manager
Melinda Ackell, Associate Managing Editor
Ellen Reed, Production Manager
Andrea Lau, Designer

Acknowledgments

Many thanks to Chad Chasteen, Karen Hoover, Bobby Hood, Spencer LeDoux, Fiona Muirhead, Shaina Walter Bowie, and Craig Patches for their invaluable work in the creation of this title.

Contents

Register Your

1 Go to **PrincetonReview.com/cracking**

2 You'll see a welcome page where you can register your book using the following ISBN: 9781101919750

3 After placing this free order, you'll either be asked to log in or to answer a few simple questions in order to set up a new Princeton Review account.

4 Finally, click on the "Student Tools" tab located at the top of the screen. It may take an hour or two for your registration to go through, but after that, you're good to go.

If you are experiencing book problems (potential content errors), please contact EditorialSupport@review.com with the full title of the book, its ISBN number (located above), and the page number of the error. Experiencing technical issues? Please e-mail TPRStudentTech@review.com with the following information:

- your full name
- e-mail address used to register the book
- full book title and ISBN
- your computer OS (Mac or PC) and Internet browser (Firefox, Safari, Chrome, etc.)
- description of technical issue

Book Online!

Once you've registered, you can...

- Access a handy spreadsheet of the LSAT scores accepted by top law schools

- See rankings of the best law schools in the country courtesy of *Best 173 Law Schools*

- Get a list of any updates to the book post-publication

The
Princeton
Review®

Chapter 1
General Information

DECODING THE LAW SCHOOL ADMISSION TEST

This book is designed to help you figure out questions on LSAT PrepTests 72–76 as part of your LSAT preparation. Each chapter tackles a different PrepTest and provides complete explanations for each question of these real Law School Admission Council (LSAC) tests. These explanations also include strategies and tips about how to eliminate certain answers.

Work through each PrepTest on your own, and then review your performance using our explanations. This will help you identify your strengths and weaknesses and better understand the logic of the LSAT. We've also categorized the various questions and labeled their corresponding explanations with tabs, to help you exploit any shortcuts or patterns you find within them.

In the following introduction, we'll look at how to identify those categories from the question stem and provide one key point about each. We'll also look at some efficient and standardized ways to approach each of the three main sections of the test: Analytical Reasoning (Games), Logical Reasoning (Arguments), and Reading Comprehension.

STRUCTURE OF THE LSAT

The LSAT is a tightly timed, multiple-choice test that almost always consists of 99 to 102 questions. By tightly timed, we mean that the test is designed so that the "average" test taker (someone scoring around the fiftieth percentile) should not be able to comfortably complete all the questions in the time allotted.

This experimental section can be Arguments, Games, or Reading Comprehension.

To be more specific, the LSAT is made up of five 35-minute multiple-choice sections and one 35-minute essay. Two of the five multiple-choice sections will be Logical Reasoning (Arguments), one will be Analytical Reasoning (Games), and one will be Reading Comprehension. The remaining section (which is usually one of the first three to be administered) will be an experimental section that will not count toward your score.

Because the essay is un-scored, this book does not include samples. However, a scan of your essay is sent to each school that you apply to, so if you're feeling uncomfortable with this section, we recommend checking out some of the successful submissions found in *Law School Essays That Made a Difference.*

As you may have already noticed, the order of these sections changes with each administered PrepTest. This is because the only consistent thing about the format of the LSAT is the 10-15 minute break given between sections 3 and 4, and that the essay will be at the end of the test. Also, bear in mind that the experimental section is not included in LSAC's official PrepTest book. If you're trying to prepare for the pacing of this test, you might consider using one or two sample tests to supplement the others. (For instance, insert the Reading Comprehension section from PrepTest 76 after the first Arguments section in PrepTest 72. Just make sure you keep track of which tests you've already taken.)

WHEN IS THE LSAT GIVEN?

The LSAT is administered four times a year—February, June, September/October, and December. Typically, students applying for regular fall admission to a law program take the test during June or September/October of the previous calendar year. You can take the test in December or February, but many schools will have filled at least a portion of their seats by the time your scores hit the admissions office.

HOW IS THE LSAT SCORED?

The LSAT is scored on a scale of 120 to 180, with the median score being approximately 152. You need to answer about 60 questions correctly (out of 99–102) to get that median score of 152, which means you need to bat about 60 percent. Very few people earn a perfect score, mainly because the test is designed so that very few people can correctly answer all the questions, let alone do so in the time allotted. Along with your LSAT score, you will receive a percentile ranking. This ranking compares your performance with that of everyone else who has taken the LSAT for the previous three years. Because a 152 is the median LSAT score, it would give you a percentile ranking of approximately 50. A score of 156 moves you up to a ranking of about 70. A 164 pulls you up to a ranking of 90. And any score over 167 puts you above 95 percent of all the LSAT takers.

As you can see, small numerical jumps (five points or so) can lead to a huge difference in percentile points. That means you're jumping over 20 percent of all test takers if, on your first practice test, you score a 150, but on the real test, you score a 155. Small gains can net big results. The following table summarizes the number of questions you can skip or miss and still reach your LSAT goal. Notice that 93 percent of those taking the test make more than 15 errors. Take this into consideration as you develop your strategy of exactly how many questions you intend to answer or skip.

Approximate Number of Errors (out of 102)	LSAT Score	Percentile Rank (approximately)
1	180	99++
5	175	99+
8	170	98+
15	165	91+
22	160	80+
32	155	66+
43	150	45+
52	145	27+
62	140	14+
69	135	5+

Because you're working with official PrepTests that have already been administered and graded, be sure to review the "Computing Your Score" pages in the *10 New Actual, Official LSAT PrepTests with Comparative Reading* book. That will give you the most precise assessment of your grade.

What Is a Good Score?

A good score on the LSAT is one that gets you into the law school you want to attend. Many people feel that they have to score at least a 160 to get into a "good" law school. That's pure myth. Remember, any ABA-approved law school has to meet very strict standards in terms of its teaching staff, library, and facilities. Most schools use the Socratic method to teach students basic law. Therefore, a student's fundamental law school experience can be very similar no matter where he or she goes to school—be it NYU or Quinnipiac Law School.

GENERAL STRATEGIES

Before we get into specifics, there are several key things you should do when taking any multiple-choice test, especially the LSAT. We recommend that you at least give all of these mantras a shot as you work to develop a test-taking method that works for you—they are the sum of more than 20 years' worth of our experience in researching and preparing hundreds of thousands of test takers to take the LSAT.

Technique #1: Don't Rush

As we showed on the scoring table, you can get into the 98th percentile even with several wrong answers in each section. Most test takers do their best when they don't try to answer every question.

Most test takers believe that the key to success on the LSAT is to go faster. Realize, though, that your accuracy is also a key factor in how well you perform. Generally speaking, the faster you work, the higher the chance of making an error. What this means is that there's a pacing "sweet spot" somewhere between working as fast as you can and working as carefully as you can. That's where official PrepTests come in handy, as they'll help you to find the proper balance for yourself in each of the three sections.

Your mantra: *I will fight the urge to rush and will work more deliberately, making choices about where to concentrate so I can answer questions more accurately and end up with a higher score.*

Technique #2: Fill in Every Bubble

Unlike some tests, the LSAT has no penalty for guessing, meaning that no points are subtracted for wrong answers. Therefore, even if you don't get to work on every question in a section, make sure to fill in the rest of the bubbles before time is called. Even if you do only 75 percent of the test, you'll get an average of five more questions correct by picking a "letter of the day" and bubbling it in on the remaining 25 questions.

Don't wait to start implementing this strategy; you should work through the PrepTests as you plan to work through the actual test. By the time you've gone through a couple of tests, this should be a habit that you employ without even thinking about it. If you're concerned that this won't show your "real" score, remember that your "real" score will come from a bubble sheet that you've (hopefully) completely filled out, so don't hold back. Use this book of explanations to ensure that you know how to solve the questions you might have guessed correctly.

Your mantra: *I will always remember to bubble in answers for any questions I don't get to, giving me better odds of getting a higher score.*

Technique #3: Use Process of Elimination

One solace (perhaps) on multiple-choice tests is the fact that all of the correct answers will be in front of you. Naturally, each will be camouflaged by four incorrect answers, some of which will look just as good as, and often better than, the credited response. But the fact remains that if you can clear away some of that distraction, the right choice is right in front of you. Don't expect that the correct answers will just leap off the page at you. They won't. In fact, choices that immediately catch your eye are often just tricky distractors.

Process of Elimination (POE) may be a very different test-taking strategy from what you are used to. If you look first at the answer choices critically, with an eye toward trying to see what's wrong with them, you'll do better on almost any standardized test than by always trying to find the right answer. This is because, given enough time and creativity, you can justify the correctness of any answer choice that you find appealing. That skill may be useful in certain situations, but on the LSAT, creativity of that sort is dangerous.

Your mantra: *I will always try to eliminate answer choices using Process of Elimination, thereby increasing my chances to get each question right and, therefore, a higher score.*

ANALYTICAL REASONING

In this section, we'll look at the broad structure of the Analytical Reasoning, or Games, section and lay out key strategies for each question type.

Games: A Step-by-Step Approach

Analytical Reasoning is deeply rooted in logic, even if no formal training in that subject is required. To that end, we've devised a series of steps to help methodically work through even the trickiest of games.

Step 1: Diagram and inventory

Your first step will be to determine the appropriate diagram for the game by evaluating both the setup and the clues. You will be given enough information to understand the basic structure of the game. Your diagram is described by the setup and will become the fixed game board onto which you will place the elements—your game pieces. You should make an inventory of the elements next to the diagram, so that you'll have everything in one place and will be able to keep track of it easily. Don't rush through this step, because this is the heart of your process. People often want to start scribbling a diagram as soon as something pops out at them from the setup. Take the time to evaluate the setup thoroughly, and you'll be well equipped for the rest of the process.

Step 2: Symbolize the clues and double-check

After you've drawn your diagram, transform the clues into visual symbols. Your symbols should be consistent with the diagram and with each other. The goal is to change the clues into visual references that will fit into your diagram. Here are the three Cs of symbolization: Keep your symbols clear, consistent, and concise. Never forget that correctly symbolizing every clue is the key to improving accuracy and efficiency.

The most valuable 30 seconds you can spend on any game is double-checking your symbols to make sure that they perfectly match all the information in the clue. Do not merely reread each clue and glance at your symbol again. If you misread the clue once, you might do it again. Instead, work against the grain when you double-check. Number each of your symbols. Then articulate in your own words what each symbol means and carry that back up to the clues you were given. When you find a match, check off that clue. Finally, be sure to go back over the information presented in the setup as well, because some games may include restrictions or extra rules that should be treated like clues. Once you're sure everything is all accounted for, you're ready to move on.

Step 3: Make deductions and size up the game

Now that you're sure you have everything properly symbolized, it's time to make any deductions that you can from the information that was given by the clues.

Look for overlap between the clues and the diagram and among the clues that share the same elements. See if there is anything else that you know for sure. Making deductions is not merely suspecting that something may be true; a deduction is something that you know for a fact. It is something that must always be true or must always be false. Add your deductions to the information you already have.

You'll notice that many deductions give you concrete limitations about where elements are restricted—where they can't go—rather than where they must go. Consider each clue individually to see what it says about the placement of an element. Then look for overlap between different clues.

Step 4: Assess the questions

Not all games questions are on the same level of difficulty. As a result, you should move through the questions from easiest to most challenging.

First, look for what we call Grab-a-Rule questions. Grab-a-Rule questions do not appear on every game, but they are common. They have historically been the first question of a game. These are questions that give you full arrangements of the elements in every answer and ask you which one doesn't break any rules. Remember, if the question does not deal with every element and every space on your diagram, it is not a true Grab-a-Rule.

Next, look for Specific questions. These questions will further limit the initial conditions of the game and provide you with more information. They will usually start with the word "if." Specific questions tend to be fairly quick since the question itself constrains some of the vagueness of the game. Once you've done all the Specific questions, you'll have a diagram with several valid permutations—or "plays"—of the game.

The third style of question you should work is the General questions. These questions are typically open-ended and ask what could happen without placing specific restrictions. These questions usually begin with the word "which." By saving these for later, you can often use your prior work from the Specific questions to eliminate bad answer choices.

The final question type that you may see is Complex questions. Complex questions can change the original game by adding, changing, or deleting a rule. They can also ask which answer choice could be substituted for a rule without changing the game. No matter what form they take, Complex questions should be saved for last since they function differently from the rest of the questions. These questions can also be very time-consuming for little gain. Never forget that the Complex question is worth the same number of points as the Grab-a-Rule. It is always worth considering how much you need to get that one question correct. For most test takers, the best strategy on these questions is to bubble in your letter of the day and move on to the next game. Remember that you can always come back and work a Complex question if you have time.

There is one last thing to know about the questions. No matter what the question type, the question stem will affect how the credited response is reached. The

You may note that we sometimes refer to questions out of chronological order. This is because we've found that there are efficient ways to use the information from one question to rule out choices in another. You'll definitely want to use our explanations to practice this and refine your notes and diagrams so that the specific premises of a Complex question are not accidentally used in another, independent problem.

four question stems are must be true, could be true, could be false, and must be false. The LSAT has a wide variety of phrasing, but every question will ultimately use one of these four stems. Make a habit now of underlining each question stem. This will help you to determine the best approach to the question and the type of answer you'll need.

Step 5: Act

Each question task requires its own strategy. Using the proper strategy leads to saving time on a given question without sacrificing accuracy. Plus, by approaching the questions in an efficient order, you'll find that the work you've done on earlier questions will often help you to find the right answer on a later question.

Step 6: Answer using Process of Elimination

Different question stems require POE to different degrees. Sometimes you'll be able to go straight to the right answer from your deductions, but often you'll need to work questions by finding the four wrong answers. As a last resort, you may need to test answer choices one at a time to find the right one.

The Structure of a Games Section

You will be given four "logic games" in a 35-minute section. Each game will have a setup and a set of conditions or clues that are attached to it. Then five to seven questions will ask you about various possible arrangements of the elements in the game. The four games are not arranged in order of difficulty.

The Four Types of Games Questions

A large part of the six-step method involves being able to quickly identify the four different question types so that they can be worked through in the most efficient way possible. As you compare your test results to our explanations, feel free to use the identifying tabs beside each question to check your process. Additionally, here's a core takeaway for each of the four question types you'll find in the Games section.

Grab-a-Rule
- Compare each of the given rules to the answer choices, looking to eliminate the choices that violate the rules.

Specific
- Work the given information into your notes/diagram and only then compare the answer choices.

General
- Use some of the valid solutions that you have already created for other question types to help narrow down choices.

Complex
- Because these questions mix up the rules, be careful to properly modify the assumptions made in your diagrams, or better still, start them from scratch (if you have the time).

THE LOGICAL REASONING SECTION

Here, we'll break down the process for working through the Logical Reasoning, or Arguments, section and present key strategies for each question type.

Working Arguments: A Step-by-Step Process

In the context of the LSAT, Logical Reasoning revolves around careful analysis, without using outside knowledge that may complicate things. For that reason, it helps to have a specific, formal process for working through even the most complex arguments.

Step 1: Assess the question

Reading the question first will tip you off about what you need to look for in the argument. Don't waste time reading the argument before you know how you will need to evaluate it for that particular question. If you don't know what your task is, you are unlikely to perform it effectively.

Step 2: Analyze the argument

You've got to read the argument critically, looking for the author's conclusion and the evidence used to support it. When the author's conclusion is explicitly stated, mark it with a symbol that you use only for conclusions. If necessary, jot down short, simple paraphrases of the premises and any flaws you found in the argument.

To find flaws, you should keep your eyes open for any shifts in the author's language or gaps in the argument. Look for common purpose and reasoning patterns. The author's conclusion is reached using only the information on the page in front of you, so any gaps in the language or in the evidence indicate problems with the argument. You should always be sure that you're reading critically and articulating the parts of the argument (both stated and unstated) in your own words.

Our explanations clearly identify each question task (Step 1) as well as the conclusion, premise, and common flaws (Step 2). If you're attempting to get a routine down, we suggest comparing your train of thought against ours, even on questions that you got right.

Step 3: Act

Each question task will have different criteria for what constitutes an acceptable answer. Think about that before going to the choices.

The test writers rely on the fact that the people who are taking the LSAT feel pressured to get through all the questions quickly. Many answer choices will seem appealing if you don't have a clear idea of what you're looking for before you start reading through them. The best way to keep yourself from falling into this trap is to predict what the right answer will say or do before you even look at the choices, and write that prediction down on your test!

Step 4: Answer using Process of Elimination (POE)

Most people look for the best answer and, in the process, end up falling for answer choices that are designed to look appealing but actually contain artfully concealed flaws. The part that looks good looks really good, and the little bit that's wrong blends right into the background if you're not reading carefully and critically. The "best" answer on a tricky question won't necessarily sound very good at all. That's why the question is difficult. But if you're keenly attuned to crossing out those choices with identifiable flaws, you'll be left with one that wasn't appealing, but didn't have anything wrong with it. And that's the winner because it's the "best" one of a group of flawed answers. If you can find a reason to cross off a choice, you've just improved your chances of getting the question right. So be aggressive about finding the flaws in answer choices that will allow you to eliminate them. At the same time, don't eliminate choices that you don't understand or that don't have a distinct problem.

The Structure of an Arguments Section

There will be two scored Arguments sections, each lasting 35 minutes, on your LSAT. Each section has between 24 and 26 questions. Tests in the past frequently attached two questions to one argument, but LSAC has more or less phased out this style of question; you will almost certainly see one question per argument. Typically, the argument passages are no more than three or four sentences in length, but they can still be very dense and every word is potentially important, making critical reading the key skill on this section. The arguments are not arranged in strict order of difficulty, although the questions near the beginning of a section are generally easier than those at the end.

The Fourteen Types of Arguments Questions

Our explanations have been tagged with different identifiers for each question type, so as to help you more readily associate the strategies you're practicing with the various questions you'll encounter. Here's a breakdown of the main takeaways for each of the fourteen question types you'll find in the Arguments section.

Main Point

Key Words in Question Stem: "main point," "main conclusion," "argument is structured to lead to which conclusion."

Strategy: Keywords and opinion language can often lead you to the main point. You can confirm you found the main point by asking why the author believes a certain statement is true. The other sentences in an argument are all premises that answer that question. We sometimes refer to this as the Why Test.

Reasoning

Key Words in Question Stem: "X responds to Y by," "claim that…plays what role," "technique/method/strategy of argumentation/reasoning."

Strategy: Try to describe the overall structure and logic to these arguments before matching an answer choice to the argument.

Necessary Assumption

Key Words in Question Stem: "assumption on which the argument depends/relies," "assumption required."

Strategy: Help these arguments by providing an important assumption. Confirm the credited response to these questions by negating the answer choices. A negated necessary assumption will make the conclusion invalid. We sometimes refer to this as the Negation Test.

Sufficient Assumption

Key Words in Question Stem: "if assumed, allows the conclusion to follow logically," "allows the conclusion to be properly drawn."

Strategy: Help these arguments by finding a credited response that will prove the conclusion is true.

Strengthen

Key Words in Question Stem: "most supports/justifies the argument above," "most strengthens."

Strategy: The best way to strengthen an argument is to fill in any gaps in logic. Identify the argument's weakness and find the answer choice that fixes it the best.

Principle-Strengthen

Key Words in Question Stem: "principle that, if valid, justifies the argument."

Strategy: Help these arguments by providing a guiding principle, or rule, that will prove the conclusion is true based on the set of facts in the argument.

Weaken

Key Words in Question Stem: "most undermines," "calls into question," "casts doubt on."

Strategy: The best way to weaken an argument is to attack it where it is weakest. Find the argument's weakness and then find the answer choice that exploits that logical mistake.

Flaw

Key Words in Question Stem: "flaw/error in reasoning," "vulnerable to criticism."

Strategy: Describe the logical error made in each of these arguments before looking at the answer choices.

Inference

Key Words in Question Stem: "statements above, if true, support," "must/could be true/false."

Strategy: The credited answer to these questions must be strongly supported by the facts in the passage. Avoid making any assumptions as you find the answer choice that is true.

Point at Issue

Key Words in Question Stem: "committed to disagreeing about."

Strategy: Compare each answer choice to each person's argument individually. The credited response will be one in which the two people take an opposing stance.

Resolve/Explain

Key Words in Question Stem: "puzzling statement," "apparent contradiction," "paradox," "resolution," "explanation."

Strategy: Identify the two sides of the issue before looking at the answer choices. The credited response will be a new piece of information that allows both statements to be true.

Parallel

Key Words in Question Stem: "most analogous," "similar pattern of reasoning."

Strategy: Diagram the main argument and each answer choice, and then choose the answer with the most similar diagram.

Principle-Match

Key Words in Question Stem: "conforms/illustrates…principle/proposition."

Strategy: Match these arguments by applying the principle rule to the argument. The best answer will work with the rule to come to the same conclusion.

Evaluate

Key Words in Question Stem: "helps to evaluate" or "most useful in evaluating."

Strategy: Treat these like any other help or hurt question by identifying the conclusion, premises, and assumptions. The credited response will ask a question for which the answer will confirm or deny the assumption.

READING COMPREHENSION

The rest of this chapter will clarify the components of the Reading Comprehension section and provide key strategies for each question type.

Reading Comprehension: A Step-by-Step Process

Whenever you're reading dense, complicated material, it helps to be methodical and to know what you're looking for. The following method helps to break things down.

Step 1: Prepare the Passage

A.   Preview the questions, looking for lead words and/or line references that tell you what parts of the passage will be especially relevant.

B.   Work the passage efficiently, focusing on the main claims made by the author.

C.   Annotate the passage, circling key words that relate to the question topics or that provide clues to the structure and tone of the author's argument, and making brief marginal notes.

D.   Define the Bottom Line of the passage as a whole: the main point, purpose, and tone of the text.

Step 2: Assess the Question

Translate exactly what each question is asking you to do with or to the passage.

Step 3: Act

Just as some Games questions require you to make new deductions before you attack the answers, or some Arguments questions are best answered by first identifying or analyzing certain aspects of the paragraph, most Reading Comprehension questions are most accurately and efficiently attacked by doing some work with the passage text before looking at a single answer choice.

Step 4: Answer

Use a combination of your understanding of the question and of the relevant part or parts of the passage to use Process of Elimination on the answer choices. Look for what is wrong with each choice, keeping in mind that one small part of the choice that doesn't match the passage and/or the question task means the choice is bad.

The Structure of a Reading Comprehension Section

In this 35-minute section, you will be given four Reading Comprehension passages of about 60 to 80 lines each. Three of the passages will be written by one author; the fourth will be a combination of two shorter passages from two different sources discussing the same general subject. In each case, between five and eight questions will be attached to each passage. This is probably something you're familiar with from the SAT, the ACT, or any of the other myriad standardized tests you might have taken over the years. These passages are not arranged in any order of difficulty.

The Five Types of Reading Comprehension Questions

Being able to quickly pinpoint strategies for each type of question should help you to more efficiently work through the Reading Comprehension section. These are the main identifiers and strategies to recognize and know:

Big Picture

- Develop your own version of the Bottom Line of a passage by putting the overall point, tone, and purpose of the passage in your own words, and then look for the answer choice that comes closest to it.

Extract-Fact

- The credited response will match something directly stated by the author in the passage, so look to the exact language of the text.

Extract-Infer
- The best answer will always be supported by the text; avoid using outside information or making assumptions.

Structure
- These questions ask about the organization of the passage or paragraph, which means you should compare each choice to the relevant section of the text.

Reasoning
- Identify the argument being made in the passage, and describe it in your own words before looking at the answer choices.

SUMMARY

For all these tips, strategies, and explanations of what to expect on the LSAT, at the end of the day, it all comes down to you and the test. The practice found in those official LSAT PrepTests should help to iron out timing issues and point out any immediate problem spots that need additional focus, and the explanations in this book should help to solidify your test-taking process and raise both your comfort level and familiarity with the test's tricks. But if a mantra or a specific technique isn't working for you, don't feel beholden to it. With five tests to work through, you have the space to try different things and the time to turn a successful strategy into a muscle memory. Once you know the test and understand the explanations, it's just a matter of doing what you've done here on one more official test. You've got this!

Chapter 2
PrepTest 72:
Answers and
Explanations

ANSWER KEY: PREPTEST 72

Section 1:
Reading
Comprehension

1. D
2. E
3. C
4. A
5. B
6. D
7. B
8. B
9. C
10. A
11. C
12. D
13. B
14. B
15. D
16. C
17. D
18. D
19. A
20. C
21. A
22. C
23. E
24. D
25. D
26. B
27. B

Section 2:
Arguments 1

1. D
2. C
3. B
4. A
5. E
6. C
7. E
8. D
9. D
10. C
11. C
12. E
13. C
14. C
15. D
16. D
17. B
18. E
19. C
20. B
21. B
22. C
23. A
24. A
25. B
26. D

Section 3:
Arguments 2

1. C
2. B
3. D
4. E
5. C
6. C
7. A
8. A
9. E
10. D
11. A
12. C
13. C
14. B
15. B
16. D
17. D
18. C
19. D
20. B
21. E
22. E
23. C
24. A
25. D

Section 4:
Games

1. B
2. E
3. B
4. D
5. A
6. E
7. E
8. C
9. D
10. A
11. E
12. B
13. B
14. A
15. E
16. A
17. C
18. C
19. A
20. E
21. C
22. E
23. E

EXPLANATIONS

Section 1: Reading Comprehension

Questions 1–6

The main point of the first paragraph is that the success in fighting wildfires in North America may actually be worse for forests, because many of them depend on periodic fires for long-term stability. The second paragraph goes on to argue that land management policies should recognize the essential role of fires in maintaining stability. The third paragraph concludes that the best method for controlling wildfires is the use of selective harvesting and prescribed fires to control the supply of fuel. The Bottom Line of the passage is that land managers should shift to a new system of wildfire management focused on using prescribed fires to control fuel supply in order to protect forests over the long term. The overall tone of the passage is persuasive: The passage criticizes the current system of wildfire management and advocates for a change to a new system.

1. **D**   Big Picture

   Use the Bottom Line to choose an answer. Watch out for answers that are too narrow (a purpose that's not primary) and answers that don't match the Bottom Line of the passage.

   A.   No. This answer does not match the overall tone of the passage. The passage does not discuss ideological dogma impeding the adoption of a new system, but rather suggests that new information is leading foresters and ecologists to consider this new system necessary.

   B.   No. This answer does not match the purpose of the passage. The passage does not merely compare the effects of two policies; it advocates for a change to a new policy.

   C.   No. This answer does not match the passage. The passage does not discuss funding or any need for a substantial increase in funding.

   D.   Yes. The first and second paragraphs discuss the current policy and evidence of its potential devastating effects, and the third paragraph advocates for a new system of wildfire management.

   E.   No. This answer does not match the passage. The passage discusses the current system for fighting wildfires and advocates for a proposed new system; the passage does not discuss two seemingly contradictory goals of one policy.

2. **E**   Extract Fact

   The question asks what the phrase "maintenance burns" in line 55 refers to. The correct answer should match the meaning of that phrase in context, likely located within five lines of line 55. In lines 51–52, the passage provides the definition: "intentional lighting of controlled burns" and "allowing fires set by lightning to burn."

   A.   No. This answer does not match the passage. Maintenance burns are controlled burns that the passage recommends as part of a new fire-management system. While they are similar to fires that regularly occurred in ancient forests, they are different in that they are managed and controlled.

   B.   No. This answer contradicts the passage. According to the third paragraph, the goal of maintenance burns is to protect mature (larger, fire-tolerant) trees from destruction.

C. No. This answer contradicts the passage. According to the second paragraph, the fires that are likely to occur today would result in total devastation.

D. No. This answer contradicts the passage. According to the first paragraph, this type of fire typically occurred at intervals between 5 and 25 years.

E. Yes. The passage describes maintenance burns in lines 51–52 as the intentional lighting of controlled burns as well as allowing fires set by lightning to burn under certain conditions.

3. **C**   Complex

The question asks which sentence would most logically complete the last paragraph. Eliminate answers that contradict the passage, bring up new topics, or do not match the Bottom Line or the overall tone of the passage.

A. No. This answer brings up a new topic. The passage does not address damage to developed property.

B. No. This answer contradicts the passage. The second paragraph states that foresters are becoming increasingly aware of the danger of too much firefighting. Nothing in the passage indicates that foresters would resist this new proposal.

C. Yes. The fourth paragraph indicates that the proposal will reduce the damage of inevitable wildfires once fuels are reduced by maintenance burns, which implies that in the meantime the risk of devastating fires will continue.

D. No. This answer brings up a new topic. The passage does not address the economic impact of the new proposal.

E. No. This answer brings up a new topic. The passage does not indicate that large financial resources will be needed for the new proposal.

4. **A**   Structure

The question asks for the function of the factors of topography, weather, and fuel in the passage. Look for the claim that these factors are used to support, likely located within 5 lines of the factors. The third paragraph mentions that topography, weather, and fuel are the factors that affect fire behavior, and concludes that, since fuel is the only factor land managers can control, they should focus on reducing fuel to control wildfires.

A. Yes. The function of topography, weather, and fuel in the passage is to support the claim of the third paragraph: that land managers should focus on reducing fuel to combat wildfires.

B. No. This answer goes too far and contradicts the passage. The passage does not state that land managers' efforts will always be somewhat ineffective.

C. No. This answer is from the wrong part of the passage. The second paragraph discusses the reason forest fires may be unnaturally devastating, but the third paragraph discusses topography, weather, and fuel.

D. No. This answer does not match the passage. The passage does not discuss the relationship of fuel types and forest densities to topography or weather.

E. No. This answer is from the wrong part of the passage. The third paragraph discusses forest fires started by lightning as part of the proposed new wildfire management system. Like the factors of topography, weather, and fuel, this answer contains additional evidence supporting the claim of the paragraph: that land managers must conserve fuel.

5. **B** **Extract / Infer**

The question asks which answer is true of ancient ponderosa forests. Ancient ponderosa forests are mentioned in line 9 of the passage. Look for an answer choice that is proved by statements in the passage about the ancient ponderosa forests, likely located within five lines up or down from line 9. Avoid answers that contradict the Bottom Line or include strongly worded language or comparisons that are not supported by statements in the passage.

A. No. This answer makes an unsupported comparison. The passage does not discuss genetic differences between ancient and modern ponderosas.

B. Yes. This answer makes a comparison that is supported by the passage. The first paragraph states that ancient ponderosa forests were stable in part because fires maintained open forests and cleared brush and young trees, while the second paragraph states that fuel builds up in modern forests.

C. No. This answer makes an unsupported comparison. The passage does not discuss differences in weather patterns in ponderosa forests.

D. No. This answer makes an unsupported comparison. The passage does not discuss differences in diversity of plant species in ponderosa forests.

E. No. This answer contradicts the passage. The second paragraph states that wildlife might escape low-intensity fires, and the passage does not state that fires helped control wildlife populations.

6. **D** **Extract / Infer**

The question asks how the author would regard a policy in which all forest fires started by lightning were allowed to burn until they died out naturally. The passage states in line 51 that fires started by lightning could be allowed to burn when the weather is damp enough to reduce the risk of extensive damage. This implies that the author believes extensive damage might occur if the weather were not damp.

A. No. This answer contradicts the passage. According to line 53 of the passage, allowing all fires to burn even when the weather is not damp would risk extensive damage to the forest, and so it would not be a viable means of restoring the forest.

B. No. This answer contradicts the passage. According to line 53 of the passage, allowing all fires to burn even when the weather is not damp would risk extensive damage to the forest, and so it would not be an essential component of a new wildfire management plan.

C. No. This answer contradicts the passage. According to line 53 of the passage, allowing all fires to burn even when the weather is not damp would risk extensive damage to the forest, and so it would not be beneficial to forests with older trees.

D. Yes. This answer matches the statement in line 53 of the passage that fires may cause extensive damage if the weather is not damp.

E. No. This answer is not supported by the passage. The passage does not discuss public perception of the consequences of fires, and it does not suggest that a solution is politically infeasible.

Questions 7–13

The main point of the first paragraph is that Mali's restrictions on exporting of cultural artifacts actually resulted in looting of artifacts, and thus the loss of important knowledge about them. The second paragraph notes that many societies condemn such looting and have adopted policies that such artifacts belong to the country where they are found. The third paragraph argues that Mali's regulations ironically resulted in lootings that led to loss of information about cultural artifacts. The fourth paragraph suggests that if Mali had actually allowed and licensed excavations rather than prohibiting them, the excavations of artifacts might be less well conducted than careful archaeological excavations, but the information gained about the artifacts might be worth it. The Bottom Line of the passage is that a system that allows and licenses the excavations of cultural antiquities, although flawed, might be preferable to the alternative, where restrictions lead to looting and loss of valuable information. The overall tone of the passage is persuasive: The passage criticizes the current system and describes an alternative solution.

7. **B**   **Big Picture**

Use the Bottom Line to choose an answer. Watch out for answers that contradict the Bottom Line, are too narrow (a point that is not the main point), or go beyond the statements in the passage.

A. No. This answer is too narrow; it matches the main point of the second paragraph only.

B. Yes. This answer matches the Bottom Line. The passage suggests in the fourth paragraph that a more flexible solution may be preferable to the damage caused by the restrictive policies described in the second and third paragraphs.

C. No. This answer does not match the tone of the passage, and it goes beyond the passage. The passage does not suggest that Mali should resist the dictates of international bodies or that Mali must find a unique solution.

D. No. This answer contradicts the passage. The passage does not suggest that only accredited archaeologists should be licensed for excavations.

E. No. This answer does not match the passage. The passage does state that Mali's restrictive policies seem to have done more harm than good, but the passage does not suggest that the idea that cultural artifacts are the property of the state does more harm than good.

8. **B**   **Extract Fact**

The question asks which answer represents a way some countries have made use of the UNESCO doctrine. Since the UNESCO doctrine is mentioned in line 17, the answer should be located somewhere in the second paragraph. Look for an answer choice that is proved by a statement in the passage about the use of the UNESCO doctrine. Avoid answers that contradict the Bottom Line or include strongly worded language or comparisons that are not supported by statements in the passage.

A. No. This answer does not match the passage. The passage does not state that UNESCO regulations require the origins of all antiquities sold to collectors to be fully documented.

B. Yes. In lines 23–25, the second paragraph states that a number of countries have declared that all antiquities originating within their borders are state property and cannot be freely exported.

C. No. This answer is from the wrong part of the passage. In the third paragraph, the author suggests that Mali could have adopted a plan that involves educating people about the proper excavation of antiquities, but this plan does not relate to the UNESCO doctrine, which concerns the sovereign power of a country over antiquities originating within its borders.

D.   No. This answer does not match the passage. The passage does not discuss countries with borders containing an ancient culture's territory.

E.   No. This answer does not match the passage. The passage does not discuss the restoration of antiquities or the commitment of substantial resources to such a plan.

9.   **C**   Structure

The question asks for the author's purpose in asking the reader to suppose that Mali had imposed a tax on exported objects. Look for the claim that this request supports, likely located within five lines of the statement. In this case, the request is made in support of the main point of the fourth paragraph: A flexible plan of licensing would be preferable to a strict prohibition on excavation and export of antiquities.

A.   No. This answer does not match the purpose of the request. While the new tax would help fund the acquisition of pieces by the national museum, the purpose of the discussion of the new task is to support the main idea of the fourth paragraph: A more flexible policy would be preferable to the more restrictive policies currently in place.

B.   No. This answer contradicts the tone of the passage. The passage is critical of the Malian government's past policies concerning cultural antiquities.

C.   Yes. This answer matches the purpose of the request. The purpose of the discussion of the new task is to support the main idea of the fourth paragraph: A more flexible, pragmatic approach may be preferable to past restrictive policies.

D.   No. This answer does not match the purpose of the request. While the passage does suggest requiring that records be kept, the purpose of the discussion of the new tax is to support the main idea of the fourth paragraph: A more flexible policy would be preferable to the more restrictive policies currently in place.

E.   No. This answer is from the wrong part of the passage. The UNESCO doctrine is discussed in the second paragraph, while the purpose of the discussion of the new tax is to support the main idea of the fourth paragraph: A more flexible policy would be preferable to the more restrictive policies currently in place.

10.   **A**   Extract
Infer

The question asks which answer the author would be most likely to agree with regarding UNESCO. Since UNESCO is mentioned in various locations in the passage, look for an answer choice that is proved by a statement in the passage about UNESCO. Avoid answers that contradict the Bottom Line or include strongly worded language or comparisons that are not supported by statements in the passage.

A.   Yes. This answer is supported by the passage. The first sentence of the fourth paragraph asks to reader to suppose that UNESCO helped Mali to exercise its rights by licensing excavations and educating people. This statement suggests that the author believes that UNESCO can play an important role in stemming abuses relating to cultural artifacts.

B.   No. This answer goes beyond the passage. The passage does not suggest that UNESCO's policies came about in response to Mali's situation.

C.   No. This answer makes an unsupported comparison. The passage does not compare UNESCO's success in single-state versus multi-state initiatives.

D. No. This answer goes beyond the passage. The passage does not discuss whether UNESCO pays enough attention to countries like Mali.

E. No. This answer goes beyond the passage. The passage does not discuss the level of funding received by UNESCO.

11. **C**   **Extract Infer**

The question asks which answer the author would be most likely to agree with regarding regulations governing trade in antiquities in countries like Mali. Since these regulations are discussed throughout the passage, look for an answer choice that is proved by a statement in the passage about the regulations. Avoid answers that contradict the Bottom Line or include strongly worded language or comparisons that are not supported by statements in the passage.

A. No. This answer contradicts the tone of the passage. The passage argues for flexible regulations, not regulations that must be approved by archaeologists.

B. No. This answer contradicts the Bottom Line of the passage. The fourth paragraph suggests that it may be preferable to allow cultural antiquities to be exported, so long as information about the artifacts is recorded and registered.

C. Yes. This answer is supported by a statement in the passage. In the fourth paragraph, lines 54–55 state that some people would still have been able to avoid the proposed regulations, and yet this may still be preferable to the actual results with the current regulations.

D. No. This answer contradicts the tone of the passage. The passage argues for flexible regulations, not for strict punishment of violators.

E. No. This answer makes an unsupported comparison. The passage does not discuss the idea that the regulations would be most effective when they are easy to understand.

12. **D**   **Extract Infer**

The question asks which statement about cultural antiquities the author would be most likely to agree with. Since cultural antiquities are discussed throughout the passage, look for an answer choice that is proved by a statement in the passage about the antiquities.

Avoid answers that contradict the Bottom Line or include strongly worded language or comparisons that are not supported by statements in the passage.

A. No. This answer goes beyond the passage. The passage suggests a policy that would provide funding for the country's national museum to acquire important pieces, but the passage does not suggest that artifacts must be owned and protected by the national museum.

B. No. This answer contradicts the Bottom Line of the passage. The passage suggests that a flexible policy allowing the export of artifacts would be preferable to restrictive policies prohibiting export of cultural artifacts.

C. No. This answer contradicts the passage. The fourth paragraph suggests that the country's national museum should acquire important artifacts.

D. Yes. This answer is supported by a statement in the passage. In the fourth paragraph, lines 51–54 state that excavations not conducted by accredited archaeologists may be inferior and less informative, which implies that excavations conducted by accredited archaeologists would be preferred.

E.   No. This answer contradicts the passage. The fourth paragraph suggests that only licensed excavations of artifacts should be permitted; the passage does not state that artifacts belong to anyone who finds and registers them.

13.   **B**   Big Picture

The question asks about the author's attitude toward foreign collectors of terra-cotta sculptures from Djenne-jeno. Look for a statement about the foreign collectors that includes words indicating the author's attitude: In line 8, the passage states that terra-cotta sculptures were sold to foreign collectors who rightly admired them, which indicates that the author believes the foreign collectors correctly thought the sculptures were admirable.

A.   No. This answer does not match the author's attitude. The author is critical of such collecting, calling it "pillaging" that is "natural to condemn" in line 13.

B.   Yes. This answer matches the author's attitude. The author states that the foreign collectors rightly admired the sculptures, which indicates that the author approved of their artistic judgment.

C.   No. This answer does not match the author's attitude. The author does not discuss the idea of foreign collectors taking action against illegal exportation.

D.   No. This answer does not match the author's attitude. The author does not discuss whether the foreign collectors are concerned for the people of Mali.

E.   No. This answer does not match the author's attitude. The author states that the foreign collectors rightly admired the sculptures, which indicates that the author approved of their artistic judgment, but this does not mean the author had sympathy with their motives.

Questions 14–21

The main idea of the first paragraph is that in a clinical trial comparing a new treatment to a currently accepted treatment, experts traditionally believed that the physicians participating in the trial should be unbiased toward each treatment option. The second paragraph suggests that this requirement of neutrality ("theoretical equipoise") may be too strict, because it is effectively an impossible standard for clinical trials to meet. The third paragraph suggests that a new standard be developed ("clinical equipoise") that eliminates unreasonable restrictions while maintaining strict ethical standards. The fourth paragraph suggests that this new standard would be possible because absence of consensus among clinical experts is enough to ensure that the process meets ethical standards. The Bottom Line of the passage is that traditional standards for clinical trials are overly restrictive, and they should be replaced with a new standard that would allow a physician to prefer one method of treatment and yet remain in the study, so long as the physician recognizes the lack of consensus among clinical experts. The overall tone of the passage is persuasive: The passage advocates for the replacement of traditional, restrictive requirements for clinical trials with new, more flexible requirements.

14.   **B**   Big Picture

Use the Bottom Line to choose an answer. Watch out for answers that are too narrow (a purpose that's not primary) and answers that don't match the Bottom Line of the passage.

A.   No. This answer does not match the purpose of the passage. The passage does not merely explain the difference between two conceptions; rather, it advocates for a change to a new conception.

B.   Yes. This answer matches the purpose of the passage. The passage advocates for a change from theoretical equipoise, a more restrictive requirement, to a new standard of clinical equipoise, which is less restrictive.

C.   No. This answer contradicts the Bottom Line of the passage. The passage argues that a change in the standards would improve the standards of clinical trials, not endanger them.

D.   No. This answer does not match the purpose of the passage. The passage does not advocate that researchers more closely examine the conceptions; rather, it advocates for a change to a new conception.

E.   No. This answer does not match the purpose of the passage. The passage does not argue for a change in the scientific methods used in clinical trials; rather, it argues for a change in the ethical standards governing the state of mind of physicians participating in clinical trials.

15.   **D**   **Structure**

The question asks for the primary purpose of the second paragraph. The second paragraph suggests that the requirement of theoretical equipoise may be too strict, because it is effectively an impossible standard for clinical trials to meet. Eliminate answers that contradict the Bottom Line or that are too narrow (i.e., that describe a purpose that is not the primary purpose of the second paragraph).

A.   No. This answer does not match the purpose of the second paragraph. The second paragraph does not provide a view that contrasts with the arguments in favor of clinical equipoise; instead, it provides reasons why theoretical equipoise may be too strict, thereby supporting the idea that clinical equipoise may be preferable.

B.   No. This answer does not match the purpose of the second paragraph. While the second paragraph does discuss the factors underlying physicians' preferences regarding treatments, this is just a topic discussed in the second paragraph. The purpose of the second paragraph is to argue that the traditional conception of equipoise is too strict.

C.   No. This answer contradicts the Bottom Line. The passage does not disagree with the moral principle that underlies theoretical equipoise; rather, it suggests a new, less restrictive standard that would still achieve the same moral principle.

D.   Yes. This answer matches the purpose of the second paragraph. The second paragraph suggests that the requirement of theoretical equipoise may be too strict, because it is effectively an impossible standard for clinical trials to meet.

E.   No. This answer does not match the purpose of the second paragraph. The second paragraph does not criticize the general notion of equipoise; rather, it argues that the requirement of theoretical equipoise imposes standards that are virtually impossible for clinical trials to satisfy.

16.   **C**   **Extract Fact**

The question asks which answer is true according to statements in the passage. Since the answer could be supported from a statement located anywhere in the passage, look for a statement in the passage that would prove an answer choice true. Eliminate answers that contradict the Bottom Line or include strongly worded language or comparisons that are not supported by statements in the passage.

A.   No. This answer contradicts the Bottom Line of the passage. The passage argues that the requirements of theoretical equipoise are effectively impossible for clinical trials to satisfy.

B. No. This answer goes beyond the passage. The passage does not discuss how often clinical researchers are forced to suspend trials in this manner.

C. Yes. This answer is supported by a statement in the passage. In lines 50–53, the passage states that even if one or more researchers has a decided clinical preference as to treatment, this situation would be no ethical bar to participation in a trial, which implies that a physician holding such a preference would not render the clinical trial unethical.

D. No. This answer contradicts the Bottom Line of the passage. The passage suggests that the standard of theoretical equipoise is too restrictive, and it proposes clinical equipoise as a less restrictive alternative; therefore, a clinical trial that meets the standard of clinical equipoise would not necessarily meet the standard of theoretical equipoise.

E. No. This answer contradicts the Bottom Line of the passage. The passage suggests that theoretical equipoise is the traditional standard applied to clinical trials, and it argues that a new standard of clinical equipoise should be adopted. However, the passage does not state that researchers already do try to conduct trials in accordance with the clinical equipoise standard.

17. **D** Complex

The question asks which answer would be significantly more likely to jeopardize theoretical equipoise than clinical equipoise. Look for an answer that describes a violation of the standard of theoretical equipoise but that would comply with the standard of clinical equipoise. According to the second paragraph, theoretical equipoise requires that the researcher consider the evidence for the treatment regimens being compared to be exactly balanced. According to the third paragraph, clinical equipoise provides that a researcher may prefer one treatment over another based on evidence, so long as clinical experts disagree as to which treatment is superior and the researcher recognizes this lack of consensus.

A. No. This answer would not achieve the goal stated by the question. If, during a clinical trial, most clinical specialists came to favor one treatment over another, there would be no lack of consensus among medical experts, and therefore this scenario would violate the standard of clinical equipoise.

B. No. This answer would not achieve the goal stated by the question. If preliminary results indicate that the two treatments are equally effective, then researchers participating in the study would have no reason to prefer one treatment over another, and this scenario would not jeopardize theoretical equipoise.

C. No. This answer would not achieve the goal stated by the question. If physicians participating in the study prefer one treatment to another, then this scenario would jeopardize theoretical equipoise, but if there is no lack of consensus among clinical experts, then this scenario would also jeopardize clinical equipoise.

D. Yes. This answer achieves the goal stated by the question. If physicians participating in the study prefer one treatment to another, then this scenario would jeopardize theoretical equipoise, but if there is a lack of consensus among clinical experts and the physicians in question recognize this, then this scenario would not jeopardize clinical equipoise.

E. No. This answer would not achieve the goal stated by the question. If physicians participating in the study believe both treatments are equally effective, then this scenario would not jeopardize theoretical equipoise.

18. **D** Big Picture

Use the Bottom Line to choose an answer. Watch out for answers that are too narrow, go too far, or contradict the Bottom Line of the passage.

A. No. This answer is too narrow. This is the main idea of the second paragraph only. It does not address the main ideas of the third and fourth paragraphs: that a new standard of clinical equipoise should be adopted instead.

B. No. This answer does not match the Bottom Line. While the passage does say in the second paragraph that the conception of theoretical equipoise is almost impossible to satisfy, the passage goes on in the third and fourth paragraphs to propose a new standard that should be adopted.

C. No. This answer is too narrow. This is the main idea of the fourth paragraph only. This answer does not address the main point, which is that the restrictive conception of theoretical equipoise should be replaced with the less restrictive conception of clinical equipoise.

D. Yes. This answer matches the Bottom Line. The second paragraph argues that theoretical equipoise is too restrictive, and the third and fourth paragraphs argue that clinical equipoise is less restrictive and therefore should be adopted.

E. No. This answer is too narrow. The passage argues that a clinical trial that does not meet the standard of theoretical equipoise but does meet the standard of clinical equipoise should not be considered unethical.

19. **A** Extract Fact

The question asks which answer represents a group of people referred to by the term "community," as used in line 41 of the passage. Look for a statement located likely within five lines of line 41 that would support the answer choice. In this case, eliminate answers that contradict the Bottom Line or include strongly worded language or comparisons that are not supported by statements in the passage.

A. Yes. This answer is supported by a statement in the passage. In lines 40–42, the passage refers to the expert clinical community and its opinions over which treatment is better for patients with a given illness. This implies that the community is a group of people who focus on a common set of problems (patients with a given illness) using a shared body of knowledge (expertise in clinical treatment of a given illness).

B. No. This answer is not supported by the passage. The passage does not discuss the geographical area where clinical experts work or live.

C. No. This answer makes an unsupported comparison. The passage does not discuss the differences of opinion of clinical experts with other groups.

D. No. This answer is from the wrong part of the passage. This answer is a paraphrase of the last sentence of the first paragraph, but the physicians and ethicists referred to by this sentence are not the community of clinical experts referred to in lines 40–41.

E. No. This answer is not supported by the passage. The passage does not indicate that the community of clinical experts are employed in unrelated disciplines.

20. **C** [Extract Fact]

The question asks which answer is true according to statements in the passage. Since the answer could be supported from a statement located anywhere in the passage, look for a statement in the passage that would prove an answer choice true. Eliminate answers that contradict the Bottom Line or include strongly worded language or comparisons that are not supported by statements in the passage.

A. No. This answer contradicts the passage. The last sentence of the second paragraph of the passage states that few trials could comply with the standard of theoretical equipoise.

B. No. This answer makes an unsupported comparison. The passage does not suggest that clinical trials would be conducted more often if a more reasonable standard were in place; rather, the passage suggests that more clinical trials would be able to satisfy that new standard than the current standard.

C. Yes. This answer is supported by a statement in the passage. The last sentence of the second paragraph of the passage states that few trials could comply with the standard of theoretical equipoise.

D. No. This answer goes too far. While the last sentence of the first paragraph does state that most physicians and ethicists have traditionally agreed that traditional equipoise is appropriate for physicians in clinical trials, the passage does go so far as to state that most of them believe the currently accepted ethical requirements are adequate.

E. No. This answer goes beyond the passage. While the third paragraph does discuss conflicts of opinion in the expert clinical community, the passage does not suggest that most comparative trials are undertaken to help resolve such conflicts of opinion.

21. **A** [Complex]

The question asks which answer, if true, would most weaken the author's argument in the third and fourth paragraphs. Treat this question the same as a Weaken question in the Arguments section. The author's conclusion in the third and fourth paragraphs is that a new standard called "clinical equipoise" should be developed. The author supports this conclusion with the premise that a physician participating in a clinical study who develops a preference for one treatment over another should be allowed to continue to participate so long as a lack of consensus exists among clinical experts, and the physician acknowledges this lack of consensus. Look for an answer that suggests a problem with this plan to develop a new standard of clinical equipoise.

A. Yes. This answer weakens the argument in the third and fourth paragraphs. If most comparative clinical trials are undertaken to prove that a treatment considered best by a consensus of relevant experts is superior, then the standard of clinical equipoise would be jeopardized, because the standard of clinical equipoise requires that a lack of consensus exist among clinical experts as to which treatment is superior.

B. No. This answer strengthens the argument. If physicians rarely ask to leave trials when they believe early data favors one treatment over another, then the study does not satisfy the requirement of theoretical equipoise. This supports the plan to develop a new standard of clinical equipoise that would allow those physicians to remain in the study so long as they acknowledge a lack of consensus among medical experts.

C. No. This answer is irrelevant. The number of clinical trials being conducted annually does not affect the decision whether to develop a new standard of clinical equipoise.

D. No. This answer is irrelevant. The opinion of medical ethicists compared with the opinion of clinical researchers is not relevant to whether a new standard clinical equipoise should be developed.

E. No. This answer is not strong enough to weaken the argument. Even if it is rare that researchers begin a trial with no preference, then later develop a strong preference, the standard of clinical equipoise would still be needed to deal with such situations; furthermore, the standard of clinical equipoise would also still be needed to deal with other situations, such as allowing researchers to participate in a trial even if they begin the trial with a preference for one treatment over another.

Questions 22–27

The main point of the first paragraph of passage A is that the flat tax seems to work fine in the real world, despite past objections that it works only in theory. The second paragraph notes that the first objection to the flat tax is generally that it is unfair because it is not progressive. The third paragraph argues that this is untrue, because the flat tax can be made progressive by exempting a certain amount of income from the tax, and then notes that high-income earners pay about the same rate under both systems, because typical progressive tax systems include numerous legal loopholes that reduce the taxes for the high-income earners. The Bottom Line of passage A is that the flat tax can be instituted fairly, despite objections to the contrary.

The first paragraph of passage B argues that a graduated tax rate is fairer than a flat tax, because people are treated equally, but dollars are not. The second paragraph argues that dollars should be treated unequally, because the first dollars earned are needed for survival expenses, while excess dollars earned are not as important. The third paragraph argues that, even if a flat tax exempts some low income levels from taxes, the higher-income taxpayers will pay less, and therefore the middle class will end up paying more. The Bottom Line of passage B is that a flat tax is unfair to the middle class.

22. C **Big Picture**

The question asks which one of the answers is addressed by both passages. Use the Bottom Line of each passage to choose an answer. Eliminate answers that are addressed by only one of the two passages or that are not addressed by either passage.

A. No. This question is addressed only by passage A. The first paragraph of passage A discusses whether a flat tax is practical in the real world, but passage B does not address whether a flat tax can be implemented.

B. No. This question is addressed only by passage B. The first paragraph of passage B states that graduated tax rates treat all taxpayers equally, but passage A does not address this issue.

C. Yes. This question is addressed by both passages. Passage A argues that a flat tax can be fair to all taxpayers, while passage B argues that a flat tax is unfair to middle-class taxpayers.

D. No. This question is addressed only by passage B. The first paragraph of passage B discusses objections to progressive taxes, but passage A discusses objections only to flat taxes.

E. No. This question is addressed only by passage A. The third paragraph of passage A discusses incentives to avoid taxes legally and illegally, and it suggests that flat tax regimes would reduce such avoidance, but passage B does not address illegal tax avoidance.

23. **E** **Structure**

This question asks which technique is used by both passages to advance their arguments. Look for supporting evidence in each passage that matches an answer choice.

A. No. This technique is used only by passage A. The second paragraph of passage A suggests that those who initially said flat taxes were impractical in the real world then offer a further instant objection that they are unfair when they see that they have been successfully implemented. This is an example of shifting one's ground (changing a position once the first position has been proved wrong). Passage B, on the other hand, does not make any similar suggestion.

B. No. This technique is used only by passage A. The first paragraph of passage A discusses historical developments in Estonia as evidence, but passage B does not discuss any specific historical developments.

C. No. This technique is used only by passage B. Passage B uses an analogy to compare the dollars earned by the working poor to the dollars earned by middle-wage earners. However, passage A does not use any comparisons to advance its argument.

D. No. This technique is used only by passage B. In lines 51–53, passage B asks this question: "…[W]hy go suddenly from one extreme…to the other..?," which is a rhetorical question. However, passage A does not use any rhetorical questions.

E. Yes. This technique is used by both passages to advance their arguments. In lines 17–19, passage A corrects the misunderstanding described in the previous paragraph (that a flat tax is unfair to lower-income taxpayers). Similarly, in lines 33–36, passage B corrects the misunderstanding described in the previous sentence (that progressive tax rates seem unfair).

24. **D** **Complex**

Treat this question like a Strengthen question in an Arguments section. The question asks which answer, if true of a country that switched from a progressive tax system to a flat tax, would support the position of passage B over passage A. The position of passage B is that switching to a flat tax will shift more of the tax burden from the high-income earners to the middle class, while the position of passage A is that the flat tax is fair and will result in high-income earners paying approximately the same amount. Look for an answer that supports the idea that middle-class taxpayers will pay a greater share of taxes under a flat tax than under a progressive tax system.

A. No. This answer is irrelevant. Whether total revenues collected will remain the same does not address the issue of whether middle-class taxpayers will pay a greater share.

B. No. This answer is irrelevant. Whether the tax codes have been simplified does not address the issue of whether middle-class taxpayers will pay a greater share.

C. No. This answer is irrelevant. Whether high-income taxpayers believe they are overtaxed does not address the issue of whether middle-class taxpayers will pay a greater share.

D. Yes. This answer supports the position of passage B over that of passage A. If middle-income taxpayers tend to pay higher taxes, this supports the position of passage B over Passage A, which indicates that high-income taxpayers would pay about the same (and therefore implies that middle-income taxpayers would pay about the same as well).

E. No. This answer is irrelevant. Whether some legislators favor a return to the former system does not address the issue of whether middle-class taxpayers will pay a greater share.

25. **D** `Extract Fact`

The question asks which answer is a conclusion for which passage A argues but that is not addressed by passage B. Look for an answer that is supported by the argument in passage A but that is not addressed in passage B. Eliminate answers that reverse the relationship or that are addressed in both passages.

A. No. This answer is addressed by both passages. The last paragraph of passage B addresses whether exempting a threshold amount enables a flat tax to avoid unfairness, so this answer does not match the requirement that the answer is not addressed by passage B.

B. No. Passage A argues against this conclusion. The main idea of the first paragraph of passage A is that the flat tax is actually practical in the real world, so this answer does not match the requirement that the answer is a conclusion argued for by passage A.

C. No. This answer is an outside knowledge trap. Neither passage addresses how taxes may inhibit investment or economic growth.

D. Yes. This answer is a conclusion argued for by passage A, and it is not addressed in passage B. The third paragraph of passage A argues for the idea that a flat tax would eliminate opportunities for high-income earners to avoid tax, but passage B does not address this issue.

E. No. This answer is not supported by either passage. Passage A argues that the flat tax is not unfair, but passage A does not argue that a progressive tax system is unfair. Passage B, on the other hand, argues that the flax tax is unfair, but it does not argue that a progressive tax system is unfair.

26. **B** `Extract Fact`

Treat this question like a Point-at-Issue question in an Arguments section. Look for an answer that is supported by the a statement in one passage but contradicted by a statement in the other. Eliminate answers that are supported by both passages or not supported by either passage.

A. No. This answer is supported by both passages. Both passage A and passage B state that a flat tax can be modified to exempt a threshold amount, which would technically make the flat tax system progressive.

B. Yes. The authors of the two passages would likely disagree over this statement. The last sentence of passage A argues that high-income earners usually pay about the same amount under a flat tax as under a progressive tax system. On the other hand, the last sentence of passage B argues that high-income earners would pay less under a flat tax than under a progressive tax system.

C. No. The authors of both passages would disagree with this statement. The last sentence of the first paragraph of passage A contradicts this statement by saying that a flat tax seems to work as well in practice as it does in theory. Passage B argues that the flat tax is unfair, and therefore the author of passage B would disagree with the idea that the flat tax is fine in theory.

D. No. The authors of both passages would agree with this statement. The second paragraph of passage A supports this statement, as does the first paragraph of passage B.

E. No. Neither passage supports this statement. The third paragraph of passage A argues that a certain portion of every individual's income should be exempt from taxation, as does the third paragraph of passage B.

27. B `Complex`

Treat this answer like a Weaken question in an Arguments section. The question asks which answer, if true, would be a reasonable response for the author of passage B to make to the final argument of passage A. The final argument of passage A is that progressive tax systems include numerous incentives for avoidance of taxes by high-income taxpayers, and these incentives would be removed by the flat tax. Look for an answer that is consistent with the Bottom Line of passage B and that suggests that the flat tax would not actually remove the incentives and opportunities to avoid taxes.

A. No. This answer does not weaken the final argument of passage A. Even if some high-income taxpayers could avoid taxes under a flat-tax system by under-reporting their income, the flat tax may still have eliminated various other incentives and methods for avoiding taxes.

B. Yes. This answer weakens the final argument of passage A. If tax avoidance is the result of tax loopholes and special deductions, and not the nature of the progressive tax system itself, then similar loopholes and tax deductions might eventually be added to the flat tax as well, which means the flat tax might not actually remove those opportunities.

C. No. This answer does not match the Bottom Line of passage B. Passage B argues that the flat tax is unfair to middle-income taxpayers, not high-income taxpayers; furthermore, the fact that people at all income levels have been known to avoid taxes is irrelevant to the comparison between the progressive tax and the flat tax.

D. No. This answer is irrelevant. Which system is preferred by more taxpayers is not relevant to the question of whether the flat tax eliminates the incentives and opportunities for high-income earners to avoid taxes.

E. No. This answer is irrelevant, and it does not match the Bottom Line of passage B. Passage B does not address the idea of taxes on consumption of goods and services; rather, passage B argues that the flat tax is unfair and that a progressive tax system is fair.

Section 2: Arguments 1

1. D `Principle Strengthen`

This argument makes the claim that you should use praise and verbal correction to train your dog rather than using edible treats. This claim is based upon the fact that even though dogs learn quickly when trained with treats, most dogs will not obey commands without seeing a treat. The argument continues that it is not possible to always have treats. The argument assumes that praise and verbal correction are both an effective alternative to training and that it is better to use a stimulus that is always available. The credited response will provide a strong general rule that forces one of these assumptions to be true.

A. No. The speed at which a dog learns and the likelihood the owner will use a certain stimulus is irrelevant to the conclusion that verbal praise and correction should be used instead.

B. No. This answer choice directly contradicts the premise that treat commands are less effective since dogs will not obey without the stimulus.

C. No. This answer choice does not fully support the claim that verbal training should be used instead of treats since treat stimulus is a somewhat effective method according to the premises. Therefore, "some circumstances" could include either the treat training or verbal training methods.

D. Yes. This is the credited response. This rule, if true, would suggest that verbal training would be better than treat training since verbal commands can be supplied in all circumstances.

E. No. The focus of this answer choice is reversed from the conclusion. The claim is about what owners should do, not what they should not do.

2. C — Weaken

The archaeologist's argument makes the claim that a similar fate of high salinity soil is likely to occur to modern civilizations that rely heavily on irrigation for agriculture. This is based upon a comparison with the ancient Sumerians who depended upon irrigation. The irrigation used by the ancient Sumerians led to a toxic buildup of salts, which in turn led to a collapse of the civilization when agriculture failed. The argument assumes that ancient Sumerians and modern practices of agriculture are similar enough to warrant comparison. The credited response will exploit this comparison flaw by suggesting some reason that agricultural practices in modern times are different from those used by the ancient Sumerians.

A. No. This answer is irrelevant since the issue in the conclusion is the likely collapse of modern civilizations that rely on irrigation, not whether they could feed themselves. If anything, this answer choice would strengthen the archaeologist's claim.

B. No. This answer is irrelevant since the question task is to weaken the claim that modern civilizations will likely collapse.

C. Yes. This is the credited response. This answer choice provides a reason to doubt the validity of the comparison between ancient Sumerian irrigation practices and modern ones.

D. No. This is irrelevant to the conclusion since the claim stipulates "civilizations that rely heavily on irrigation." Just because many do not rely heavily on irrigation does not weaken a claim about those that do.

E. No. This answer is irrelevant to the conclusion since the premises state explicitly that the practice of irrigation led to the buildup of toxicity in the soil. The presence of toxic compounds in the soil before irrigation does not weaken the comparison.

3. B — Strengthen

This argument makes the claim that mineralized dinosaur bones and dinosaur tracks in dried mud flats are rarely found together. The only evidence supplied for this claim is that scavengers most likely went to mud flats to find carcasses. The researcher assumes that the cause of the lack of tracks and bones together was scavengers and ignores other possible causes for the observed phenomenon. The credited response will strengthen the causal assumption by providing some proof that scavengers could in fact cause a lack of fossilized bones in mudflats or will rule out an alternative cause for the tracks and bones being found separately.

A. No. This is irrelevant since the claim is focused on what occurs in the mud flats.

B. Yes. This answer choice provides additional information on scavenger habits that would strengthen the claim that they are a reason for the lack of bones where dinosaur tracks are found.

C. No. This is irrelevant since the claim is focused on the fact that fossilized tracks and bones are rarely found together. The relative frequency of tracks to bones does not strengthen this claim.

D. No. This answer is irrelevant since it discusses items that are neither tracks nor bones.

E. No. While this answer choice provides a difference between tracks and bones, it does not strengthen the claim that it is scavenger activity that led to the two items rarely occurring together. If anything, this answer choice would weaken that claim.

4. A **Main Point**

This argument concludes that stovetop burners would cause fewer fires if the burners were limited to a temperature of 350 degrees C. This claim is based upon the premise that this would provide enough heat for cooking while remaining below the ignition temperatures of cooking oil and common fibers. The author assumes that at least some fires are caused by stovetops igniting cooking oil or fibers. The credited response will identify the conclusion and will match it in both tone and scope.

A. Yes. It matches the argument's conclusion in both tone and scope.

B. No. This is a premise in support of the claim that limiting burners to 350 degrees would cause fewer fires.

C. No. This is a premise in support of the claim that limiting burners to 350 degrees would cause fewer fires.

D. No. This is a premise in support of the claim that limiting burners to 350 degrees would cause fewer fires.

E. No. This claim is not found within the argument.

5. E **Flaw**

This argument opens by summarizing a statement made by Jenkins that his movie was not intended to provoke antisocial behavior and that a director's best interest is to prevent that behavior. The author concludes that this claim by Jenkins must be rejected. As evidence, the author claims that the movie produced antisocial behavior. The speaker assumes that the new evidence is sufficient to cast doubt on Jenkins's claim. There is a language shift from an intended action to a result. Specifically, the speaker assumes that since the movie had a certain effect (antisocial behavior) that this effect must have been intended. The credited response will identify some weakness in the new evidence.

A. No. This choice describes an ad hominem flaw, which is not found in the argument.

B. No. This describes a correlation as causation flaw, which is not found in the argument.

C. No. This describes a part to whole comparison flaw, which is not found in the argument.

D. No. This answer has the wrong focus of people acting in a way contrary to the intentions that they themselves stated. The argument confuses intentions with effects upon others.

E. Yes. This is the credited response. It describes the confusion between the actual effects of the film with the intended effects of the film's director.

6. **C** **Principle Strengthen**

This argument claims that the word "loophole" should not be used in news stories unless there is evidence of wrongdoing. This conclusion is based upon the premise that "loophole" is a partisan word and that its use causes news stories to read like editorials. Since the conclusion is a conditional statement, it can be diagrammed as "If use loophole → evidence." The contrapositive is "if ~evidence → ~ use loophole." There is also a language shift in this argument between the perceptions of the word "loophole" and evidence mentioned in the conclusion. The credited response should provide a strong general rule that forces evidence to be required before the word "loophole" is used in a news story.

A. No. This answer wrongly focuses on wrong doing or scandal. It is irrelevant to the conclusion that evidence is necessary for the use of the word.

B. No. This answer choice compares editorials and news stories. This principle cannot be applied to the conclusion that the use of "loophole" requires evidence.

C. Yes. This is the credited response. This answer choice states a general rule that new stories must provide evidence for suggestions of wrong doing. Since the premises stated that the word loophole suggests wrongdoing, this principle is applicable.

D. No. This principle would actually contradict the conclusion that reporters should provide evidence in this situation.

E. No. Public interest is not an issue in the argument, so this principle cannot be applied to the conclusion.

7. **E** **Strengthen**

This argument concludes that widespread food shortages are inevitable. This argument opens by stating a claim by some people that there is no reason for concern over food supplies since food production currently increases faster than population. The expert then suggests that the current resources can increase only a little more than their current levels after which no increase is possible. The expert makes a time comparison flaw by assuming that since a trend has occurred in the past, it will continue to occur in the future. To support this comparison, the credited response should provide some reason that this time comparison is valid by ruling out alternatives or by providing additional evidence for its validity.

A. No. Whether or not food sources are renewable is irrelevant to the claim that shortages are inevitable.

B. No. Whether ocean resources will be fully utilized does not support the claim that shortages are inevitable. This can be viewed as a premise restatement since the expert has already claimed that food can be produced only a few times higher than the current amount.

C. No. This answer choice would weaken the argument by providing a reason that the time comparison is invalid.

D. No. The occurrence of regional shortages in the past is irrelevant to the claim that widespread food shortages in the future are inevitable.

E. Yes. This is the credited response. This answer choice shows that the current trends in both food production and population growth will continue to a point at which population growth outpaces food production.

8. **D** **Sufficient Assumption**

The argument concludes that in respect to technical sophistication, newer video games are less compelling to players. This is based upon a brief comparison between the earliest video games and newer ones in which newer video games have more detailed characters. The argument states that players cannot identify as well with newer game characters since they can clearly see that these characters represent other people. There is a language shift from "identify" to "compelling" games. The credited response should help the conclusion by building a bridge between one's ability to identify with a character and how compelling that makes a video game. The credited response should move from the premises to the conclusion.

A. No. This response focuses on one of the premises rather than on the conclusion. It is irrelevant.

B. No. This response discusses compelling aspects of video games other than technological sophistication. This answer choice is irrelevant.

C. No. This answer choice is necessary for the conclusion to be true, but it is not sufficient to force the conclusion that technological sophistication makes games less compelling.

D. Yes. This is the credited response. This answer choice links the premises about a player's ability to identify with a character and how compelling that makes the game.

E. No. This answer choice moves in the wrong direction, moving from the conclusion to the premises. Thus, it does not support the conclusion.

9. **D** **Resolve/ Explain**

This states that many regions in North America would be suitable for pumpkin crops where pumpkins would be able to grow without danger of destruction by frost. The argument then poses a paradox by stating that instead, pumpkin production is located in regions of North America where there are long winters and a high degree that the crops will be destroyed by frost. The credited response will provide a viable explanation for why pumpkins are grown in regions with long winters rather than in more temperate regions.

A. No. This would not explain why pumpkins are grown predominately in colder regions.

B. No. This would not explain why pumpkins are grown predominately in colder regions. If anything, this answer would make the discrepancy worse.

C. No. This would not explain why pumpkins are grown predominately in colder regions. If anything, this answer would make the discrepancy worse.

D. Yes. This answer choice provides a reason why colder climates would be preferable for pumpkin crops despite the danger of early frost.

E. No. This would not explain why pumpkins are grown predominately in colder regions. If anything, this answer would make the discrepancy worse.

10.   C   **Weaken**

The argument concludes that it is necessary to adopt an alternative code of procedure. This claim is based upon the fact that the current code has many obscure and unnecessary rules that cause fighting and a loss of public confidence. The speaker acknowledges that the code is entrenched but counters by stating the public confidence is necessary for their endeavors. The speaker assumes that the proposed solution is complete and effective. The speaker also assumes that the solution is the sole possible manner in which the problem can be addressed. Specifically, the council chair assumes that the only viable option for fixing the problem of fighting and loss of confidence is the alternative code. To weaken this claim, the credited response will provide either a problem with the alternative code or suggest a different possible solution to the issue at hand.

A.   No. This answer choice suggests that the problems might not be common. However, it does not weaken the claim that the alternative code should be adopted.

B.   No. While this answer suggests that the alternative code has been used for personal ends, it does not clearly show that the reason for this is inherent to the alternative code. As a result, this answer choice is not strong enough to cast doubt on the claim that the alternative code should be adopted.

C.   Yes. This is the credited response. This answer choice suggests that an alternative solution to the problem is under consideration casting doubt on the necessity of adopting the alternative code.

D.   No. This answer choice is irrelevant to the conclusion. Just because it is not always necessary to adopt an alternative does not preclude the necessity to do so in this specific situation. This answer choice is too softly worded to cast doubt on the conclusion.

E.   No. This answer choice moves in the wrong direction. It would strengthen the claim that the alternative code should be adopted.

11.   C   **Resolve/ Explain**

This argument says that among similar businesses, those that used customer surveys to improve profits saw a decline in profits when they used the surveys. Businesses that did not employ the surveys did not see a corresponding drop in profits. Since the businesses are of the same type, the credited response will state some reason that helps explain why the use of surveys seemed to lead to the opposite of the desired effect.

A.   No. This answer choice is irrelevant since it does not mention surveys.

B.   No. This is stated in the argument. The general use of surveys does not explain why profits dropped among those who did use them.

C.   Yes. This is the credited response. This answer choice resolves the dilemma by showing that the use of surveys is motivated by complaints, which could lead to a decline in sales and profits. If a business has no complaints, it would have no reason to use a survey.

D.   No. Whether the surveys are accurately completed does not explain why businesses who use them see a drop in profits.

E.   No. This answer choice addresses only one side of the issue. It might explain why those who used the surveys saw a drop in profits but does not explain why businesses who do not use surveys saw no drop in profits.

12. **E** **Necessary Assumption**

This argument claims that humans are unable to choose more wisely. The premises state that human emotional tendencies are essentially unchanged from the earliest members of our species. The argument allows that technology broadens our range of social and individual choices. The language shift in this argument is the notion of choosing wisely. The author assumes there is a link between emotional tendencies and wise choices and that this assumed link is not affected by technological advances. The credited response will provide a link between the premises and the conclusion or will rule out an alternative interpretation of the premises.

A. No. This is irrelevant to the conclusion about wise choices. This is also a broader version of the first premise.

B. No. While this statement mentions both wise choices and emotions, it is not necessary to the argument since there is no information about being in control of those emotions.

C. No. This answer choice has the wrong scope and is thus irrelevant. This answer choice discusses becoming wiser and the emotional predisposition to be so. However, the conclusion discusses making wise choices, which is not the same as becoming wiser.

D. No. This is too strongly worded to be necessary to the argument. This answer choice states that humans choose on the basis of emotions alone. This is not necessary to the conclusion that humans are generally unable to choose more wisely.

E. Yes. This is the credited response. This answer choice says that a change in humans' emotional disposition is necessary for wise choices. This answer choice builds a bridge between the conclusion and premises. Negated, this answer choice would read "A change in human emotional disposition is NOT necessary for wise choices," which would destroy the conclusion.

13. **C** **Reasoning**

This argument concludes that songbirds are threatened by deforestation and that, despite reforestation, the situation continues to get worse. This claim is based upon the premises that open spaces caused by deforestation reduce the distance between songbird nests and their predators. The role that reforestation plays in the argument is as a premise in support of the second conclusion that the situation is getting worse. The credited response should match this claim in tone and scope.

A. No. This does not match the argument since extinction is not mentioned.

B. No. This answer choice contradicts the argument that songbirds are threatened.

C. Yes. This is the credited response. Reforestation is something that occurs but is still compatible with the conclusion that songbirds continue to be threatened.

D. No. This is not the conclusion of the argument, so this does not match.

E. No. The claim is about songbirds, not their predators.

14. **C** **Flaw**

This argument concludes that by reducing excessive chocolate consumption, adults can almost certainly improve their mood. The premises state that a diverse sample of 1,000 adults was studied and that those who ate the most chocolate were the most likely to be depressed. There are several possible flaws here. The first is a causal flaw the argument assumes because the two things (chocolate consumption and depression) occurred together that one must cause the other. This could be either reverse causation, in which depression could cause chocolate consumption, or correlation equals causation, in which the two things share no direct causal relationship. Another possible flaw is survey sample. The premises state that the group is diverse, but that doesn't preclude all pertinent information being gathered. The credited response will point out either the causal flaw or a problem with the methodology of the survey.

A. No. This answer seems close on first read. However, it does not correctly match the conclusion. The conclusion states "improve their mood," while this answer choice states "eliminate that condition."

B. No. While there is a sample group under study, the premises state that it is a diverse group so it is likely to be representative.

C. Yes. This answer choice correctly identifies the correlation equals causation flaw.

D. No. This answer choice describes a necessary as sufficient flaw, which is not what this argument does.

E. No. This is not the flaw in the argument.

15. **D** **Necessary Assumption**

This argument concludes that scientific fraud is a widespread problem among authors who submit to a particular journal. This is based upon the premise that after careful examination by computer software, dozens of digital images had been manipulated in ways that violated the journal's submission guidelines. The major flaw in this argument is the language shift from manipulation of images to "scientific fraud." The author assumes that manipulation occurs, at least in part, to defraud the scientific findings. The credited response will build a bridge between the conclusion and the premises.

A. No. This answer choice is not necessary to the conclusion that scientific fraud is widespread.

B. No. The presence of digital images in all articles is not necessary to the conclusion. This answer choice is too strongly worded.

C. No. The argument does not assume that digital imagery is necessary for fraud to be possible. This is too strongly worded.

D. Yes. This answer correctly builds the bridge between premises and conclusion. When negated, it would state, "NONE of the scientists who...." This would destroy the conclusion.

E. No. This answer choice is not necessary to the conclusion that scientific fraud is widespread in this journal. It is too strongly worded.

16. **D** **Flaw**

This argument concludes that contemporary artists, who believe their works enable others to feel aesthetically fulfilled, are mistaken. This is based upon the premise that there are more works in the world than anyone could appreciate and that those works are capable of satisfying any taste imaginable. The author assumes that the existence of artworks is alone sufficient to lead to aesthetic fulfillment instead of being necessary to that fulfillment. The credited response will either identify this flaw in abstract language or will identify some situation in which this factor alone is not sufficient for aesthetic fulfillment.

A. No. This directly contradicts the conclusion and thus is not the flaw.

B. No. This does not match the conclusion, which states that art "enables" people. The author does not assume that all people will actually become aesthetically fulfilled.

C. No. The value of an artwork is not mentioned. This is irrelevant.

D. Yes. This answer choice demonstrates that access to all non-contemporary art is also a necessary precondition for aesthetic fulfillment by showing that contemporary art might be one of only a few types of art accessible.

E. No. This does not match the argument. The author does not assume that contemporary art is less fulfilling due to the volume of other art.

17. **B**   **Inference**

This argument states that the government will not pay for the anti-flu medication until the drug company provides information on cost-effectiveness. The drug company responds by arguing that that information will require massive clinical trials, which in turn require widespread circulation which itself requires government funding for the drug. These statements can be diagrammed as follows:

Govt: ~pay → ~ info on cost effectiveness;
Drug Co: info → trials → widespread circulation → govt. funding.

These two conditional chains are mutually exclusive meaning that both situations can never occur simultaneously. The credited response will identify this.

A. No. This is a bad contrapositive of the first statement. It is too strongly worded.

B. Yes. This correctly describes the conflicting conditional statements.

C. No. Whether patients will pay is new/unsupported information.

D. No. What the government should do is unsupported.

E. No. The cost-effectiveness of the drug is an unsupported evaluation.

18. **E**   **Flaw**

This argument concludes that dislike of vegetables is genetically determined. This is based upon a study taken from a large, diverse group of participants. All of the participants in one group enjoyed eating vegetables, but all of those in the other group disliked them. After analyzing blood samples from the group that disliked vegetables, all of the volunteers in that group had a gene in common. The flaw in the argument is a survey/sample flaw. The premises state that the sample is representative; however, pertinent information is missing that would allow for a more accurate evaluation of the study. The credited response will identify some relevant information that is missing.

A. No. This does not match the conclusion.

B. No. This contradicts the first sentence of the argument.

C. No. Translate the abstract language if necessary to read "ignores the possibility that even when dislike of vegetables is genetically predetermined, dislike of vegetables can occur for other reasons." This is granted by the conclusion, which states "at least in some cases."

D. No. This does not match the conclusion since the conclusion does not assume monocausality.

E. Yes. From the premises it is unknown whether the vegetable liking group had this gene. This is missing pertinent information.

19. **C** Point at Issue

Ana concludes that she opposes the ban on smoking since it is not the government's place to prevent people from harming only themselves. Pankaj points out that the ban is limited only to public spaces and that people could smoke at home. Ana and Pankaj disagree about whether the ban prevents smokers from harming themselves or not.

A. No. Ana would agree with this statement, but there is not enough information to determine Pankaj's position.

B. No. It is not known whether either person would agree with this.

C. Yes. Ana would agree with this statement based on her premise; Pankaj would disagree since smokers can still smoke at home.

D. No. Pankaj would definitely agree with this. There is not enough information to make a clear statement about Ana.

E. No. It is not known whether either person would agree with this.

20. **B** Flaw

The agricultural scientist concludes that apples were probably not cultivated 5,000 years ago on the grounds that wild apples are much smaller than cultivated apples. The apples found from a time close to the beginning of cultivation are no larger than those that grow wild. The assumption in this argument is a time comparison. The agricultural scientist assumes that there are no changes to cultivated apples that occurred after these apples but before modern supermarket ones. The credited response will identify some reason to doubt this comparison.

A. No. This does not match the conclusion that specifically states "this region."

B. Yes. This is a reason that the time comparison is not valid. If size changes took place gradually, then cultivated and wild apples would not immediately appear different.

C. No. This does not match the argument, which compares apples from only a specific region.

D. No. This is not found in the argument.

E. No. This common flaw (circular reasoning) is not found in this argument.

21. **B** Necessary Assumption

This argument concludes that the happy life tends to be the good life. The premises define the good life as a morally virtuous life and that genuine happiness derives from a sense of approval of one's character and projects. The hole in the argument is the jump between approval of one's character and morally virtuous life. The credited response will link these premises together.

A. No. This is too strongly worded to be required by the argument.

B. Yes. This correctly bridges the two premises. The negation of this answer destroys the conclusion.

C. No. This is not relevant to the argument's conclusion.

D. No. This is not relevant to the argument's conclusion.

E. No. This is not relevant to the argument's conclusion.

22. **C** Parallel Flaw

This argument concludes that returning organic wastes to soil is a good solution for waste disposal problems small-scale organic farms face. This is based upon the premise that this good solution requires that wastes be non-toxic and have low transport energy requirements. The premises then state that these conditions are met by small-scale organic farms. These premises can be diagrammed as follows:

P1: Good solution → non toxic AND not too much energy;
P2: non toxic AND not too much energy → Conclusion: good solution.

The diagrams make it clear that this is a necessary as sufficient flaw in which the statement was flipped but not negated. The credited response must have the same flaw. If two answer choices share this flaw, then the argument will also match structure and scope.

A. No. This argument claims that greenhouse plants are healthy because they have moisture, light, and nutrients. The premise states that if they have these three things they will thrive. This is a valid argument.

B. No. This argument concludes that the desired results will be seen in 20 years, based on the premise that every country will be globalized in 20 years, so every country will have a way to optimize its resources. This is a language shift, which is a different type of flaw.

C. Yes. This argument claims your idea has three conditions, so it is viable. In this conclusion, the three conditions are treated as sufficient. The premise states those three conditions are necessary factors for a viable idea.

D. No. This argument claims your idea has three conditions, so it is viable. In this conclusion, the three conditions are treated as sufficient. The premise states those three conditions are necessary factors for a viable idea.

E. No. This argument concludes that what I ate was not nutritious. The premises state that carbohydrates and protein are requirements for nutritious meals and that 80 percent of the calories in the lunch were from fat. This argument shifts from needing carbohydrates and protein to fat content, so it does not match the original flaw.

23. **A** Strengthen

This argument concludes that phenazines serve as molecular pipelines that give interior bacteria essential nutrients from the area around the colony. The premise states that some bacteria produce antibiotic molecules known as phenazines. The flaw in the argument is that there is no support at all for phenazines to serve as nutrient pipelines. The credited response will strengthen this claim by either providing evidence that phenazines do in fact involve nutrient transfers or that a lack of phenazines can lead to a lack of nutrients.

A. Yes. This answer choice indirectly supports the conclusion by suggesting that bacteria without phenazines have an alternative method of providing nutrients to interior bacteria.

B. No. The rate of production is not relevant to the claim that they are nutrient pipelines.

C. No. This answer choice would weaken the claim by suggesting that phenazines are not necessary for nutrients.

D. No. A bacteria's ability to fend off other bacteria is not relevant to the conclusion.

E. No. This answer choice would weaken the claim by suggesting that phenazines do not transport nutrients to interior bacteria.

24. **A** Inference

This argument deals with how quantity statements interact. The argument states that most of the culturally significant documents will be restored, some questionable authenticity documents will be restored, only manuscripts whose safety will be restored, and no infrequently consulted manuscript will be restored.

A. Yes. Since at least one suspect document will be restored and since frequently consulted documents will be restored, this must be true.

B. No. This is too strongly worded to be supported.

C. No. The argument does not state that all safe to restore manuscripts are also frequently consulted. This is too strongly worded to be supported.

D. No. Information about manuscripts susceptible to deterioration is unsupported.

E. No. Which manuscripts are rarely consulted is unsupported information.

25. **B** Strengthen

This argument concludes that the perception of direct mail being bad for the environment is misguided. This is based on the premise that most of the products advertised are for the home and that because of direct mail, millions of people buy products over the phone or online rather than driving to the store. The premises establish a causal link between home purchases and direct mail; however, the argument assumes that there are no other factors that need to be considered. The credited response will either limit other possible interpretations of the premises or will establish that direct mail has only the one effect.

A. No. This answer would weaken the claim by suggesting that more people might drive rather than less.

B. Yes. This answer strengthens the argument by limiting the scope of direct-mail purchases to needed goods, thus making the advertising for them necessary rather than superfluous.

C. No. Magazine advertisements are irrelevant to the conclusion that direct mail is not bad for the environment.

D. No. Why the advertisements are sent is not relevant to the claim that they are not bad for the environment.

E. No. Just because more products are being purchased from home than were before does not strengthen the claim that direct mail is not bad for the environment. This is irrelevant.

26. D | Parallel |

This argument concludes that if a country is new, it is probably not ruled by a monarch. This is based upon the premise that most countries are not ruled by monarchs and that the older a country is, the more likely it is to be ruled by a monarch. This can be abstracted to read as follows: more A then more likely B. B is rare. Conclusion: if ~A then likely ~B. The credited response will match this structure but not necessarily the order of this argument.

A. No. The structure of this argument reads "B is rare. More A then more likely B. Conclusion: ~A so likely ~C." The conclusion introduces a new piece, so this is not parallel.

B. No. The structure of this argument reads "B is rare. More A then more likely B. Conclusion: More A then more likely B." The conclusion in this argument does not align with the original conclusion.

C. No. The structure of this argument reads "B is rare. If less A then less likely B. Conclusion: If more A then more likely B." Neither the second premise nor the conclusion aligns with the original argument.

D. Yes. The structure matches exactly: "B is rare. If more A then more likely B. If ~A then likely ~B.

E. No. The structure reads "B is rare. More A then likely more B. Conclusion: ~A so likely B." The conclusion does not align with the original conclusion.

Section 3: Arguments 2

1. C | Resolve/ Explain |

In this question, the credited response will explain how two seemingly disparate statements can both be true. The dentist states that brushing after a meal will remove sugars that cause tooth decay but if brushing is not an option, the dentist suggests chewing gum to prevent tooth decay, even if the gum contains sugar. The credited response will show why gum with sugar is better than the alternative when brushing is not an option.

A. No. The fact that gum contains any sugar makes gum a confusing recommendation since sugar causes tooth decay.

B. No. This choice does not explain the recommendation to chew gum despite the fact that gum contains sugar, which causes tooth decay.

C. Yes. This choice explains the recommendation to chew gum since by showing that it provides a benefit that reduces tooth decay.

D. No. This choice does not explain the recommendation to chew gum despite the fact that gum contains sugar, which causes tooth decay.

E. No. While this choice references beneficial effects of chewing gum, it does not explain the recommendation to chew gum despite the fact that gum contains sugar, which causes tooth decay.

2. **B** Weaken

In this question, the credited response will hurt the conclusion by attacking the flaw in the argument. The author disagrees with the theory that New Zealand's bird population exists due to a lack of competition from mammals, based on evidence that states that fossils have been found that prove the existence of indigenous mammals in New Zealand. The author assumes that the existence of indigenous mammals proves that those mammals competed with birds, but the evidence is not strong enough to prove that claim.

A. No. This choice would strengthen the claim that mammals competed with birds.

B. Yes. This choice would hurt the argument by showing that the mammals did not compete with birds in New Zealand.

C. No. Other types of animal fossils discovered at the site are not directly relevant to the question of whether mammal species competed with birds in New Zealand.

D. No. This would strengthen the claim that mammal species compete with birds.

E. No. What is true of other islands is not relevant to what is true of New Zealand.

3. **D** Main Point

In this question, the credited response will match the conclusion of the argument. The restaurant owner claims that the newspaper reporter who panned the restaurant is not a true restaurant critic. The premises state that the reporter has no special expertise in food and that one cannot be called a drama critic if one does not have special training in theater. Use the Why Test to confirm that the conclusion is supported by the other facts in the argument.

A. No. This is a premise.

B. No. This is a premise.

C. No. This is a premise.

D. Yes. This matches the conclusion of the argument.

E. No. This is a premise.

4. **E** Necessary Assumption

In this question, the credited response will help the argument by filling in the gap. The argument concludes that the hypothesis that our solar system was formed from a cloud of dust and gas produced by a supernova is false. This is based on the premise that if the hypothesis is correct, there would be iron-60 present in the early history of the solar system but that scientists have not found iron-60 in early meteorites. The argument assumes that if iron-60 were present in the early history of the solar system that it would be found in early meteorites so the credited response will address this assumption.

A. No. The argument does not assume that early meteorites did not contain elements from the supernova. It actually assumes the opposite.

B. No. The material used to form other solar systems is not relevant to whether the meteorites indicate that our solar system was formed from dust and gas from a supernova.

C. No. Other types of iron than iron-60 are not relevant to whether the lack of iron-60 in meteorites indicates that our solar system was formed from dust and gas from a supernova.

D. No. Late forming meteorites are not relevant to whether the early meteorites indicate that our solar system was formed from dust and gas from a supernova.

E. Yes. This helps the argument. Use the Negation Test. If this were not true, then the failure to find iron-60 in meteorites would not itself disprove the original hypothesis.

5. C **Resolve/ Explain**

In this question, the credited response will explain how two seemingly disparate statements can both be true. The argument states that tuna is sometimes treated with carbon monoxide to prevent it from turning brown as it ages. On one hand, the argument states that carbon monoxide in this usage is not harmful to humans. On the other hand, people are more likely to get sick from eating tuna that has been treated with carbon monoxide.

A. No. This does not explain why people are more likely to get sick from eating tuna that has been treated with carbon monoxide.

B. No. This does not explain why people are more likely to get sick from eating tuna that has been treated with carbon monoxide.

C. Yes. This explains how eating tuna that has been treated with carbon monoxide could cause people to get sick even though carbon monoxide used in this way is not itself dangerous.

D. No. Other ways to prevent tuna from turning brown would not explain why people are more likely to get sick from eating tuna that has been treated with carbon monoxide.

E. No This does not explain why people are more likely to get sick from eating tuna that has been treated with carbon monoxide.

6. C **Sufficient Assumption**

In this question, the credited response will help the conclusion by providing strong evidence that the assumption is valid. The astrophysicist claims that the descriptive labels "long" and "short" used to describe Gamma ray bursts are not useful. This is based on the premise that a "long" GRB has many characteristics of "short" GRBs. The argument assumes characteristics of GRBs other than duration are important.

A. No. This choice does not link the possibility of unique characteristics with the "short" or "long" descriptions in the argument.

B. No. This would hurt the argument by showing that duration alone is important in some situations.

C. Yes. This choice states the assumption in the argument. If true, the argument's conclusion must also be true.

D. No. This choice states another factor that is not important, which provides more evidence for the claim that duration alone is important.

E. No. The argument is not concerned with the ability to label with non-descriptive labels.

7. **A**   Flaw

In this question, the credited response will hurt the argument by describing the flaw. The conclusion states that hospital patients with a greater tendency to laugh are helped more when they laugh a little than other patients who laugh more. The premises refer to a study that indicated that immune systems grew stronger when patients watched comic videos indicating that laughter can aid recovery. The study also noted that immune system gains were stronger in people who had a greater tendency to laugh. The argument is flawed in that it assumes that the patients who had a greater tendency to laugh did not in fact laugh more at the comic videos in the study than did others.

A. Yes. This describes the flaw in the argument.

B. No. The conclusion argues that the comic movie helped aid the recovery process regardless of the level of immune system that a patient started with.

C. No. The conclusion is not about the general population since it is specifically about hospital patients.

D. No. There is no concern about the direction of causality since the gains in the immune system came after the comic movie was shown.

E. No. The argument states that these patients were aided more, but there is no evidence that those patients recovered more quickly.

8. **A**   Strengthen

In this question, the credited response will help the conclusion of the argument by providing additional evidence. The conclusion states that a male guppy will change its courting patterns based on feedback from a female. The premises state that females preferred male guppies with more orange showing and that males tended to show females their more orange side when courting. The argument assumes a causal relationship between male and female preferences by establishing a correlation.

A. Yes. This would strengthen the claim by showing that the female feedback was responsible for the behavior of male guppies since it shows that a lack of female feedback results in no shift in behavior by the male guppies.

B. No. The preferences of females of other species of guppies are not relevant to the behavior of males of this species.

C. No. The lack of research into this question is not relevant to the argument's study.

D. No. The coloration of female guppies is not directly relevant to the behavior of males of this species.

E. No. This would weaken the argument by showing that the behavior may have been caused by an inability to interact.

9. **E**   Main Point

In this question, the credited response will match the conclusion of the argument. The politician concludes that acting on the basis of an argument that proposes to unilaterally reduce nuclear arms is dangerous. This is based on premises that state that the argument for unilateral nuclear arms reductions does not consider countries that are on the verge of civil war and that those countries cannot be relied upon to conform to an international policy.

A. No. There is no direct evidence that these countries would not agree to an international policy; the premises state that these countries cannot be trusted to follow through with the agreement.

B. No. This is contradictory to the claims of the argument.

C. No. There is no mention of disclosure of nuclear capabilities in the argument, so this cannot be the main point.

D. No. There is no direct evidence that countries would not agree to an international policy; the premises state that some countries cannot be trusted to follow through with the agreement.

E. Yes. This choice matches the conclusion of the argument.

10. **D** Weaken

In this question, the credited response will address the flaw. The advertisement concludes that you should take the full LIC treatment after any accident that involves a fall or a head bump. This is based on premises that state that many types of accidents can produce the types of motion that cause whiplash. The advertisement assumes that the types of motion that cause whiplash occur in accidents that involve a fall or a head bump.

A. No. The conclusion does not state that people shoved from behind should go through the treatment for whiplash.

B. No. This would help the argument by linking auto accidents to the types of motion that cause whiplash.

C. No. Other causes of whiplash wouldn't hurt the argument that people should go through treatment for accidents involving the most common types of motion that cause whiplash.

D. Yes. This would weaken the argument by showing that accidents that involve falls or head bumps are unlikely to cause whiplash and would not need treatment for whiplash.

E. No. The methods of treatment are not relevant to the question of whether a person who experiences certain accidents should go through the treatment for whiplash.

11. **A** Flaw

In this question, the credited response will describe the flaw in the argument. The argument concludes that a development proposal should move forward since the objections of a citizen group to developing a hiking trail are groundless and that most trail users would be hikers who care about the environment. The argument assumes that the only reason the proposal may not move forward would be if the citizen group's argument is valid when there may be other reasons to avoid the development of hiking trails.

A. Yes. This describes the flaw. An argument is not necessarily correct just because opponents of the argument are wrong.

B. No. This argument does not have a part-to-whole comparison flaw.

C. No. This argument is not circular because the premises are different from the conclusion.

D. No. The argument states that a majority of users of the trail will share a certain characteristic.

E. No. There is no attack on the members of the citizen group.

12. **C** Strengthen

In this question, the credited response will help the conclusion, which states that those people who predict a catastrophic shortage of scientists and engineers are wrong based on premises that state that there is little upward pressure on salaries for these positions and unemployment is as high in these fields as others. The argument assumes that a lack of upward pressure on salaries and "normal" unemployment are indications of a field that is not in danger of imminent shortage.

A. No. The proportion of research done by corporations is not relevant to the question of whether upward salary pressure or unemployment are indications of an imminent shortage of researchers.

B. No. Financial success is not directly relevant to the question of whether upward salary pressure and unemployment are indications of an imminent shortage of researchers since there is no information about the financial success of researchers.

C. Yes. This would provide an additional reason to support the claim that there is no imminent shortage because the number of people in the field has increased.

D. No. Specializations within the field of science are not directly relevant to the question of whether upward salary pressure and unemployment are indications of an imminent shortage of researchers since the argument talks about the field of science generally.

E. No. Professional development is not relevant to the question of whether upward salary pressure and unemployment are indications of an imminent shortage of researchers.

13. **C** Principle Strengthen

In this question, the credited response will help both arguments. Rhonda argues that you should use your time, energy, and money to help others as long as the cost isn't too great. She bases this on the premise that charitable people live richer lives than miserly hermits. Brad argues that you should focus generosity on friends and relatives because they will remember sacrifices and return kindness.

A. No. This would not help Brad's argument since his argument says to ignore complete strangers.

B. No. The golden rule does not help Brad's argument since his argument says to ignore complete strangers.

C. Yes. This would help Rhonda's argument because she says that charitable people live richer lives so helping oneself in that situation would be to act charitably in order to live richer. This would help Brad's argument by showing that helping friends and relatives would lead to returned kindnesses for oneself in the future.

D. No. This would not help Rhonda's argument because she does not indicate whether charitable people lead richer lives due to their returning kindness.

E. No. Neither Rhonda nor Brad discuss pride.

14. **B** Flaw

In this question, the credited response will hurt the argument by describing the flaw. The columnist disagrees with the position of wildlife activists who claim that cable TV lines should not be strung along with electric wires above ground. As a premise, the columnist cites the fact that animals are electrocuted by power lines even when cable TV lines are above ground. The argument assumes that because the wildlife activists' argument would not completely address the issue of electrocuted animals that the proposal is invalid.

A. No. The argument does not confuse necessary and sufficient conditions.

B. Yes. This describes the flaw in the argument.

C. No. Advantages to the proposal are not directly relevant to the logic of the argument.

D. No. The author does not criticize the wildlife activists.

E. No. The author does not discuss other proposals that would be effective.

15. **B** Reasoning

In this question, the credited response will describe the role of the sentence in question. The argument concludes that *Thrinaxodon* was probably warm-blooded. This conclusion is based on premises that state that *Thrinaxodon* had skull features that suggest it had whiskers, and that if it had whiskers, it probably also had hair on other parts of its body that would serve as insulation to regulate body temperature and insulation would not be useful to a cold-blooded animal. The credited response will state that the sentence in question is a premise that supports the conclusion.

A. No. The conclusion does not state that insulation would not be useful to a cold-blooded animal.

B. Yes. This describes the role of the sentence in the argument.

C. No. The sentence is not the conclusion.

D. No. The author agrees with the sentence.

E. No. The sentence is used as a premise to support the conclusion.

16. **D** Inference

To determine the answer to this question, fill in the blank with an answer choice that is supported by the remaining text. The economist states that countries use taxation to fund expenditures but an income tax does not promote savings and investment whereas taxing consumption encourages savings. The economist also states that the only way to improve economies for most countries is to increase savings rates.

A. No. The author does not discuss taxing savings or investments.

B. No. There is no evidence that the rate of economic improvement would be rapid.

C. No. There is no evidence that taxing consumption alone would be enough to fund government.

D.   Yes. This conclusion is supported by the text since one way to accomplish the important goal of improving economies is to encourage savings by taxing consumption instead of income.

E.   No. The author says taxing income does not help a country's economy, but the passage does not state that taxing income would be harmful.

17.   **D**   Weaken

In this question, the credited response will hurt the argument by attacking its flaw. Meade argues that governments are justified in outlawing behavior that puts one's own health at risk because people who are injured due to risky behavior inevitably impose emotional and financial costs on others. The argument is flawed in that it assumes that the government is justified in passing laws that prevent certain behaviors to protect others.

A.   No. The ability to harm oneself is not in question.

B.   No. Personal obligations are not relevant to the question of whether the government can pass laws that prevent certain behaviors in order to protect others.

C.   No. This would strengthen the argument by connecting the government actions to the premises.

D.   Yes. This choice would hurt the argument by showing that the law is not justified only because it protects harm to others.

E.   No. This would strengthen the argument by showing that harm to others is more important than personal freedom.

18.   **C**   Necessary Assumption

In this question, the credited response will help the argument by providing an important assumption. The conclusion states that Sanderson's omission was morally wrong. This is based on premises that lying is morally wrong, an intentionally misleading statement is a lie, and that there is no moral difference between a statement and an omission done with the same intent. The argument assumes that Sanderson's omission was intentionally misleading.

A.   No. What Sanderson's cousin wanted is not relevant to the argument.

B.   No. What other people did or did not say is not relevant to whether Sanderson was morally wrong.

C.   Yes. Use the Negation Test. If Sanderson did not believe that the overheard statement was correct, then his omission was not intentionally misleading.

D.   No. Hypothetical situations are not required assumptions.

E.   No. Use the Negation Test. If Sanderson did not have something to gain, the act of omission could still have been intentionally misleading.

19.   **D**   Principle Match

In this question, the credited response will match the principle in the argument, which states that a judge must follow precedent that is not contrary to basic moral values and that in the absence of precedent judges may use their own legal views to decide a case as long as those views are not contradictory to widespread public opinion.

A. No. By deciding the case on his own legal views that contradict public opinion, Judge Swoboda did not use the principle as stated.

B. No. By deciding the case on his own legal views that contradict public opinion, Judge Valenzuela did not use the principle as stated.

C. No. By deciding the case without applying the precedent that doesn't violate basic moral values, Judge Wilson did not use the principle as stated.

D. Yes. Judge Watanabe used her own legal view in a situation where there was no precedent and her own legal view did not contradict any widespread public opinion.

E. No. By deciding the case without applying the precedent that doesn't violate basic moral values, Judge Balila did not use the principle as stated.

20. **B** **Inference**

In this question, the credited response will be supported by the text of the passage. The passage states that in a study of people with amusia, volunteers were unable to tell the difference between tones when there was a shift in pitch. The volunteers were able to perceive changes in timing.

A. No. There is no evidence that there is a compensatory relationship between perceiving shifts in tone and changes in timing.

B. Yes. This must be true because volunteers with amusia were unable to perceive shifts in tone but were able to perceive changes in timing.

C. No. There is no evidence that there is a compensatory relationship between perceiving shifts in tone and changes in timing.

D. No. There is no evidence that the perception of a melody has no relationship with discerning timing.

E. No. There is no evidence for the reasons behind people's ability to perceive timing or shifts in pitch.

21. **E** **Principle Strengthen**

In this question, the credited response will help the conclusion by providing a rule that would make the conclusion true. The literary critic argues that there is little of social significance in contemporary novels. This is based on the premise that readers can't get into a literary world unless they can experience that world through the moral understanding of its characters and contemporary novels have sensationalistic spectacles that serve only to make readers wonder what will happen next. There is a gap between the conclusion about social significance and the premises based on experiencing a world.

A. No. This would hurt the argument by showing that what is true of classic literature may not be true of contemporary literature.

B. No. This goes in the wrong direction and discusses the wants of a novelist rather than the existential question of whether novels have social significance.

C. No. There is no indiciation that a novel is to be considered a work of art.

D. No. While attractive, this conditional is the opposite of what is needed. To strengthen the argument, this choice would have to say "If a novel does NOT allow a reader to understand injustice, it will not be socially significant."

E. Yes. This links the premises with the conclusion.

22. **E**   Flaw

In this question, the credited response will hurt the conclusion by describing its flaw. The argument concludes that the recommendations for avoiding infection is counter-productive because people who follow the recommendations are more likely to contract diseases from those pathogens than those who deviate considerably from the recommendations. The argument assumes that there is no other causal factor that would make a person who follows the recommendations to become infected.

A. No. Foods that are not meat-based are not relevant to this argument.

B. No. The argument states that is true so it cannot assume this fact.

C. No. The recognizability of the symptoms is not directly relevant to the argument without also assuming that people that do not follow the recommendations are sick without knowing it.

D. No. The argument says that following the recommendations causes a greater number of infections, so it does not assume that people who follow the recommendation will not be infected.

E. Yes. This choice says that the people who are most likely to follow the recommendations are the same people who are most likely to become infected due to a susceptibility to infection.

23. **C**   Parallel

In this question, the credited response will match the structure of the original argument. The argument states that no nonfiction book published by Carriage Books has been profitable and that they made a profit on every book published last year and concludes from these premises that Carriage Books must not have published a nonfiction book last year. This is a logically appropriate argument that uses elimination of alternatives to draw a conclusion. The credited response will match this structure.

A. No. This argument is invalid because the premises are contradictory. There are no circumstances in which it is possible that no actor has ever played an important role and that every actor last year played an important role.

B. No. This argument does not match because it is linear and does not eliminate alternatives to draw a conclusion.

C. Yes. This argument matches. It states that Pranwich Corporation has never given a bonus to its marketing division but that it did give bonuses to every analyst last year. Therefore, it is not possible that an analyst worked in its marketing division.

D. No. This argument does not match because it is linear and does not eliminate alternatives to draw a conclusion.

E. No. This argument does not match because it does not eliminate alternatives to draw a conclusion. Also, this argument is flawed because it assumes that if it has never done something in one area that it has never done that thing anywhere.

24. **A** Inference

In this question, the credited response will be supported by the text of the passage, which states that all unemployed artists are sympathetic to social justice and that no employed artist is interested in great personal fame.

A. Yes. If there are artists that are interested in great personal fame, they are unemployed and therefore must be sympathetic to social justice.

B. No. There is no evidence that artists uninterested in personal fame (those that are employed) are sympathetic to social justice.

C. No. There is no information about how unemployed artists feel about great personal fame.

D. No. It is possible that employed artists are also sympathetic to social justice.

E. No. It is possible that some employed artists are neither interested in personal fame nor sympathetic to social justice.

25. **D** Parallel Flaw

In this question, the credited response will have a flaw that matches the flaw in the original argument. The argument claims that there are two suspects for a burglary and that since one of them has an alibi that the other must be the burglar. The argument assumes that the burglar must be one of the suspects and not some other person. The credited response will have an argument where there are two likely possibilities, but one is found to be not possible so the other must be chosen without considering a third alternative.

A. No. This argument is the opposite of the original argument because it assumes that since one option will be chosen, the other option will not also be chosen.

B. No. This argument confuses necessary and sufficient conditions to draw its conclusion.

C. No. This is a valid argument so it does not contain a flaw that matches the flaw in the original argument.

D. Yes. This matches the original argument. Baxim Corporation has two choices that are likely, but since one option has been ruled out, the other option must be true. Like the original argument, this choice assumes that no other option is possible.

E. No. This argument states that there are only two possible situations, so this is a valid argument and does not have a flaw that matches the original argument.

Section 4: Games

Questions 1–6

This is a grouping game with two groups and a twist. The groups are segment 1 and segment 2—put these on top of the diagram. Segment 1 has three spaces and segment 2 has two spaces. The inventory consists of 5 reports—I and N are general and S, T, and W are local. Since there are two groups and more than one category in the inventory, this sets up just like a 2D In/Out game. The twist is that order matters in each group. Programs proceed from longest to shortest in each group, so label the first space in each group "longest" and the last spot in each group "shortest." The first two clues contain information about how to set up the diagram, and the remaining clues are fixed and range. There is one wildcard.

Clue 1. Use this information to set up your diagram.

Clue 2. Mark the first spaces in each group as "longest" and the last space in each group as "shortest."

Clue 3. Local in both segments; this can be noted as ~TWS in segment 1.

Clue 4. NG longest

Clue 5. SL shortest

Clue 6. IG—WL

Deductions: Since NG is the longest program, it will have to go first in whatever segment it is in. You can note this on top of your diagram. Since SL is the shortest, it will have to be in the last space in whatever segment it is in. You can also note this on top of your diagram. It is important to note that clue 6 comes into play only if both IG and WL are in the same segment. Also note that NG and IG cannot be together in segment 2 since there are only two spaces in segment 2 and both segments must contain a local report (clue 3). So one, or both, of them must be in segment 1. TL is the least restricted element.

Here's the diagram:

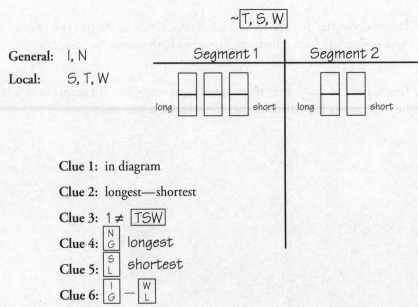

1. **B**   Grab-a-Rule

Use rules to eliminate answer choices; then choose the remaining answer.

A. No. This violates clues 2 and 4 because N is longer than I.

B. Yes. This choice does not violate any of the clues.

C. No. This violates rules 2 and 5 by putting S before T.

D. No. This violates rules 2 and 6 by putting W before I.

E. No. This violates rule 3 since there is no room for a local report in segment 2.

2. **E**   Specific

Make a new line in your diagram and add the new information. If T is the last report in the first segment, then according to the deductions, S must be in the last spot in the second segment, making (E) the credited response.

3. **B**   Specific

Make a new line in your diagram and add the new information. If N is the first report in the second segment, then I is forced into the first segment and one of S, T, or W is the second report in the second segment. Eliminate (E) because there are only five reports and N is in the second segment. Eliminate (D) because S must be in the last spot in a segment (clues 5 and 2). Now, since I is in the first segment, if W is in the same segment, it cannot be first because of clue 6. Eliminate (C). So, the first spot in the first segment cannot be N, S, or W. That leaves I and T. If I is first, then W can be second and S can be third, pushing T into the second segment. This is just one possibility, but since it works, try putting T in the first spot in segment 1. If T is first, I would be second and S or W would be third. This works as well, so eliminate (A) and select (B), the credited response.

4. **D**   General

Use the deductions, prior work, and trying the answers to determine which answer choice must be false.

A. No. I was one possibility for the first report in the first section in question 3.

B. No. N was in the first spot in the first segment in the credited answer to question 1.

C. No. N was in the first spot in the second segment in the question stem of question 3.

D. Yes. Since N must be the first report in one of the segments, if W is the first report in segment 1, then N is the first report in the second segment. Since the second report must be local (clue 3), this forces I into the first segment, and according to clue 6, I is longer than W, so putting W in the first spot violates clue 2.

E. No. W is in the last spot in segment 2 in the credited response to question 6.

5. A **General**

Use the deductions, prior work, and trying the answers to determine which answer choice provides enough information to lock each report into exactly one position.

A. Yes. If I is the last report in the first segment, then S must be the last report in the second segment (clues 5 and 2) and W must be in the second segment as well because of clue 6. This forces N into the first spot of the first segment, leaving T in the second spot in the first segment.

B. No. N was in the first spot of the first segment in question 2 and there were multiple possible arrangements of the other elements.

C. No. N was in the first spot of the second segment in questions 3 and 6 and there were multiple possible arrangements of the other elements.

D. No. S was in the last spot of the second segment in question 2 and there were multiple possible arrangements of the other elements.

E. No. W could have been in the last spot in the first segment in questions 4 and 6 with multiple possible arrangements of the other elements.

6. E **Specific**

Make a new line in your diagram and add the new information. If T is the first report in the first segment, then N has to be the first report in the second segment (clues 2 and 4). This will force I into segment 1 since clue 3 dictates that there must be a local report in each segment. You are looking for what could be true, so cross off anything that must be false.

A. No. I must be in the first segment.

B. No. N could never be the second report. This would violate clue 4.

C. No. Since I must also be in the first segment, W cannot be the second report in the first segment.

D. No. N must be the first report of the second segment (clues 2 and 6).

E. Yes. S, T, and W can all be the last report of the second segment, so this could be true.

Questions 7–12

This is a 1D order game with 1-1 correspondence. There are five houses—Q, R, S, T, and V—shown one at a time, so put 1–5 across the top of the diagram. There are no wildcards.

Clue 1. R = 1 or 2

Clue 2. T = 1 or 5

Clue 3. 3 = Q or V

Clue 4. ~QS ~SQ

There is not much to work with here, but make sure to put the information from the clues into the diagram. The elements are very restricted by the clues, so once you start filling in information from the questions they should fall into place with only a few possibilities.

Here's the diagram:

Q, R, S, T, U

	1	2	3	4	5
			Q/V		

R (over 1-2)

Clue 1: R = ½
Clue 2: T = ⅕
Clue 3: 3 = Q/V
Clue 4: QS or SQ

---

7. E — *Specific*

Make a new line in your diagram and add the new information. If Q is in spot 4, then according to clue 3, V must be in spot 3, making (E) the credited response.

8. C — *General*

Use the deductions, prior work, and trying the answers to determine which answer choice forces each inventory element into only one space.

A. No. If Q is in spot 3, then S cannot be in spots 2 or 4 (clue 4), but it can be in either spot 1 or spot 5, interchangeable with T, without violating any other clues.

B. No. If R is in the first spot, then T is in spot 5. Q cannot be in the third spot as this would leave only spots 2 and 4 open, which would force S next to Q (rule 4), so Q must be in either spot 2 or 4, interchangeable with S.

C. Yes. If S is second, then R must be first (clue 1), T must be fifth (clue 2), V must be third (clues 3 and 4), and Q must be fourth.

D. No. If Q is in spot 3, then S cannot be in spots 2 or 4 (clue 4), but it can be in either spot 1 or spot 5, interchangeable with T, without violating any other clues.

E. No. This scenario was demonstrated as having multiple options in question 9.

9. D — *Specific*

Make a new line in your diagram and add the new information. If S must be shown before Q, and S and Q cannot be consecutive (clue 4), then the new clue should look like S _ –Q. This means that Q cannot be first or second, and S cannot be fourth or fifth. Try putting Q in 3. This would force R and S into the first two spots, which in turn would force T into spot 5 and V into spot 4. Now try Q in spot 4. This would force V into spot 3, R and S into the first two spots, and T into spot 5. If you try to put Q in spot 5, then the first three spots would still have to be R, S, and V since S cannot be immediately next to Q (rule 4), and that would force T into spot 4, which violates clue 2. So, T must be in spot 5, making (D) the credited answer.

10. **A** General

Use the deductions, prior work, and trying the answers to determine which answer choice could be true. Eliminate any answer choice that must be false.

A. Yes. This scenario was demonstrated in Question 11.

B. No. If Q is fifth, then T is first (clue 2), R is second (clue 1), and V is third (clue 3). The only spot left for S is fourth, right next to Q, which doesn't work (clue 4).

C. No. If V is first, then R is second (clue 1), Q is third (clue 3), and T is fifth (clue 2). The only spot left for S is fourth, right next to Q, which doesn't work (clue 4).

D. No. If V second, then R is first (clue 1), Q is third (clue 3), and T is fifth (clue 2). The only spot left for S is fourth, right next to Q, which doesn't work (clue 4).

E. No. If V is fifth, then T is first (clue 2), R is second, (clue 1), and Q is third (clue 3). The only spot left for S is fourth, right next to Q, which doesn't work (clue 4).

11. **E** Specific

Make a new line in your diagram and add the new information. If V is third and R is first or second (clue 1), then either Q or S must be before T because if T is first, then Q and S will be forced together in violation of clue 4. So, no matter what, T must be in spot 5 (clue 2), making (E) the credited response.

12. **B** Complex

This question is asking for a replacement clue for R, which must be first or second. The credited response will force R to be first or second.

A. No. Just because R can't be fourth doesn't mean it can't be fifth. Try it. If R is in 5, then V could be third, T could be first, and Q and S can be in either spots 2 or 4.

B. Yes. If R must be earlier than V, then if V is third, this forces R into spots 1 or 2, and if V is fourth, then Q is third (clue 3) and R must still be in spots 1 or 2.

C. No. Without any other constraints on R, just limiting V to spot 3 or 4 does not limit R to spots 1 or 2.

D. No. With this new clue, if Q is third, then R must be second, which is too limiting since R cannot also be first.

E. No. This would be a good replacement for clue 2, but you need a replacement for clue 1. As it is, if the first clue is not in effect, then this new information does nothing to limit R.

Questions 13–18

This is a grouping game with three groups—Iceland, Norway, and Sweden—which should go across the top of the diagram. The inventory consists of five artifacts—V, W, X, Y, and Z—which are each used exactly once. While this game seems very straightforward, there is a twist that if missed, can make this game quite difficult. It is possible for Norway, and even Sweden, to be empty and all the artifacts to be in just two groups. There are no wildcards.

Clue 1. WY

Clue 2. X = N or S

Clue 3. I > N

Clue 4. VI → ZS ; ~ZS → ~VI

Deductions: The trick here is to note that there is nothing that prevents N or S from being an empty group. I cannot be empty because of the third clue. If there are always more artifacts from I than from N, then I cannot be empty. Since X must be in N or S, I cannot have all 5 artifacts. Note that X cannot be in I on your diagram. According to clue 4, if V is in I, then Z is in S. This means that I can have at most three artifacts—W, Y, and V or Z. According to clue 3, since I > N, that means N can have 0, 1, or 2 artifacts. There are not any restrictions on what can go in S, but the maximum number of artifacts that S can have is 4 since I must have at least 1.

Here's the diagram:

V, W, X, Y, Z

Clue 1: WY
Clue 2: X = N/S
Clue 3: I > N
Clue 4: V = I → Z = S
~Z = S → ~V = I

I | N | S

13. **B** **Grab-a-Rule**

Use the rules to eliminate wrong answers and be left with the credited response.

A. No. This violates clue 1 since W and Y are not from the same country.

B. Yes. This does not violate any clues.

C. No. This violates clue 3 because I and N have the same number of artifacts.

D. No. This violates clue 4. V is in I, but Z is in N, not S.

E. No. This violates clue 2 since X must be in N or S, not I.

14. A Specific

Make a new line in your diagram and add the new information. If both Y and Z are in I, then W is also in I (clue 1). V cannot be in I since that would force Z into S (clue 4), but V could be in N, as could X (clue 2). So, all of the artifacts could be from I and N, which means that there is no minimum number that must be in S. Choice (A) is the credited response.

15. E General

Use the deductions, prior work, and trying the answers to determine which answer choice must be false. Eliminate any answer that could be true.

A. No. If V and X are in N, then W, Y, and Z would have to be in I (rule 3). This does not violate any other rules and so could be true.

B. No. V and Y (with W) can be in I as per the discussion above in the deductions.

C. No. Question 14 demonstrates that both W and Z can be in I.

D. No. If W and Z are in S, Y is also in S, then V would have to be in I (clue 3) and X would have to be in S (clue 3). This could be true.

E. Yes. If W and Y are in N, then according to clue 3, the remaining artifacts would have to be in I. However, if V is in I, then Z is in S (clue 4), which means that W and Y cannot ever be in N.

16. A Specific

Add a new line to the diagram and fill in the new information. If W and X are in S, then Y is in S (clue 1), which leaves only V and Z to go elsewhere. Since I must have more artifacts than N (clue 3), one of V or Z must go in I and the other must go in S. N cannot have any artifacts, making (A) the credited response.

17. C General

Use deductions, prior work, and trying to put the elements into N to determine how many artifacts could be in N. X can be in N according to clue 2 and demonstrated in questions 14 and 15. V can also be in N as shown in the same questions. Z can be in N as long as V is not in I (clue 4). If W and Y are in N, then according to clue 3, the remaining artifacts would have to be in I. However, if V is in I, then Z is in S (clue 4), which means that W and Y cannot ever be in N. So, the maximum number of artifacts that could be in N is three, making (C) the credited response.

18. C General

Use deductions, prior work, and trying the answers to determine what must be false. Eliminate any answers that could be true.

A. No. This choice is demonstrated to be possible in question 16.

B. No. This could be true. If V and Z are in S, then X is in N (clue 2) and W and Y are in I (clues 1 and 3).

C. Yes. This must be false. If W and Y are in S, then X must be in N (clue 2) and V and Z in I (clue 3). But if V is in I, then Z is in S (clue 4), so this does not work.

D. No. This could be true. If X and Z are in S, then W, Y, and V could all be in I together. There are other possible combinations, but you need only one to prove that this could be true.

E. No. This could be true. If V, W, Y, and X are in S, then Z is in I (clue 3).

Questions 19–23

This is a mapping game that requires you to keep track of whom each of 4 employees—J, K, L, and M—can pass a project to from day to day. While order seems to be a factor (Monday through Thursday), it isn't really since every employee must have a project and pass a project every day.

Clue 1. ~JM

Clue 2. ~KJ

Clue 3. ~LJ

Since the clues all indicate who cannot pass to whom, it is important to determine who can pass to whom. There are only 4 employees, so just go through them systematically.

J—can pass to K and L

K—can pass to L and M

L—can pass to K and M

M—the only one who can pass to J, so ALWAYS passes to J since every employee must receive a project every day.

Indicate these connections on your test. It may be useful to use a standard diagram with M—F across the top to keep track of multiple exchanges.

Here's the diagram:

Clue 1: ~ JM
Clue 2: ~ KJ
Clue 3: ~ LJ

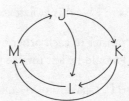

19. **A** Grab-a-Rule

A. Yes. This does not violate any clues.

B. No. This violates the rule given in the setup that an employee can work on only one project on any given day.

C. No. This violates the third clue by passing a project from L to J.

D. No. This violates the second clue by passing a project from K to J.

E. No. This violates the first clue by passing a project from J to M.

20. **E** **General**

Don't let the wording confuse you. No projects are passed on the beginning of Monday—that is, the first day each employee works on his own project before passing it to someone else on Tuesday, and so on. From the deductions, you know that M is the only one who can pass to J and so must pass to J every day, making (E) the credited response.

21. **C** **Specific**

Use your map to interpret the new information given. If one project gets passed back and forth between only two people, the only two who can pass to each other are K and L, making (C) the credited response.

22. **E** **Specific**

Use your map to interpret the new information given. If L works the same piece on Tuesday and Thursday, then it must have received it from K or L on Tuesday and then passed it to K on Wednesday. Since L can pass only to K or M, if L passed the piece to M, then M would pass it to J, since M cannot pass to anyone else (deductions). So, in order to get the piece back on Thursday, it must pass the piece to someone who can pass the piece back—K. This makes (E) the credited response.

23. **E** **General**

Use your map, deductions, and prior questions to help eliminate answers that must be false since you are looking for what could be true about Tuesday.

A. No. If J passes to K, K passes to M, and M can pass only to J (deductions), so L is left out of the loop.

B. No. If J passes to L, L passes to M, and M can pass only to J (deductions), so K is left out of the loop.

C. No. J cannot pass to M—this violates the first clue.

D. No. If K and L transfer to each other on the same day, then M would pass to J, but J cannot pass to M (clue 1) so J would be left unable to pass on his piece.

E. Yes. If K passes to L, L passes to M, and M passes to J (deductions), then J can pass to K. NO one is left out of the loop or left not being able to pass.

Chapter 3
PrepTest 73:
Answers and
Explanations

ANSWER KEY: PREPTEST 73

Section 1:
Reading
Comprehension

1. A
2. B
3. D
4. B
5. A
6. E
7. C
8. B
9. A
10. D
11. C
12. E
13. E
14. B
15. B
16. C
17. B
18. E
19. A
20. E
21. A
22. B
23. A
24. D
25. E
26. D
27. A

Section 2:
Arguments 1

1. C
2. E
3. A
4. D
5. D
6. D
7. C
8. B
9. C
10. A
11. B
12. A
13. B
14. E
15. B
16. A
17. B
18. E
19. B
20. E
21. E
22. A
23. C
24. D
25. C

Section 3:
Games

1. B
2. C
3. B
4. E
5. E
6. D
7. A
8. A
9. B
10. A
11. C
12. C
13. E
14. A
15. D
16. D
17. B
18. E
19. A
20. B
21. E
22. A
23. C

Section 4:
Arguments 2

1. D
2. D
3. E
4. C
5. A
6. E
7. E
8. D
9. D
10. E
11. B
12. A
13. B
14. C
15. A
16. E
17. C
18. C
19. B
20. D
21. E
22. D
23. E
24. E
25. E
26. A

EXPLANATIONS

Section 1: Reading Comprehension

Questions 1–7

The main point of the first paragraph is that, despite Charles Darwin's objection, strict construction Darwinians believe that natural selection explains all biological phenomena. The second paragraph explains what natural selection is and what the consequences of a strict constructionist view would be, and it introduces that there are many counterexamples. The main point of the third paragraph is that population genetics shows that most mutations are nonadaptive and not explainable by natural selection. The main point of the fourth paragraph is that paleontological studies of mass extinctions also undermine the strict constructionist view. The Bottom Line of the passage as a whole is that the strict constructionist view that natural selection is responsible for all biological phenomena is false. The overall tone of the passage is negative toward the strict constructionist claim.

1. **A**   Big Picture

   Use your Bottom Line of the passage to help you to evaluate the choices. The correct answer will describe the main point of the passage.

   A.   Yes. The author uses evidence from population genetics and paleontology to dispute the strict constructionist point of view.

   B   No. While strict constructionist Darwinians do claim that natural selection is responsible for the success or failure of the species, the main point of the passage is to disagree with such claims.

   C   No. The passage states at the end of the third paragraph that natural selection does not explain neutral, nonadaptive mutations.

   D.   No. While this answer choice accurately captures what strict constructionists believe, the main point of the passage is to disagree with strict constructionists.

   E.   No. The author does not dispute that natural selection exists, only that the strict constructionist view that it is responsible for all evolution.

2. **B**   Extract Fact

   The question is asking what the author said about why mammals were able to survive catastrophic environmental changes. This is discussed in the last paragraph of the passage. The correct answer will be explicitly mentioned in the passage.

   A.   No. This is contradicted by the passage in line 55.

   B.   Yes. In lines 43–44, the passage states that "smaller animal species are generally better able to survive."

   C.   No. Intelligence of mammals is not mentioned in the passage.

   D.   No. The environments of mammals were not mentioned in the passage.

   E.   No. Mammal reproduction was not mentioned in the passage.

3. **D** **Extract Fact**

The passage is asking for something that the author states about mutations of genetic material. The correct answer will be explicitly supported by the passage.

A. No. This is not supported by the passage. Persistence from one generation to the next is mentioned at the end of the third paragraph, but the other does not claim that a majority of mutations are not passed on.

B. No. The passage does not discuss when mutations occur.

C. No. The passage does not discuss whether mutations affect behavior or appearance, only whether they enhance reproductive success.

D. Yes. This is explicitly stated in lines 31–33.

E. No. The passage does not discuss the relative occurrence of mutations in larger and smaller species.

4. **B** **Extract Infer**

The correct answer will be the statement that is best supported by evidence within the passage text.

A. No. While the author refutes the strict constructionist view by providing evidence of exceptions, he or she does not claim that those exceptions account for the majority of traits in existing species.

B. Yes. In the fourth paragraph, the author discusses that the success of small mammals in the Cretaceous period was a result of "dumb luck" rather than adaptation to environment.

C. No. The author discusses in the third paragraph many neutral, nonadaptive mutations persist from one generation to the next but are not explainable by natural selection.

D. No. Watch out for deceptive language. The author claims that smaller species are generally better able to survive catastrophic climate changes, but catastrophic changes are not the same thing as harsh environmental conditions.

E. No. The author defines natural selection as generally held to shape both form and behavior.

5. **A** **Extract Infer**

The correct answer will be the statement that is best supported by evidence within the passage text and will agree with the Bottom Line and the overall tone of the passage.

A. Yes. At the end of the second paragraph, the author introduces that there are numerous examples that refute the strict constructionist Darwinian view and the third and fourth paragraphs detail two of those examples.

B. No. The author spends the bulk of the passage refuting the strict constructionists. This answer choice is not strong enough.

C. No. The author takes a position against the strict constructionists.

D. No. The author takes a position against the strict constructionists.

E. No. The author takes a position against the strict constructionists.

6. **E** Structure

The question is asking for the role that the second paragraph plays. The correct answer will discuss the strict constructionists' claims and the introduction of the evidence against those claims.

A. No. This paragraph introduces objections to the strict constructionists, not their objections.

B. No. The evidence against the strict constructionists' claims is laid out in the third and fourth paragraphs.

C. No. While the paragraph does describe the strict constructionists' view, there is no discussion of whether the evidence in the subsequent paragraphs has received any attention.

D. No. The passage does not discuss any arguments for the strict constructionist view, only the evidence against that view.

E. Yes. This accurately captures the discussion of the strict constructionists' claims and the introduction of the evidence against those claims.

7. **C** Big Picture

Use your Bottom Line of the passage to help you to evaluate the choices. The correct answer will describe the primary purpose of the passage to refute the strict constructionists' claims.

A. No. The passage is disputing the strict constructionists' claims.

B. No. This answer choice is too neutral. The author disagrees with the strict constructionist point of view.

C. Yes. This accurately captures that the author is refuting the strict constructionists' claims.

D. No. While the author is criticizing a theory, the strict constructionists' view is not a traditional theory.

E. No. The author mentions that the strict constructionist view is rising to prominence, but does not discuss why.

Questions 8–15

The main point of the first paragraph is that Julia Margaret Cameron's "fancy-subject" pictures derive their peculiar charm from their less-than-seamless elements. The main point of the second paragraph is that the realism of photography lends a depth to the pictures and captures the "doubleness" of imaginary and real personas that is not possible in theater or narrative painting. The main point of the third paragraph is that Cameron's pictures succeed because of their combination of amateurism and artistry, with *The Passing of Arthur* as an example. The Bottom Line of the passage as a whole is that the combination of reality and fantasy in Cameron's fancy-subject pictures results in peculiar treasures of photography. The overall tone of the passage is positive toward Cameron's work.

8. **B** Big Picture

Use your Bottom Line of the passage to help you to evaluate the choices. The correct answer will describe the main point of the passage.

A. No. While this answer is partly true, the passage does not discuss Cameron's intentions and this answer does not capture the author's appreciation of Cameron's work.

B. Yes. This is an accurate paraphrase of the Bottom Line.

C. No. The author's attitude toward the fancy-subject pictures is positive.

D. No. The passage discusses that the charm of Cameron's pictures is derived in part from the obviousness that the sitters are actors along with the imaginary scenes.

E. No. The passage discusses that the charm of Cameron's pictures is derived from both the sitters and the imaginary scenes.

9. **A** Structure

The question is asking why the author brought up the props in the picture. The passage states that they are obviously broomsticks and muslin, but that those details are insignificant, supporting the paragraph's claim that the combination of amateurism and artistry is what makes the pictures special.

A. Yes. The author introduces *The Passing of Arthur* with "for example," and the broomsticks and muslin support the claim of amateurism.

B. No. The transformative power of theater is discussed in the second paragraph.

C. No. The author never discusses Cameron's ingenuity.

D. No. The passage never claims that Cameron's work is intended to be ironic.

E. No. The author has a positive appraisal of the work, calling it magical and mysterious.

10. **D** RC Reasoning

The question is asking for an additional piece of information that will support the claim that we can suspend our disbelief when we look at a narrative painting but we cannot when we look at a photograph.

A. No. The length of sitting time does not impact the viewer's willingness to suspend disbelief.

B. No. This would make the viewer less likely to suspend disbelief when viewing paintings.

C. No. This has no impact on the viewer's reaction to a painting.

D. Yes. This is in line with the author's discussion of the difference between paintings and pictures: In pictures there is always the doubleness of reality and fantasy, but that is not the case in paintings. The suppression of conflicting details would allow a viewer to more easily suspend disbelief.

E. No. This has no impact on whether the viewer would be likely to suspend disbelief.

11. **C** `RC Reasoning`

The question is asking for an analogous relationship to that between Cameron and her fancy-subject pictures. Cameron uses ordinary people in costume to portray scenes from literature.

A. No. The author does not claim that Cameron tried to preserve an aesthetic distance between her characters and the audience.

B. No. The author does not claim that Cameron designed her pictures to subvert the meaning of the works she portrays.

C. Yes. Cameron's works use ordinary people in costumes to portray grand scenes from literature.

D. No. The author does not claim that Cameron's work was designed to be functional.

E. No. The author does not claim that Cameron's goal was to give the appearance of authenticity.

12. **E** `Extract Infer`

Four of the answer choices will be supported by the passage text, and the correct answer will disagree with the passage.

A. No. In the second paragraph, the author states that we can more easily suspend our disbelief when we look at a narrative painting than we can with a photograph.

B. No. In the third paragraph, the author claims that amateurism is part of what gives Cameron's pictures their special quality.

C. No. In the first paragraph, the author states that the comical conditions under which the pictures were taken are what give the pictures their charm.

D. No. In the second paragraph, the author states that theater transcends its doubleness only some of the time.

E. Yes. At the end of the first paragraph, the author discusses that the charm of Cameron's work is due in part to the fact that she did not succeed in making seamless works of illustrative art.

13. **E** `Extract Infer`

The correct answer will be the statement about the Victorian era that is best supported by evidence within the passage text.

A. No. The passage does not discuss what people were interested in during Cameron's time.

B. No. The passage does not discuss photographers other than Cameron and gives no indication of her socioeconomic standing.

C. No. The passage never mentions publicity stills, nor does it discuss what was popular in the Victorian era.

D. No. The fact that Cameron used ordinary people does not necessarily mean that there were no professional models available.

E. Yes. In the second paragraph, the author mentions that the subjects of Cameron's pictures were "trying desperately hard to sit still," which implies that taking a picture took some time.

14. **B** Structure

The question is asking why the author brings up the suspension of disbelief in the second paragraph. The suspension of disbelief is brought up to contrast how people view narrative paintings and narrative photographs.

A. No. The main conclusion of the passage is that Cameron's work succeeds because of its peculiar combination of reality and fantasy.

B. Yes. The author discusses the suspension of disbelief to contrast how people view narrative paintings and narrative photographs and how that contrast adds to our appreciation of the photographs.

C. No. The author views Cameron's work positively.

D. No. There is no criticism of Cameron's work in the passage.

E. No. The contrast is between narrative paintings and narrative photographs.

15. **B** Big Picture

Use your Bottom Line of the passage to help you to evaluate the choices. The correct answer will describe the primary purpose of the passage to praise Cameron.

A. No. The passage discusses attributes of Cameron's pictures and *The Passing of Arthur* in particular, but it does not discuss her development.

B. Yes. This accurately paraphrases the Bottom Line of the passage.

C. No. The passage does not argue that Cameron's vision is essentially theatrical.

D. No. This answer choice is too extreme. There is no indication that Cameron's goals were doomed, only that they did not, in fact, succeed.

E. No. The passage does not mention distractors of *The Passing of Arthur* and the discussion of that picture is only one part of the passage.

Questions 16–21

The first paragraph introduces Herbert Marcuse's critique of advertising: that it creates false needs and leads people to succumb to oppression. The main point of the second paragraph is that Marcuse claims that advertising links real needs to products, resulting in people never really being satisfied. The main point of the third paragraph is that Marcuse's distinction between real and false needs, and therefore his critique, is extremely problematic. The fourth paragraph argues that people are savvier than Marcuse gives them credit for and that advertising does not subvert free will. The Bottom Line of the passage as a whole is that Marcuse's critique of advertising is problematic because it does not account for the fact that adults are not passive victims; rather, they makes choices about how to obtain fulfillment and can find a kind of fulfillment in products. The overall tone of the passage is critical of Marcuse.

16. C **Big Picture**

Use your Bottom Line of the passage to help you to evaluate the choices. The correct answer will describe the main point of the passage.

A. No. While the passage does mention that consumers sometimes get enjoyment from advertisements, this is not the main point of the passage.

B. No. The passage argues that consumers understand and recognize forces of persuasion and do not passively react to them.

C. Yes. This accurately paraphrases the Bottom Line.

D. No. While this answer choice is tempting, the author discusses only Marcuse's critique of advertising and does not generalize to what other critics typically do.

E. No. The author's criticism of Marcuse does not focus on the distinction between real and false needs; rather, it targets the assumption that people are unwittingly manipulated by advertising.

17. B **Extract Fact**

The correct answer will be directly supported by evidence in the passage. The author discusses what Marcuse believed in the first and second paragraphs.

A. No. The passage never mentions psychological research findings.

B. Yes. The author attributes this to Marcuse in lines 17–21.

C. No. This is something the author believes, not something that Marcuse believed.

D. No. The passage does not discuss what Marcuse believed about independent decision making.

E. No. The passage says that Marcuse accused advertisers of creating false needs, but there is no mention of whether advertisers accept or deny that accusation.

18. E **Structure**

The question is asking how the first paragraph fits into the passage as a whole. The correct answer should reflect that the first paragraph introduces Marcuse's theory.

A. No. The first paragraph does not discuss political or economic context.

B. No. This is discussed in the second paragraph.

C. No. This is not discussed in the passage.

D. No. The first paragraph discusses only one view.

E. Yes. This accurately captures the main point and purpose of the first paragraph.

19. **A** Extract
Fact

The correct answer will be directly supported by evidence in the passage. The author discusses what Marcuse believed in the first and second paragraphs.

A. Yes. The author attributes this to Marcuse in lines 6–9.

B. No. The passage does not discuss earlier societies.

C. No. This is more in line with what the author believes than with what Marcuse believes.

D. No. While Marcuse does think that advertising can be a tool of oppression, there is no discussion of totalitarian political regimes.

E. No. Marcuse criticizes false needs, not real needs.

20. **E** Extract
Infer

The question is asking what "forces of persuasion" refers to. The correct answer will be best supported by evidence in the third paragraph, which discusses separating real needs from those false needs created by the manipulation of advertisers.

A. No. The passage does not claim that advertisers' claims are intentionally dishonest.

B. No. The passage discusses that these forces might inform our instinctive judgments, not that they are them.

C. No. The passage says that these forces are prevalent in society, but that does not mean they are exerted by society.

D. No. There is no claim that the state is involved in indoctrination.

E. Yes. This accurately captures the author's discussion of Marcusian theory in the second and third paragraphs.

21. **A** Big Picture

Use your Bottom Line of the passage to help you to evaluate the choices. The correct answer will summarize the author's argument.

A. Yes. This accurately captures that the author disagrees with Marcuse but does not take a position on whether advertising is actually harmful.

B. No. The author does not agree that Marcusian claims are justified.

C. No. This is outside the scope of the passage. The author does not discuss the perception of human nature held by corporate leaders.

D. No. The author does not claim that advertising has numerous social benefits. There is only a minor mention that some advertising can be entertaining.

E. No. The author does not argue that advertisers exert economic power.

Questions 22–27

Passage A

The first paragraph introduces the principles of justice in acquisition and justice in transfer with respect to property. The second paragraph explains these principles. The third paragraph discusses the principle of rectification that should apply when situations don't conform to the previous two principles. The Bottom Line of passage A is that these three principles are fundamental to a theory of justice regarding property. The overall tone of the passage is neutral.

Passage B

The first paragraph introduces the Indian Nonintercourse Act as a way for Native Americans to hold onto their lands. The second paragraph discusses how an argument could be made that land that was wrongfully taken from Native Americans should be returned. The Bottom Line of passage B is that one might argue that land should be returned to Native Americans to the degree feasible in order to right the original wrong. The overall tone of the passage is neutral. Here's the relationship between the passages: Passage A outlines general principles, while passage B discusses a specific case involving those principles.

22. **B** **Big Picture**

The correct answer will reflect the Bottom Line of each passage.

A. No. While the principle of rectification in passage A arguably offers a solution to a moral problem, passage B does not criticize a solution.

B. Yes. This accurately describes the general nature of passage A and the specific application in passage B.

C. No. The description of passage A is too narrow—it does not reflect the principle of rectification— and passage B does not claim that the Native American case is ideal.

D. No. Passage A describes principles but does not argue for them, and passage B does not discuss any assumptions.

E. No. Passage A describes principles but does not argue for them, and passage B does not discuss a counterexample.

23. **A** **Extract Fact**

The correct answer will be directly supported by evidence in the passage.

A. Yes. Transfer of property is mentioned in lines 6–8 in passage A and in lines 37–39 of passage B.

B. No. This is discussed in passage B, but not in passage A. Passage A discusses only principles.

C. No. This is discussed in passage A, but not in passage B.

D. No. This is discussed at the end of passage B, but not in passage A.

E. No. This is discussed in passage B, but not in passage A.

24. **D** **Big Picture**

The question asks for the relationship between the two passages. The correct answer will reflect that passage A outlines general principles and the second paragraph of passage B discusses remedying previous illicit taking of land.

A. No. Passage B involves specific details, and passage A involves general principles.

B. No. Passage A does not make an argument; it merely outlines a principle.

C. No. Both passages share the same subject matter—justice with respect to land ownership.

D. Yes. This accurately describes the relationship between the passages. The principle of rectification in passage A supports passage B's claim about what should happen with the land.

E. No. Passage B is consistent with passage A.

25. **E** **RC Reasoning**

The question is asking for an analogous relationship to that of passage A and passage B, specifically that passage A outlines general principles and passage B discusses a specific case involving those principles.

A. No. These two documents disagree with one another.

B. No. These two documents disagree with one another, and the first document is too specific.

C. No. These two documents are on different topics.

D. No. These two documents disagree with one another, and the first document is too specific.

E. Yes. The first document outlines general ideas, and the second document applies those ideas to a specific project.

26. **D** **Extract Infer**

The question is asking for the point of view of passage A with respect to the Indian Nonintercourse Act. Since the Act is in line with the principle of justice in transfer outlined in passage A, passage A would characterize the act positively.

A. No. The purpose of the Act is to protect Native American land.

B. No. The purpose of the Act is to remedy the results of past laws.

C. No. The Act is in line with the principle of justice in transfer, not acquisition.

D. Yes. This accurately captures the function of the Act.

E. No. The Act is in line with the principle of justice in transfer, not rectification.

27. **A** **Big Picture**

The question is asking about the relationship between the two passages. The correct answer will reflect that passage A outlines general principles and the second paragraph of passage B discusses remedying previous illicit taking of land. Both passages are neutral in tone.

A. Yes. This answer accurately describes the purpose of each passage.

B. No. Passage A does not discuss competing views.

C. No. Passage A does not make a policy recommendation.

D. No. Passage A does not make an argument.

E. No. Passage A does not make an argument.

Section 2: Arguments 1

1. **C** — Necessary Assumption

This argument makes the claim that the city hired a contractor with 60 percent unqualified technicians. This is based upon the fact that only 40 percent of the technicians employed have a certification from the Heating Technicians Association. There is a language shift between having a certification and being unqualified. The credited response will link the premise to the conclusion explicitly.

A. No. The amount technicians are paid is irrelevant to the claim that some are unqualified.

B. No. Other contractors are not at issue in this argument, so this is irrelevant.

C. Yes. This answer choice correctly links a lack of certification to being unqualified.

D. No. The original installers of the heating systems are not at issue here. This is irrelevant.

E. No. The contractor having ties to the city is not required for the employees to be unqualified. This is irrelevant.

2. **E** — Resolve/Explain

This argument notes a discrepancy in the way that people respond in different situations. In the argument, people tend to respond to a "Thank you" from a salesperson with another "Thank you," while they respond with "you're welcome" to thanks from a friend. The credited response will build a bridge between these two responses by establishing a situation for both responses to occur.

A. No. This is too one-sided and doesn't explain the difference.

B. No. This says only that customers are free to respond in any form, but it does not explain why people respond differently.

C. No. The focus of the argument is on what customers, not salespeople, say.

D. No. Just because their response is dictated by habit does not explain why people have different responses for two different situations.

E. Yes. This provides a reason why a person might say "Thank you" in a sales situation, but not in a favor situation.

3. **A** Flaw

This argument claims that selling movie rights to popular video games is rarely a good idea. This is based upon an example of a video game, *Nostroma*, being sold and disliked by both critics and the public. There is some additional information given that future sequels of the game sold poorly. There are two problems with this claim: causal and survey/sample. The author provides no causal connection between the movie being disliked and the future low sales. Also, the broad claim "rarely a good idea" is supported with only this single example, which may not be representative. The credited response will identify one of these flaws.

A. Yes. This answer choice describes a sampling flaw by stating that the claim is based upon only one example.

B. No. The claim is not focused on who disliked the game.

C. No. This is not circular reasoning.

D. No. This does not match the argument since the video game was popular while the movie was disliked.

E. No. This is not a necessary as sufficient factor flaw.

4. **D** Principle Match

This principle is an if…then statement that can be diagrammed. If the consultant has business interests with the company, then the executive is likely to be overcompensated. The contrapositive is as follows: If the executive is not likely to be overcompensated, then the consultant does not have business interests at the company. The credited response will describe a situation that matches this conditional statement.

A. No. The principle cannot be applied to this answer since there is no mention of a consultant.

B. No. The principle cannot be applied to this answer since there is no mention of a consultant.

C. No. The principle cannot be applied to this answer since it cannot be determined what might occur if a company does not hire a consultant.

D. Yes. This answer choice correctly matches the conditional since it claims the executive is likely overpaid since the firm used a consultant who has many other contracts with the company.

E. No. This is too strongly worded. The principle is not sufficient to guarantee the executive is not overpaid; it can suggest only that the executive is not likely to be overpaid.

5. **D** Flaw

This argument makes the claim that Lemaître's theory must be considered inadequate. The argument describes Lemaître's theory and establishes that its predictions are valid. However, it then introduces an alternative theory that makes the same prediction. The flaw in the argument is that the writer provides no evidence against Lemaître's theory other than the existence of the alternative. The credited response will point out some form of a lack of evidence for the conclusion.

A. No. This answer choice describes an appeal to authority, which is not the flaw in the argument.

B. No. This answer choice describes equivocation, which is not the flaw in the argument.

C. No. This answer choice describes a causal flaw, which is not the flaw in the argument.

D. Yes. This answer choice points out that the existence of one theory with correct predictions cannot be used as evidence against the validity of another theory with the same correct predictions.

E. No. This argument does not establish an either/or situation with the two theories since the author uses the new theory as evidence against the old one.

6. **D** Principle Strengthen

This argument claims that the criticism of a popular comedy for being unrealistic is misguided. This is based upon the premise that the stylized characters are not problematic for a comedy since the result is funny, which is what matters. The credited response will describe a general rule that forces the conclusion to be true.

A. No. This answer choice would actually weaken the argument since the premises state that the characters were too stylized.

B. No. This answer choice is not relevant to the conclusion. The issue is not the popularity of the film but whether the film was successful as a comedy.

C. No. This answer choice cannot be applied to the conclusion. The fact that film comedies find their humor in stylistic portrayals does not make the criticism misguided.

D. Yes. This answer choice makes the criticism misguided by establishing that since the stylized characters made the film funny, and since the film is a comedy, the film has been successful.

E. No. The specific genre of film is not at issue here. This answer choice is irrelevant.

7. **C** Parallel Flaw

This argument proceeds by noting that Party X has been accused of illegal actions by Party Y. The argument then concludes that these accusations are ill-founded based upon the fact that three years ago Party Y itself was involved in a scandal. The flaw here is an appeals and attacks flaw. The argument attacks the Party Y itself without addressing the specific argument against Party X. The credited response must match an attack flaw above all other considerations. The credited response should also match the other pieces and tone of the original argument.

A. No. This argument does not make an attack against the accusing party.

B. No. This argument makes an attack on the plaintiff; however, the conclusion is focused upon the plaintiff being hypocritical rather than the argument being unfounded. Therefore, this answer choice is not fully parallel with the original.

C. Yes. This argument concludes that the plaintiff's accusations are ill founded since the plaintiff recently did the same thing that the defendant had done.

D. No. The premise in support of the accusations being ill-founded does not attack the plaintiff.

E. No. This argument describes an attack flaw without actually making one.

73

8. **B** Necessary Assumption

This argument claims that eyes are adapted only to an animal's needs rather than to some abstract sense of how a good eye should be designed. This is based upon the fact that box jellyfish have eyes capable of forming sharp images with fine detail; however, their retinas are too far forward, causing their vision to be blurry and lacking fine detail. There is a language shift from the function of the box jellyfish's eyes and the notions of adaptation to need. The credited response will build a bridge from the premises to the conclusion.

A. No. Whether this is true only of the box jellyfish is irrelevant to the conclusion that adaptations are based only upon need.

B. Yes. This answer choice links the notion of need to the specific adaptations found in the box jellyfish eye. When negated, this answer would destroy the conclusion.

C. No. This answer choice would undermine the conclusion if anything by suggesting that the needs of the jellyfish are not met by its adaptations.

D. No. The origin of current box jellyfish is irrelevant to the claim about adaptations occurring based upon an animal's needs.

E. No. This answer choice does not explicitly link this method of identifying prey to a need of the jellyfish, so this answer choice is irrelevant to the conclusion.

9. **C** Weaken

This argument claims that there are grounds for disputing claims made by tobacco companies that advertising has no causal impact on smoking. This is based upon research that has shown that there has been a significant reduction in smoking in countries that have also imposed restrictions on advertising. This argument assumes the correlation between the advertising restrictions and the reduction of smoking is actually a causal relationship. The credited response will weaken the causal flaw in some way.

A. No. This answer choice does not weaken the claim that advertising has a significant effect on smoking since it focuses only on existing smokers. The argument specifically mentions first-time smokers.

B. No. How stringent the restrictions are in different media does not weaken the claim that advertisement restrictions cause a reduction in smoking.

C. Yes. This answer choice weakens the conclusion by introducing an alternative cause for both the reduction in smoking and for the advertising restrictions.

D. No. This answer choice is irrelevant since it does not deal with smoking advertising.

E. No. This answer choice is irrelevant. The argument is concerned about those that advertising affects.

10. **A** Sufficient Assumption

This argument makes the claim that Brecht's plays are not genuinely successful dramas. This is predicated upon the fact that the roles in these plays are so incongruous that audiences and actors find it difficult to discern the characters' personalities. The argument then states that for a play to be successful, audiences must care what happens to some of its characters. The gap in this argument is between the

inability to discern personalities of characters and caring about those characters. The credited response will provide an answer that makes the reasoning solid and forces the conclusion to be valid.

A. Yes. This answer choice establishes a link between discerning a character's personality and caring for that character.

B. No. What determines a character's personality is not relevant to the claim that the plays are not successful.

C. No. While this answer choice does establish that a lack of caring about a character is directly related to the lack of success of a play, this answer choice does not connect these ideas to Brecht's plays specifically. Therefore, this answer choice is not sufficient to force the conclusion.

D. No. This answer choice essentially rephrases the known premises as an if...then statement. However, the premises already state that both actors and the audience find it difficult to discern the motives. Linking these two things is not sufficient to force the conclusion.

E. No. This is irrelevant since the claim is about Brecht's plays being unsuccessful.

11. **B** Main Point

This argument claims that there would be no problem in accepting the mayor's proposal to accept a gift of lights despite fears that the company wants to influence the city. This conclusion is supported by a speculation on a single ulterior motive. The argument claims that favoritism is not an issue with the gift due to a competitive-bidding procedure. The credited response will paraphrase the conclusion and match it in both tone and scope.

A. No. This answer choice is too strongly worded to match the conclusion. The argument states that there is no problem with accepting the lights, not that the fear itself is unfounded.

B. Yes. This answer choice correctly paraphrases the conclusion.

C. No. This answer choice is the opposite of what the argument is claiming.

D. No. This is a premise in support of the claim that accepting the lights is not problematic.

E. No. This is a premise in support of the claim that accepting the lights is not problematic.

12. **A** Sufficient Assumption

This argument claims that the chairperson should not have released a report to the public. This is based upon the fact that the chairperson did not consult any other commission members before releasing it. There is a language shift here between not consulting with other members and not releasing the report. The credited response will link these two ideas and make it clear that the chairperson should not have released the report.

A. Yes. This answer choice makes the consent of a majority of the commission members a prerequisite for the report's release. Since this prerequisite was not met according to the premise, then the release of the report could not have been permissible.

B. No. This answer choice moves in the wrong direction. The credited response should make it wrong for the chairperson to release the report.

C. No. The issue at hand is not whether the commissioner was justified, but whether the report should have been released at all.

D. No. The issue at hand is not whether the commissioner was justified, but whether the report should have been released at all.

E. No. This answer choice is not strong enough to force the conclusion. Just because at least one member was against the report's release does not mean that it was wrong to do so.

13. **B** | Flaw

This argument concludes that putting more people into prison cannot help to reduce crime. This is based upon a survey that shows that there has been no significant reduction in the crime rate in the last 20 years, despite increases both in the population and in the amount spent on prisons. There are two flaws in this argument. The first is a survey/sample flaw in which relevant information might be left out. The next flaw is a causal flaw in which the author assumes that because there has not been a decrease, then there is no link at all between the current incarceration rate and the crime rate. The credited response will identify one of these commonly occurring flaws.

A. No. This is not a flaw that occurs in the argument. There is no causal link assumed between the population and the reported statistics.

B. Yes. This answer choice points out that the author ignores the fact that the current imprisonment rate might be having some effect on crime.

C. No. This is a premise explicitly stated in the argument.

D. No. The reformer does not make any alternative suggestion. Instead, the reformer merely concludes that imprisonment cannot help reduce crime.

E. No. This flaw is not found in the argument.

14. **E** | Reasoning

Inez makes the claim that we cannot afford not to invest in space exploration. She bases her claim on the premise that space programs lead to many technological advancements with everyday applications, making the cost of a space program affordable. Winona rebuts this argument by arguing that technology should be funded directly, noting that it is absurd to justify an expenditure in space programs for a side effect of that program. The credited response will match a paraphrase of how Winona addresses Inez's argument.

A. No. Winona does not dispute Inez's claim that space exploration leads to technological development.

B. No. Winona does not suggest that there is direct evidence against the space program.

C. No. Winona does not point out a contradiction in Inez's premises.

D. No. Winona does not mention that technological innovations are too expensive.

E. Yes. Winona points out that the same goal Inez desires can be reached more directly than through the space program.

15. **B** | Flaw

The marketing consultant concludes that the marketing campaign is ill-conceived. This argument is based upon the fact that the consultant predicted that this campaign would be unpopular and ineffective. The consultant then points out that this season's sales figures are down, especially for LRG's new products. The flaw in the argument confuses the correlation of these two events with a causal relationship. The credited response will point out some form of causal flaw or will mention an alternative causal factor that has been ignored or overlooked.

A. No. The claim is that the competitor's campaign was ill-conceived, not whether sales would have been even lower. This is not the flaw in the argument.

B. Yes. This answer choice identifies that the downturn in sales could have been driven by an alternative economic cause rather than the unpopular advertisement campaign.

C. No. The author does not assume this.

D. No. The conclusion is on the ill-conceived advertising campaign, not on the sales of existing products. This answer choice is irrelevant.

E. No. The marketing consultant does not make a necessary as sufficient flaw.

16. **A** Reasoning

This argument concludes that it would be better to award the top prize in architecture to the best building rather than to the best argument. This claim is based upon an analogous comparison with the movie industry by arguing that buildings, like movies, are collaborative efforts and not like scientific discoveries. The argument also notes that the Pritzker Prize is currently analogous to the Nobel Prize. The credited response will identify the pattern of reasoning in this argument.

A. Yes. This answer choice correctly identifies the analogy that occurs in the argument between the movie industry practice and what the writer feels should occur with the architecture prize.

B. No. The distinction made in the argument between science and movies is not used to attribute value. This is not in the argument.

C. No. This answer does not match the conclusion in the argument. The argument does not try to apply the criticism of the movie industry to those of the architecture prize.

D. No. The argument does note that the science industry is disanalogous to the architecture industry, but the argument does not try to refute claims related to these two fields.

E. No. This answer does not match the argument. The argument does not focus on what is inappropriate but on what is appropriate.

17. **B** Parallel

This argument opens with a conditional statement that if Suarez is not the most qualified for sheriff, then Anderson is. The argument concludes that if the most qualified candidate is elected and if that is not Suarez, then it will be Anderson. This argument can be abstracted as Premise: ~A most → B most; Conclusion: If most chosen and ~A chosen → B chosen. The credited response will match this pattern in tone, scope, and direction.

A. No. The premise does not align because it does not set up Caldwell as only one of two lowest bidders.

B. Yes. The premise establishes either Ramsey or Dillon as the lowest bidder. Premise: ~A lowest → B lowest. The conclusion states if the conclusion goes to the lowest and it is not Dillon, it will be Ramsey. Conclusion: If lowest chosen and ~A chosen → B chosen.

C. No. This argument is not parallel in tone since it does not establish either Kapshaw or Johnson as being the lowest or highest bidders.

D. No. This argument does match the direction of the original argument. The original argument was who would receive the contract, not who would not.

E. No. This conclusion does not align with the original argument. This conclusion does not contain the sufficient condition "if awarded to the lowest."

18. **E**   Flaw

This argument opens by summarizing an art historian's position that fifteenth-century painters had a greater mastery of painting than did those of the sixteenth century since their paintings were more planimetric. The critic concludes that this is wrong and supports this claim with the premise that the degree to which a painting is planimetric is not relevant to mastery. This is a disagreement flaw in which the critic assumes that the new evidence is sufficient to disprove the old position. Specifically, this is an absence of evidence argument. The critic assumes because some of the support for the art historian's claim is not valid, then the entire argument is invalid. The credited response will describe a common flaw that is found in the argument.

A. No. This answer choice describes an ad *hominem* attack. This flaw is not in the argument.

B. No. This answer choice describes equivocation. This flaw is not in the argument.

C. No. This answer choice describes a necessary as sufficient flaw. This flaw is not in the argument.

D. No. The conclusion that the art historian is wrong is based upon a single claim.

E. Yes. This answer choice describes an absence of evidence flaw.

19. **B**   Weaken

This argument concludes that a carved flint object found in a Stone Age tomb in Ireland must be the head of a speaking staff. This is based upon the premises that it is too small to be a warrior's mace, and because the shape is that of a head with an open mouth speaking. Finally, the premises describe a speaking staff as a communal object. This argument is predicated upon several assumptions. First, the author assumes that because the object seems analogous to a talking head, it must belong to a speaking staff. Additionally, the author assumes that because it is too small to be a mace, it must be a speaking staff without providing clear justification for this. The credited response will weaken this claim by either suggesting an alternative detail or by providing another consideration that would cast doubt on the claim.

A. No. A lack of weapons in the tomb has no bearing on what this object is. This is irrelevant to the conclusion.

B. Yes. This answer choice presents an alternative consideration. If communal objects were passed from one generation to the next, it casts doubt on the claim that it is such an object since it was found in a tomb.

C. No. The level of artistry in the object is not relevant to the object's function.

D. No. If anything, this answer choice would lend support to the claim that it is a speaking staff.

E. No. The symbolism inherent in a speaking staff is not relevant to the interpretation of the object from the tomb.

20. **E** Necessary Assumption

This argument claims that farmers will need to abandon the use of chemical fertilizers in order to improve the soil structure. This conclusion is based upon the premises that due to fertilizer use, farmers have abandoned the planting of "green-manure" crops to improve soil. This in turn has hurt the soil structure in the region. There is a language shift in the conclusion that farmers must "abandon" the use of fertilizers. The credited response will either build a bridge from the premises to the conclusion or will rule out an alternative possibility.

A. No. This answer choice goes in the wrong direction. This is sufficient, but not necessary, for the conclusion to be true.

B. No. The effect of fertilizers on green-manure crops is not something assumed by the argument.

C. No. This answer choice is irrelevant to the conclusion that farmers need to abandon fertilizer use.

D. No. This answer choice is not relevant to the claim that they need to abandon fertilizer use in order to improve soil structure.

E. Yes. The answer choice establishes that abandoning chemical fertilizers is a necessary factor of growing green-manure crops.

21. **E** Inference

This argument contains two quantity statements. First, most of the students in Spanish 101 attended every class last semester. Second, each student who received a grade lower than a B minus missed at least one class. The credited response will be the answer choice that must be true based on the statements in the argument. Specifically, the quantity statements must be supported.

A. No. There is not enough information in the argument to support a statement about students who scored an A minus.

B. No. This statement goes in the wrong direction. The final sentence can be diagrammed as follows: "if <B minus → miss at least one." This answer is a bad contrapositive.

C. No. This information is unsupported because the argument does not stipulate how many students made a B minus exactly.

D. No. This is unsupported. There is nothing in the argument that will support a statement about students who miss a class and who scored higher than a B minus.

E. Yes. This is the valid contrapositive of the final statement: "if <B minus → miss at least one" becomes "if miss none → not lower than a B minus (B minus or higher)."

22. **A** Strengthen

This argument claims that each of the sockeye salmon populations has adapted genetically to its distinct habitat. This is based upon the fact that the populations split into two non-interbreeding groups that now differ genetically. This argument is predicated upon a causal assumption that the sole cause of the different genes is due to adaptation to the environment. The credited response either will introduce some new evidence in support of this causal link or will rule out an alternative possible cause.

A. Yes. This answer choice rules out an alternative possibility for the different genes by stating that neither population has interbred with the native salmon population.

B. No. This answer choice is irrelevant to the conclusion, which is about how the current salmon population has different genes.

C. No. This answer choice is irrelevant to the conclusion. Where salmon spend their time does not affect the conclusion since a premise states that the two populations do not interbreed.

D. No. The similarity of one of the current groups to the originally introduced salmon does not strengthen the claim that they have adapted. This is irrelevant.

E. No. The size of the current salmon population is not relevant to the claim that the two salmon populations have genetically adapted.

23. **C** Inference

This argument states that if business people invest in modern industries that have not been pursued in a country, then that country can substantially increase its economic growth. However, the argument notes that there is high risk to the endeavor and little incentive for business people to take the risk. The credited response will be the answer choice that is most strongly supported by the facts. Unsupported information should be crossed off.

A. No. This answer choice is an unsupported prediction. There is not enough information in the argument to make a statement about what will happen after the first modern industry has been started.

B. No. This is an unsupported comparison. There is not enough information to support a statement about which industries have the most competition.

C. Yes. This answer choice is supported. The argument states that economic growth is the result of investment by businesspeople but there is little incentive for them to do so. This statement suggests that if incentives are increased, then the country will increase the chance of the first statement occurring.

D. No. This is too strongly worded to be supported. This statement makes investment in modern industries a requirement for economic growth rather than being a factor sufficient to cause growth.

E. No. This is an unsupported comparison. There is not enough information to support a statement about when industries have little risk.

24. **D** Resolve/ Explain

On the one hand, almost all of a city's concertgoers were dissatisfied with the local hall and wanted wider seats and better acoustics. However, even though they were told that it was not feasible to modify the existing hall, most were opposed to the idea of tearing it down and replacing it with a new one. The credited response will provide a reason why concertgoers do not want the hall torn down despite their dissatisfaction with it.

A. No. This answer choice does not resolve the problem because it does not explain why the concertgoers would be against the hall being torn down.

B. No. The survey deals with concertgoers, not with residents in the vicinity of the hall.

C. No. The benefits to the city do not explain why the concertgoers were against the hall being torn down. If anything, this answer choice would make the situation worse.

D. Yes. This publicized plan suggests a reason that concertgoers would not want the hall to be torn down despite their dissatisfaction with it. This plan would suggest a valid alternative use that the concertgoers might support in lieu of tearing down the building.

E. No. This answer choice does not explain why the concertgoers were against the hall being torn down. If anything, this answer choice would make the situation worse.

25. C **Main Point**

This argument states several premises and asks for the ultimate conclusion to be identified in the answer choices. This argument states that without a book, a citation would not be accurate, which in turn is necessary for the inclusion of a quotation. However, the paper will be much better with the quotation. The credited response will properly conclude this argument and will match the tone and scope of the premises.

A. No. This violates the premise that the student will be unable to include the quotation without the accurate citation.

B. No. The final sentence states that the research paper will be completed. This violates a premise.

C. Yes. This answer choice sufficiently concludes the argument. The paper would be better with the quotation; however, without the book the quotation cannot be included. This is the credited response.

D. No. This violates the premise that the student cannot include the quotation without an accurate citation.

A. No. This violates the premise that the student will produce a completed paper.

Section 3: Games

Questions 1–7

This is a 1D ordering game with all range clues, so it is a ranking game. The inventory consists of five songs—R, S, T, V, and W—with 1-to-1 correspondence and no wildcards.

Clue 1: S—V

Clue 2: T—R & S OR R & S—T

Clue 3: W—R & T OR R & T—W

Deductions: From clue 1 you know that S cannot be last and V cannot be first. Put this information straight into your diagram. Since clue 2 and clue 3 have two scenarios each, there will be multiple possible arrangements.

Here's the diagram.

R, S, T, V, W

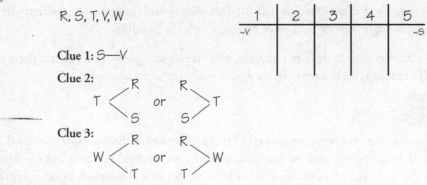

Clue 1: S—V

Clue 2:

Clue 3:

73

1. **B** Grab-a-Rule

A. No. This violates clue 2 because T is between R and S.

B. Yes. This choice does not violate any of the clues.

C. No. This violates clue 3 because W is between R and T.

D. No. This violates clue 1 because V is before S.

E. No. This violates clue 2 because T is between S and R.

2. **C** Specific

Make a new line in your diagram and add the new information. If S is fourth, then V is fifth (clue 1). S is also in clue 2. Since T cannot be after S, then T must be before S and before R. That means that (C) is the credited response.

3. **B** Specific

Make a new line in your diagram and add the new information. Combining clues 2 and 3: R must come before both T and W. Write deductions into the diagram. S must have T, W, and V after it, so it cannot be 3, 4, or 5. This means S must be second. T cannot be first, second, or last, so it must be either third or fourth. V cannot be first or second, so it can be third, fourth, or fifth. W cannot be first, second or third, so it must be either fourth or fifth. You are looking for what could be true, so eliminate anything that must be false.

A. No. T cannot be second because both R and S must come before T.

B. Yes. V could be third, which would make T fourth and W fifth. This does not violate any clues.

C. No. W cannot be third because R, S, and T must all come before W.

D. No. S cannot be fourth because T, W, and V must all come after S.

E. No. T cannot be last because W must come after T.

4. **E** Specific

Make deductions into the diagram. If T is second, then W must be first. R cannot be first or second, so it could be third, fourth, or fifth. S cannot be first, second, or fifth, so it must be either third or fourth. V cannot be first, second, or third, so it must be either fourth or fifth.

A. No. S cannot be first because it must come after T.

B. No. R cannot be first because it must come after T.

C. No. V cannot be third because W, T, and S must all come before it.

D. No. W cannot be fourth because it must come before T.

E. Yes. R can be last. The line-up would be W, T, S, V, R. This does not violate any clues.

5. **E** General

Use the deductions, prior work, and trying the answers to determine which answer choice could be the first two pieces, in order.

A. No. This would cause V to be before S, which violates clue 1.

B. No. This violates clues 2 and 3 because it would force T to be between R and S and force W to be between R and T.

C. No. This violates clue 2 by forcing T to be between S and R.

D. No. This violates clue 3 by forcing W to be between T and R.

E. Yes. This does not violate any rules and can be seen in the setup for question 7.

6. **D** Specific

Make a new line in your diagram and add the new information. If V is second, then S has to be first (clue 1). This will force R to be before T. W can be either before R and T or after R and T. This means there are only two possible orders.

A. No. S must be first, not W (clue 1).

B. No. S must be first (clue 1).

C. No. If T is third, then it is between S and R, which violates clue 2.

D. Yes. This is the first order in the diagram above.

E. No. This would force T to be between S and R, which violates clue 2.

7. **A** Specific

Make deductions into the diagram; then look for something that cannot be true in either scenario. The first deduction, with T before R and S, was used in question 4, so you don't need to write it out again. The second deduction, with T after R and S, has not been used in a prior question, so you need to work it out. R cannot be first or last, so it could be second, third, or fourth. T cannot be first, second, or third, so it must be either fourth or fifth. S cannot be first, fourth, or fifth, so it must be either second or third. V cannot be first or second, but it could be third, fourth, or fifth.

A. Yes. T cannot be third in either scenario described above.

B. No. V could be third in the second scenario described above.

C. No. S could be fourth in the first scenario described above and in question 4.

D. No. V could be fourth in the first scenario described above and in question 4.

E. No. T could be fifth in the second scenario described above.

Questions 8–13

This is a 2D order game. There are five speakers—L, M, X, Y, and Z. Each speaker gives one speech at either 1 P.M. or 2 P.M. in either the Gold Room or the Rose Room. One person will give a speech at 3 P.M. Since order matters, put the times across the top of the diagram and the rooms on the side. This will give you six spaces for five inventory elements—one space at 3 o'clock is not used. There is a mix of range and conditional clues. There are no wildcards.

Clue 1: M—L same room

Clue 2: Z—X & Y; Z & X—Y; OR Z & Y—Y

Clue 3: LG → XR and ZR

XG or ZG → LR

Since M must be before L, note that M cannot be at 3 P.M. and L cannot be at 1 P.M. Also, since Z must always be before X or Y or both, note that it, too, cannot be at 3 P.M. Since M and L must always be in the same room, that means some combination of at least two of X, Y, and Z must be in the other room (clues 1 and 3). If all three are in the same room, then Z must be at 1 P.M. (rule 2). If Z is in the room with one other, then it must still be at 1 P.M. (rule 1), and if X or Y is at 1 P.M., then Z must still be at 1 P.M.

Here's the diagram.

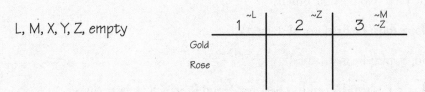

Clue 1: M—L same room

Clue 2:

Z⟨X over Y⟩ or ⟨Z over X⟩Y or ⟨Z over Y⟩X

Clue 3: LG → XR and ZR
XG or ZG → LR

8. A Grab-a-Rule

   A. Yes. This arrangement does not violate any clues.

   B. No. This violates clue 2 since X is earlier than Z.

   C. No. This violates clue 3 since L and X are in the same room.

   D. No. This violates clue 1 because L is earlier than M.

   E. No. This violates clue 1 because L and M are not in the same room.

9. B General

Use the deductions, prior work, and trying the answers to determine which pair of speeches cannot happen at the same time (1 P.M. or 2 P.M.).

   A. No. Draw this one out. Both L and Y could be at 2 P.M. if M and Z are at 1 P.M. and X is at 3 P.M.

   B. Yes. Since M must always be before L, then L can never be at 1 P.M. (clue 1), and since Z must always be at 1 P.M. (deduction), then L and Z can never be at the same time.

   C. No. Both M and X could be at 2 P.M. as seen in question 12.

   D. No. Both X and Y could be at 2 P.M. as seen in question 11.

   E. No. Both Y and Z could be at 1 P.M. as seen in question 12.

10. A Specific

Make a new line in your diagram and fill in the information given. If X is at 3 P.M., it could be either with M and L or with Y and Z. Either way, M and Z are at 1 P.M. and Y and L are at 2 P.M. You are looking for what must be false, so eliminate anything that can be true.

   A. Yes. L cannot be in the same room with Y since L must also be with M, which would mean X would have to be at 2 P.M. in the same room with Z.

   B. No. This could be true. See the description above.

   C. No. This could be true. See the description above.

   D. No. This could be true. See the description above.

   E. No. This could be true. See the description above.

11. C General

This is a partial Grab-a-Rule. The answers do not involve all the inventory in all the spaces, but you may still be able to eliminate some of the answers that directly violate a rule. Then try any remaining answers and eliminate ones that don't work.

   A. No. This answer violates clue 1 because L is before M.

   B. No. This rule violates clue 1 because it includes M but not L.

C. Yes. This does not violate any clues. If M, Y, and L are in G in that order, then Z and X are in R at 1 P.M. and 2 P.M. respectively.

D. No. This violates clue 2 since Y is before Z.

E. No. This violates clue 3 since Z is listed with M and L in G.

12. **C**   Specific

Make a new line in your diagram and fill in the information given. If Y is at 1 P.M. and Z must also be at 1 P.M., then Y must be with M and L, which will be at 2 P.M. and 3 P.M., respectively; therefore, Z and X must be in the other room at 1 P.M. and 2 P.M., respectively.

A. No. L must be at 3 P.M. in both scenarios.

B. No. L must be at 3 P.M. in both scenarios.

C. Yes. M is at 2 P.M. regardless of which room M is in.

D. No. X must be at 2 P.M., not 3 P.M.

E. No. X must be at 2 P.M., not 1 P.M.

13. **E**   Complex

This is a complex question that asks for a parallel clue, and it can be very time consuming. Try the answer choices until you find one that gives you the same deductions you got at the beginning of the game, but without the second clue. First, take stock of your remaining clues and deductions: Clues 1 and 3 are still in effect, so all you are missing is something that will force X and Y to not be before Z.

A. No. Forcing L to be at 3 P.M. does nothing to the relationship between X, Y, and Z.

B. No. This would mean that Z could never be at 3 P.M., but it has no impact on the relationship between X, Y, and Z.

C. No. This is on the right track but doesn't go far enough. If one of X or Y must be after Z, one of them could still be before Z.

D. No. This does nothing to force Z ahead of X and Y. One of them could still be before Z.

E. Yes. This is exactly what you deduced at the beginning of the game. If Z must be at 1 P.M., then there is no way for either X or Z to be before it.

Questions 14–18

This is a group game with fixed assignment. The inventory consists of five buildings—F, G, I, M and S—which are each assigned to one of three families—T, W, and Y. Every family owns at least one building and the clues are a mix of spatial, anti-blocks, and conditional clues. There is one wildcard.

Clue 1: W > Y

Clue 2: ~FI & ~FM

Clue 3: ~St → Iy
      ~Iy → St

Deductions: Since W has more buildings than Y, then W must have at least two buildings, and Y can have only one building. This now accounts for four out of the five buildings. The last building can belong either to T, meaning T = 2, W = 2, and Y = 1, or to W, meaning T = 1, W = 3, and Y = 1. Next, combine this information with clues 2 and 3 to limit the possible scenarios. Since Y can own only one building, if it's I, then F and M must be split up between T and W. S can be in W, meaning that G can be in either T or W, or S can be in T, forcing G to be in W.

If S is the only building in T, then there must be three buildings in W. Since F and M cannot be in the same group and F and I cannot be in the same group (clue 2), then M, G, and I must be in W and F must be in Y. This is the only way to keep F away from both I and M.

If S and one other building are in T, then there will be two buildings in W. There are many possible arrangements in this scenario.

If S is in T and I is in Y, then F and M still need to be split between T and W, and G will have to be in W in order for W to have more buildings than Y (clue 1).

Here's the diagram.

F, G, I, M, S

	T	W	Y
(1)	__ __	__ __	__
(2)	__	__ __ __	__

Clue 1: W > Y

Clue 2: F̸I̸ F̸M̸

Clue 3: S ≠ T → I ≠ Y
        I ≠ Y → S ≠ T

14. **A** Grab-a-Rule

    A.   Yes this does not violate any clues.

    B.   No. This violates clue 3 because S was not in T and I was not in Y.

    C.   No. This violates clue 2 because F is with M.

    D.   No. This violates clue 1 since there are fewer buildings in W than in Y.

    E.   No. This violates clue 1 since there are the same number of buildings in W and Y.

15. **D** General

    Use the deductions, prior work, and trying the answers to determine which answer choice contains two buildings that CANNOT be together in T.

    A.   No. If F and G are in T, then I must be in Y (clue 3). This leaves M and S together in W, which is consistent with the first scenario in the diagram above.

    B.   No. If G and M are in T, then I must be in Y (clue 3). This leaves F and S together in W, which is consistent with the first scenario in the diagram above.

C. No. If S and G are in T, then I must be in W (if it's in Y, it would force F and M to be together in W, which violates clue 2). So, M and I must be in W and F must be in Y.

D. Yes. If I and M are in T, there is no way to fulfill the requirement of clue 3. There is no room to add S to T, and I can't be in Y if it's in T.

E. No. If I and S are in T, then I is not in Y, which means that M and F have to be split between W and Y, leaving G to be in W.

16. **D** Specific

Make a new line in your diagram and fill in the information given. If M is in Y, then S must be in T (clue 3). You now have to find places for F, I, and G. F and I cannot be in the same group (clue 2), so one of them must be in T and the other in W. Since W must have more spaces than Y, that means G must be in W. This makes (D) the credited response.

17. **B** Specific

Make a new line in your diagram and fill in the information given. If G and I are in the same group, then they cannot be in Y, which has only one space. This will force S into T (clue 3) and G and I into W since T cannot have three spaces. F and M are unaccounted for, but they cannot be in the same group. So one of F/M is in Y. The other of F/M could be in W (M in W and F in Y) or in T. Since everything is locked in place except for F and M, look for an answer that involves one of these buildings. This makes (B) the credited response.

18. **E** Specific

Make a new line in your diagram and fill in the information given. If T has one space, then W has three. The question asks for a list of buildings that could each be in T alone. Clue 3 means that S must be on that list, so eliminate (A), (B), and (D). Choice (C) does not work because if I is not in Y, then S must be in T (clue 3). I cannot be the only building in T because I could not be in Y and S could not be in T. Eliminate (C). This leaves (E) as the credited response.

Questions 19–23

This is a group game with variable assignments. The groups consist of three bouquets—1, 2, and 3—and the inventory is made up of five kinds of flowers—L, P, R, S, and T. The inventory can be repeated across the groups or left out entirely. Each group has at least one space, but could potentially have up to five. While it is sometimes easier to work a variable assignment game by putting the inventory on top of the diagram to create smaller potential groups, the clues are mainly about the relationships between the bouquets rather than the flowers, meaning it will be easier to symbolize and work with the clues if you use a more traditional diagram. There are no wildcards.

Clue 1. $1 \rightarrow {\sim}3$
$3 \rightarrow {\sim}1$

Clue 2. 2 and 3 exactly 2 spaces in common

Clue 3. S = 3 put into diagram

Clue 4. L → R and ~S
        S or ~R → ~L

Clue 5. T → P
        ~P → ~T

Deductions: Since S is in group 3 (clue 3), it cannot also be in group 1 (clue 1) and L cannot be in group 3 (clue 4). Since groups 2 and 3 have two flowers in common, that means those groups have at least two spaces each. You cannot conclude that S must be in group 2, because the two flowers in common could be other than S and each group could have more than two flowers. There is not much else to conclude up front, and there are many possible combinations of flowers among the groups.

Here's the diagram:

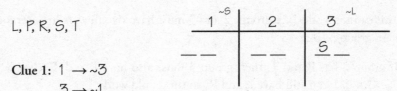

L, P, R, S, T

Clue 1: 1 → ~3
        3 → ~1

Clue 2: 2 & 3 exactly
        2 in common

Clue 3: S = 3

Clue 4: L → R and ~S
        ~R or S → ~L

Clue 5: T → P
        ~P → ~T

19. **A** Grab-a-Rule

A. Yes. This arrangement does not violate any clues.

B. No. This violates clue 1 because groups 1 and 3 both have P.

C. No. This violates clue 5 since group 2 has T but no P.

D. No. This violates clue 4 because group 3 has L and S.

E. No. This violates clue 3 because group 3 does not have S.

20. **B** Specific

Make a new line in your diagram and fill in the information given. If L is in group 1, then so is R (clue 4). This means that R cannot be in group 3 (clue 1). Since S is already in group 3, this means that the only other flower options are P and T. You need exactly two spaces in common between groups 2 and 3 (clue 2) so one of them might be S, and if there is only one other flower, then it would have to be P, since P does not guarantee T. If S is not one of the flowers in common, then groups 2 and 3 would both have to have T and P since L and R cannot be in group 3. Either way, the only thing that must be true in both scenarios is that P must be one of the common elements in the two groups, making (B) the credited response.

21. **E** **Specific**

Make a new line in your diagram and fill in the information given. If T is in group 1, then so is P (clue 4) and neither of them can be in group 3 (clue 1). Since group 3 cannot have L (clue 4) and now cannot have T or P, that leaves just S and R to be the two flowers that groups 2 and 3 have in common (clue 2). There is nothing restricting group 2 from having more flowers, but the list cannot include L (clue 4). You are looking for a list of one potential flower combination that could occur in group 2. Since the group must include S and R, you can eliminate (A), (B), (C), and (D), leaving (E) as the credited response.

22. **A** **General**

Use the deductions, prior work, and trying the answers to determine which answer choice CANNOT be the only flowers in group 2.

A. Yes. This cannot work since groups 2 and 3 must have two flowers in common (clue 2) and L cannot be in group 3 (clue 4).

B. No. If group 2 has P and T, then group 3 must also have P and T (clue 2) and group 1 cannot (clue 1). Group 1 can still have L and R, so this could work.

C. No. This combination was in group 2 in question 23. If P, R, and S are the flowers in group 2, then S must be one of the shared flowers in group 3. Group 3 cannot have more than 2 flowers though since group 1 cannot have any flowers in common with group 3 (clue 1). So, if group 3 has R, then group 1 can have T and P, and if group 3 has P, then group 1 can have L and R. This could work.

D. No. This combination was in group 2 in question 19.

E. No. If group 2 contains P, R, S, and T, then group 3 can have only two of those flowers (clue 2) and it already has S (clue 3). It cannot have T since that will require it to also have P (clue 5), but it can have P without T, as seen in question 20. This would leave L and R to be in group 1, so this could work.

23. **C** **General**

Use the deductions, prior work, and trying the answers to determine which answer choice must be false.

A. No. This combination could be true as seen in question 20.

B. No. This combination could be true as seen in question 21.

C. Yes. If group 2 has L, P, and R, then group 3 will have to have P and R along with S since it cannot have L (clue 4). This means that group 1 cannot have S, P, or R (clue 1). All that remains is T, which needs P to be with it (clue 5), or L, which needs R to be with it (clue 4). This combination does not work.

D. No. This combination was seen in question 22.

E. No. This combination was seen in question 20.

Section 4: Arguments 2

1. **D** `Weaken`

The argument concludes that chocolate interferes with one's ability to taste coffee. This is based on an experiment of ten people in which a group of five people who ate chocolate with coffee were unable to taste differences, while those that did not have chocolate were able to taste differences. The argument assumes that there is no other factor that caused the chocolate group to taste no difference and that the study was valid. The credited response will hurt the conclusion.

A. No. Random assignment despite group requests would not address the validity of the study and would not hurt the conclusion.

B. No. This would strengthen the argument by improving the validity of the study.

C. No. The state of matter of each item in the study is not relevant to the validity of the study.

D. Yes. This would hurt the conclusion because it would indicate that chocolate was not the cause of the inability to taste the difference in chocolate.

E. No. The significance of the difference is not relevant to determining whether there was a noticeable difference.

2. **D** `Principle Strengthen`

The argument states that residents are opposed to the building of a large house because it will alter the pristine landscape and hence damage the community's artistic and historic heritage despite the fact that the house will not violate any town codes. The credited response will help the reasoning by providing a rule that indicates a house that would alter the artistic heritage of a community should not be built.

A. No. There is no mention of historic buildings in the argument.

B. No. Since the purchase of the land by the community is not mentioned in their argument against the building of the house, this choice would not help their argument.

C. No. The argument is about the community opposing the building on the land, not the artist, so this rule would not support the community's argument.

D. Yes. If this is true, then the community would be supported in their claim that the family should not build the house.

E. No. There is no mention that the building of the house would limit access to historic sites.

3. **E** `Flaw`

Moore argues that sunscreens, which are designed to block skin-cancer-causing ultraviolet radiation, do not do so effectively because people who use these products develop as many skin cancers as those who do not use them. The argument assumes that people who use these products would not develop more skin cancers if they did not use the sunscreen.

A. No. The argument's conclusion is specifically about the ability of sunscreen lotions to block skin-cancer-causing UV radiation.

B. No. The severity of the cases of skin cancer are not relevant to whether the sunscreens block skin-cancer-causing UV radiation.

C. No. The argument's conclusion is specifically about the ability of sunscreen lotions that claim to block skin-cancer-causing UV radiation.

D. No. The evidence used to support the claim is not based on probability since it is based on actual numbers of people with skin cancers.

E. Yes. The argument assumes that the people who use the sunscreen lotions in question do not have more instance of skin-cancer-causing experiences.

4. **C** Reasoning

The psychologist disagrees with a position held by some people that Freudian psychotherapy is most effective because it is difficult and time-consuming. The psychologist offers another situation in which the same explanation would be invalid. The credited response will describe the psychologist's argument by pointing out that it uses a comparison.

A. No. The psychologist does not offer a contradictory principle.

B. No. The psychologist does not attack the premises of the argument with which he disagrees.

C. Yes. The psychologist uses an analogy to make the argument.

D. No. The psychologist uses an analogy in his own argument but does not claim that the point with which he disagrees is based on a similar analogy.

E. No. The psychologist does not address a causal argument.

5. **A** Main Point

The argument claims that biodiversity does not require the survival of every currently existing species because while biodiversity requires there to be various ecological niches that must be filled, many niches can be filled by more than one species. The credited response will match the conclusion of the argument.

A. Yes. This matches the conclusion of the argument.

B. No. This is a premise.

C. No. This is a premise.

D. No. This is a premise.

E. No. The argument does not mention any specific species that fill multiple niches.

6. **E** Evaluate

The clinician argues that patients should take this new drug in addition to the drug that helps to preserve existing bone. This conclusion is based on premises that state that a new drug that helps grow bone cells has been developed and that patients with immune disorders take drugs that increase the risk of osteoporosis. The argument assumes that these patients need to grow bone cells in addition to preserving existing bone and that the combination of the drugs would not impede the effectiveness in curing osteoporosis.

A. No. The size of the class of drugs that increase the risk of osteoporosis is not relevant to the question of whether patients need to grow bone in addition to preserving existing bone.

B. No. The reason patients take drugs that cause osteoporosis is not relevant to the question of whether patients need to grow bone in addition to preserving existing bone.

C. No. The price of the drug is not relevant to the question of whether patients need to grow bone in addition to preserving existing bone.

D. No. The length of time of use of a drug is not relevant to the question of whether patients need to grow bone in addition to preserving existing bone.

E. Yes. The answer to this question would provide information about the assumption that would allow you to evaluate the argument.

7. **E**   Principle Match

The critic argues that while the city's concert hall is located on a hilltop, it does not fulfill the purpose of a civic building because it is located far from the city center. The art museum that is in a densely populated area is a more successful civic building that promotes social cohesion and makes the city more alive. The credited response will be a rule that matches the argument.

A. No. While the passage mentions the "city on a hill," it does not indicate that civic buildings should be situated on an elevated location.

B. No. The passage is about what makes a civic building successful.

C. No. The passage does not indicate that the spectacular site is connected to a building's success.

D. No. The passage is not about how a downtown should be designed.

E. Yes. This matches the passage that says that the art museum is a more successful civic building and that it promotes social cohesion.

8. **D**   Inference

The passage states that fluoride enters a region's groundwater when rain dissolves fluoride-bearing minerals in the soil and that fluoride concentrations in groundwater are significantly higher in areas where the groundwater also contains a high concentration of sodium.

A. No. There is no evidence that fluoride comes from other sources.

B. No. The study held rainfall constant, so there is no way to know if rainfall has an effect on fluoride concentrations in groundwater.

C. No. Since the passage does not indicate why concentrations of fluoride and sodium were higher in some places, there is no evidence that sodium-bearing minerals dissolve faster than fluoride-bearing minerals.

D. Yes. Since fluoride is elevated in locations that have high concentrations of sodium, and fluoride enters groundwater by dissolving, it must be true that sodium increases the amount of fluoride that is dissolved.

E. No. There is no mention of a pathway for sodium to enter groundwater in a region, so it cannot be known whether sodium-bearing minerals are present in a location based on the text of the passage.

9. D Reasoning

The argument concludes that Fraenger's assertion is unlikely to be correct. Fraenger's assertion is that Bosch belonged to the Brethren of the Free Spirit. This is based on premises that state that there is evidence that Bosch was a member of a mainstream church, and no evidence that he was a member of the Brethren. The credited response will indicate that sentence in question is a premise.

A. No. The sentence is a premise, but there is no guarantee of the falsity of Fraenger's assertion.

B. No. That there is evidence Bosch was a member of a mainstream church is a premise.

C. No. The argument does not question Fraenger's credibility.

D. Yes. The argument states that there no evidence that he was a member of the Brethren as a note that the evidence to support Fraenger's assertion is insufficient.

E. No. The argument does not attempt to say that Bosch's choice of subject matter remains unexplained.

10. E Flaw

The salesperson concludes that the Super XL vacuum is a better vacuum because it picked up dirt that was left behind by the other vacuum. The argument assumes that the Super XL vacuum would have picked up the dirt the other vacuum picked up in addition to the extra dirt that was picked up by the Super XL.

A. No. The argument does not assume that the Super XL picked up all dirt, only that it picked up dirt the other vacuum did not.

B. No. The argument does not assume that the Super XL will be a better vacuum cleaner in the future.

C. No. The argument does not state that Super XL is the best vacuum cleaner available.

D. No. The argument does not compare the relative amounts of dirt picked up by the two vacuum cleaners to determine the better cleaner.

E. Yes. In stating that the Super XL is better because it picked up dirt left behind by the other vacuum cleaner, the author assumes that the other vacuum cleaner would not have performed better had the order of cleaning been reversed.

11. B Main Point

The manager argues that it would be irresponsible not to address today a problem that will occur in the future. The manager bases the argument on an analogy that a financial planner who made a similar argument about not worrying about a future problem would be guilty of malpractice.

A. No. This is a premise.

B. Yes. This matches the conclusion.

C. No. This is a premise.

D. No. The argument makes an analogy to financial planners that is a premise.

E. No. The manager is not making an argument about what financial planners should advise.

12.   A   **Inference**

The passage states that more books were sold worldwide last year than any previous year and that most of these books were cookbooks, and rather than books for beginners, more cookbooks than ever were purchased by professional cooks. Additionally, one of only a few books available on all continents is a cookbook for beginners. The credited response will be supported by the text of this passage.

A.   Yes. This must be true if "For the first time ever, most of the cookbooks sold were not intended for beginners."

B.   No. There is no evidence that the book available on all continents was the best-selling cookbook.

C.   No. There is no evidence that sales of cookbooks for beginners was not also higher than previous years despite the claim that more cookbook sales were not for beginners. It is possible that the overall sales of cookbooks was significantly greater than in previous years and that both books for beginners and books for professionals increased (and that sales of books for professionals increased at a greater rate).

D.   No. There is no mention of other types of books, but it is possible that books not purchased for beginners were predominantly purchased by experienced home cooks.

E.   No. The passage does not state how many copies of *Problem-Free Cooking* were sold.

13.   B   **Necessary Assumption**

The argument states that any methane in the Martian atmosphere must have been released into the atmosphere relatively recently. This is based on premises that state that scientists detected methane in the atmosphere of Mars and that Methane is a fragile compound that falls apart when hit by the ultraviolet radiation in sunlight. The argument assumes that ultraviolet radiation in sunlight would destroy methane on Mars that was not released relatively recently.

A.   No. The argument does not make any claims about the atmosphere on Mars prior to discovery of Methane there in 2003.

B.   Yes. This is required by the argument. Use the Negation Test. If not all methane in the Martian atmosphere is exposed to sunlight, then it not necessary for Methane to have been released recently since it might not break down due to radiation.

C.   No. The argument assumes that the methane on Mars had not fallen apart due to UV radiation.

D.   No. The argument indicates that Methane exposed to UV radiation would fall apart, so it does not assume that the Methane on Mars had been exposed.

E.   No. What happens to methane in Earth's atmosphere is not relevant to the argument about methane on Mars.

14.   C   **Inference**

The environmentalist states that consumers would pollute less if gasoline prices were higher because the cost of pollution from gasoline burned by cars is not included in the price of gasoline so does not affect consumer's decisions to drive. The credited response will be supported by the text of this passage.

A.   No. The author does not indicate a reason why the cost of pollution should be built into the price of gasoline, only that if it were, that consumers would pollute less.

B. No. The environmentalist does not state a reason that higher taxes would cause consumers to pollute less, only that it will.

C. Yes. This must be true since higher taxes would reflect the cost of pollution and that these higher taxes would cause a reduction in pollution.

D. No. There may be other factors considered by drivers such as length of time in the car or amount of wear and tear on the vehicle. All that is known is that pollution caused by gasoline is NOT a factor since it is not included in the cost of gasoline.

E. No. The passage provides one way to accomplish a reduction in pollution but does not indicate that it is the only way to reduce pollution.

15. A **Resolve/ Explain**

The argument states that the larvae of Hine's dragonfly survives in water where they are subject to predation by species including the red devil crayfish. At the same time, the dragonfly populations are more likely to be healthy in areas where red devil crayfish are present. The credited response will explain why populations are more likely to be healthy in areas with red devil crayfish.

A. Yes. If the crayfish dig holes that fill with water, the larvae that are not preyed on could survive when the surrounding areas dry up.

B. No. This would not explain why the total population is healthier when a species that preys upon larva is present.

C. No. This would make the problem worse by eliminating a possible reason that larva survive in areas with red devil crayfish: that the crayfish eliminate other threats to the larva.

D. No. The fact that the red devil crayfish is found in locations where Hine's dragonflies do not exist does not explain why the dragon flies are healthier in areas where both are located.

E. No. This fact alone does not explain why the dragonfly populations are more likely to be healthy in areas where red devil crayfish are present. It would need to assume the red devil crayfish prefer to prey on other species than Hine's dragonfly.

16. E **Inference**

The passage states that stress is a common cause of high blood pressure, that some people can lower their blood pressure by calming their minds, and that most people can calm their minds by engaging in exercise. The credited response will be supported by this text.

A. No. The passage does not state that blood pressure causes or relieves stress.

B. No. The passages states that some people can do this, but there is no evidence that most people with high blood pressure could do so.

C. No. The passage indicates that exercise can help reduce stress, but it does not state that a lack of exercise causes higher stress.

D. No. The passage states that exercise can cause some people to calm their minds and thereby reduce stress, which can cause a reduction in blood pressure. The relationship between exercise and blood pressure is therefore not a direct one.

E. Yes. This must be true since exercise can cause some people to calm their minds and thereby reduce stress, which can cause a reduction in blood pressure.

17. **C**   Weaken

The argument states that soot itself probably does not cause a certain ailment since cities with large amounts of soot in the air usually have high concentrations of other pollutants. The argument assumes that other pollutants could be the cause of the ailment.

A. No. This would strengthen the argument by proving that other pollutants are more likely the cause of the ailment.

B. No. The argument says the opposite of this is true.

C. Yes. This would weaken the argument by showing that other pollutants are not likely the cause of the ailment since the ailment occurs in areas that do not contain other pollutants.

D. No. This would strengthen the argument by showing that other pollutants could be the cause of the ailment.

E. No. This would strengthen the argument by showing that other pollutants could be the cause of the ailment.

18. **C**   Parallel Flaw

The argument claims that it will probably rain in the valley in the next week because there has been no rain in the valley this summer, there is usually a few inches of rainfall each summer, and there is only one week left in summer. The argument assumes that what is usually true of a summer will probably be true of this summer. The credited response will make a similar assumption.

A. No. This argument says that there are *sometimes* errors and that there *may* be errors in the unchecked pages, which does not match the original argument.

B. No. This argument claims that there are no errors in the unchecked pages despite the fact that there are generally few errors. This is the opposite of the claim the original argument makes.

C. Yes. This argument claims that there are usually errors in the pages of the magazine and that there will probably be errors in the unchecked pages. This matches the original argument.

D. No. This argument states that there are usually no errors and there probably won't be errors in a future issue. This argument has a comparison flaw, which does not match the original argument.

E. No. This argument assumes that since Aisha has found no errors, that she is mistaken, not that there are likely errors in unchecked pages; this does not match.

19. **B**   Necessary Assumption

The argument claims that we must enable our children to believe that better futures are possible. This is based on premises that state that young people believe efforts to reduce pollution, poverty, and war are doomed to failure; that people lose motivation to work for goals they think are unrealizable, and we must do what we can to prevent this loss of motivation; and that pessimism is probably harmful to humanity's future. The argument assumes that enabling children to believe that better futures are possible will prevent the loss of motivation that is harmful to our future.

A.   No. The author's argument does not address how he or she believes we can enable children to believe in better futures.

B.   Yes. Use the Negation Test. If enabling people will not prevent the loss of motivation, then there is no valid reason to say that we must enable people to believe in better futures.

C.   No. Optimism about an illusory future is not directly relevant to enabling children to believe in better futures.

D.   No. The author's argument does not address the need to eliminate war, poverty, or pollution.

E.   No. The author makes no assumptions about the reasons for current war or poverty.

20.   **D**   **Strengthen**

The argument concludes that glutamate leaking from damaged or oxygen-starved nerve cells is a cause of long-term brain damage resulting from strokes. This conclusion is based on premises that state that those who showed continued deterioration of the nerve cells in the brain after the stroke also had the highest levels of glutamate in their blood and that glutamate can kill surrounding nerve cells if it leaks from damaged or oxygen-starved nerve cells. There is a language shift that shows that the argument assumes that the glutamate in the blood is leaked from damaged or oxygen-starved nerve cells.

A.   No. Other types of neurotransmitters are not relevant to the argument about glutamate.

B.   No. This would weaken the claim by offering other possible reasons for long-term brain damage.

C.   No. Other neurotransmitters that leak from damaged or oxygen-starved nerve cells are not relevant to the argument about glutamate.

D.   Yes. If the only source for the increased glutamate in the blood of patients is from leaking damaged or oxygen-starved nerve cells, then it is more likely that the glutamate in these patients is causing long-term brain damage.

E.   No. The author does not make any assumptions about the cells that leak glutamate.

21.   **E**   **Parallel**

The argument concludes that if the next song Amanda writes is not a blues song, it probably will not involve more than three chords. This is based on premises that state that the only songs Amanda has ever written are blues songs and punk rock songs and that most punk rock songs involve no more than three chords. The credited response will match this argument.

A.   No. This does not match because the beginning of the conclusion that refers positively to parrots instead of saying "not a fish."

B.   No. This argument does not match because it draws a conclusion about pets the Gupta family has already owned rather than a pet they will own in the future.

C.   No. This does not match because it draws a conclusion about any pet the Gupta family will ever own and not just the next pet the Gupta family owns.

D.   No. This does not match because the conclusion should refer to a parrot by saying "not a fish."

E.   Yes. This matches the structure of the original argument.

22. D **Resolve/Explain**

The argument states that advertising usually has a greater influence on consumer preferences on yogurt than on milk but that LargeCo's advertising has increased sales of its milk brand more than its yogurt brand. The credited response will explain the difference for LargeCo.

A. No. Since there is no information about milk, this does not explain why the advertising caused a greater increase in the sale of its milk brand than its yogurt.

B. No. Since there is no information about how the advertising impacts shoppers, this does not explain why the advertising caused a greater increase in the sale of its milk brand than its yogurt.

C. No. Since both milk and yogurt are dairy products, this does not explain why the advertising caused a greater increase in the sale of its milk brand than its yogurt.

D. Yes. A national trend away from the sale of yogurt would correspond with a similar trend at LargeCo and could explain why the advertising caused a greater increase in the sale of its milk brand than its yogurt.

E. No. Since both the milk and yogurt in question are store brand, this does not explain why the advertising caused a greater increase in the sale of its milk brand than its yogurt.

23. E **Principle Strengthen**

The problem states that Shayna will either misrepresent her feelings toward Daniel or hurt his feelings. The principle states that one should not be insincere except possibly when the recipient would prefer kindness to honesty. The credited response will show how Shayna may choose to misrepresent her feelings in order to avoid hurting Daniel's feelings as long as Daniel prefers kindness to honesty.

A. No. The principle requires that Shayna believe Daniel prefers kindness to honesty to congratulate him and this is not known based on this answer choice.

B. No. The principle requires that Shayna believe Daniel prefers kindness to honesty to congratulate him and this is not known based on this answer choice.

C. No. The principle requires that Shayna believe Daniel prefers kindness to honesty to congratulate him and this is not known based on this answer choice.

D. No. The principle requires that Shayna believe Daniel prefers kindness to honesty to congratulate him and this is not known based on this answer choice.

E. Yes. In this case, Shayna does not believe Daniel prefers kindness to honesty so it would be inappropriate for her to congratulate him and misrepresent her feelings.

24. E **Sufficient Assumption**

The argument concludes that a democracy cannot thrive without effective news media. This is based on premises that state that a democracy cannot thrive without an electorate that is knowledgeable about important political issues, and an electorate can be knowledgeable in this way only if it has access to unbiased information about the government. The argument assumes that because one way to achieve the goal of having a knowledgeable electorate is to have an effective news media, that such a news media is required in order to have a knowledgeable electorate.

A. No. This choice does not improve the argument because it does not address the necessary/sufficient relationship between having a knowledgeable electorate and having an effective news media.

B. No. This choice does not improve the argument because it does not address the necessary/sufficient relationship between having a knowledgeable electorate and having an effective news media.

C. No. This choice does not improve the argument because it does not address the necessary/sufficient relationship between having a knowledgeable electorate and having an effective news media.

D. No. This choice does not improve the argument because it does not address the necessary/sufficient relationship between having a knowledgeable electorate and having an effective news media.

E. Yes. This choice proves that an effective news media is required to have a knowledgeable electorate.

25. **E**   Flaw

The argument concludes that Roberta is almost certainly irritable because she is irritable and loses things only when she is tired and she's been yawning all day and lost her keys. The argument would correctly conclude that Roberta is tired, but in concluding that she is irritable, the argument assumes that she is always irritable when she's tired (which may or may not be true based on the facts of the argument).

A. No. The argument would correctly conclude that Roberta is tired since she lost her keys and she loses things only when she is tired.

B. No. The conclusion confuses necessary and sufficient conditions, but it is not circular.

C. No. The argument uses what is always true to make a conclusion about a specific instance.

D. No. The argument does not confuse necessary and sufficient around losing things. It would properly conclude that because Roberta lost her keys that she is tired.

E. Yes. The premises state that she is irritable only when she is tired, but the conclusion states that because she is tired, she must be irritable.

26. **A**   Necessary Assumption

The argument concludes that using genetically engineered crops more widely is likely to help wildlife populations to recover. This is based on premises that state that crops genetically engineered to produce toxins that enable them to resist insect pests do not need to be sprayed with insecticides and that excessive spraying of insecticides has harmed wildlife populations near croplands. The argument assumes that there are no downsides to the possible solution of using more genetically engineered crops.

A. Yes. This choice helps the argument by providing the assumption. Use the Negation Test. If using more genetically engineered crops would not result in less harm to wildlife, it would be inappropriate to claim that genetically engineered crops will help wildlife populations.

B. No. The ability of wildlife populations to recover without genetically engineered crops is not relevant to the argument about genetically engineered crops helping wildlife populations to recover.

C. No. This choice is too extreme. Use the Negation Test—the fact that crops could sometimes be sprayed with insecticides would not hurt the argument because it might reduce the overall amount of insecticides.

D. No. The costs of pesticides are not relevant.

E. No. Use the Negation Test. Hypothetical situations are not assumed by the argument.

Chapter 4
PrepTest 74:
Answers and
Explanations

ANSWER KEY: PREPTEST 74

Section 1:
Arguments 1

1. C
2. C
3. B
4. C
5. C
6. A
7. E
8. A
9. E
10. E
11. D
12. E
13. A
14. D
15. E
16. D
17. A
18. A
19. A
20. E
21. B
22. E
23. D
24. B
25. D

Section 2:
Games

1. C
2. D
3. E
4. A
5. E
6. E
7. B
8. E
9. A
10. A
11. A
12. C
13. E
14. D
15. B
16. A
17. E
18. D
19. B
20. B
21. A
22. B
23. C

Section 3:
Reading
Comprehension

1. D
2. E
3. A
4. A
5. B
6. B
7. B
8. D
9. C
10. B
11. D
12. A
13. D
14. E
15. A
16. D
17. B
18. A
19. B
20. C
21. C
22. E
23. A
24. B
25. B
26. D
27. E

Section 4:
Arguments 2

1. B
2. C
3. E
4. D
5. D
6. B
7. A
8. B
9. B
10. C
11. A
12. D
13. D
14. A
15. C
16. E
17. E
18. E
19. C
20. D
21. A
22. C
23. E
24. D
25. A
26. B

EXPLANATIONS

Section 1: Arguments 1

1. **C** **Sufficient Assumption**

This argument makes the claim that children should be dissuaded from reading Jones's books. This claim is based upon an analogy with candy, which has short-term benefits but is not sufficiently nourishing. The argument also states that candy diminishes one's taste for superior foods. The argument assumes that Jones's books share the same characteristics as candy. Thus, the credited answer will fill in the blank by stating that Jones's books have similar characteristics, but with regard to books and reading.

A. No. This answer focuses on the premise, eating candy, rather than the conclusion. It is irrelevant.

B. No. This answer is too extreme to match the conclusion in tone and scope.

C. Yes. Impeding appreciation for more challenging literature is analogous to losing one's taste for better-quality food. This is the credited response.

D. No. Parents are not mentioned in the argument. This answer is irrelevant.

E. No. This answer is too extreme to match the conclusion in tone and scope.

2. **C** **Strengthen**

The author hypothesizes that, in order to carve Parthenon's columns with identical bulges in the center, stonemasons might have referred to a scale drawing. This is based on the discovery of such a drawing etched into a temple at Didyma, which depicts a column surrounded by a grid. The grid allows the correct width to be found at every height of the column. The author assumes that the Parthenon's stonemasons would have had access to a scale drawing and that the drawing would have helped them carve the columns identically. The credited answer will provide additional evidence that the stonemasons used a scale drawing or that such a drawing would be useful.

A. No. Modern attempts are irrelevant to the conclusion.

B. No. The hypothesis states that stonemasons referred to a similar drawing to the one at Didyma, not necessarily the same drawing. This answer is irrelevant.

C. Yes. If scale drawings were commonly used, that increases the likelihood that the Parthenon's stonemasons would have used one. This is the credited answer.

D. No. The actual columns at Didyma are not relevant to the hypothesis.

E. No. The stonemasons' level of experience is not relevant to whether or not they referred to a scale drawing.

3. **B** **Principle Match**

Match the answer choices to the editorialist's argument. The editorialist argues that the government should not fund essential health services with lottery revenues because those funds could decline in the future. The credited response will match this argument.

A. No. The discussion of essential versus non-essential services is not mentioned in the argument, so this does not match.

B. Yes. This matches the argument that says the government should not fund essential services with unreliable funding sources.

C. No. This does not match because the argument does not discuss all types of government services.

D. No. The argument discusses types of funding for essential services. A discussion of what is essential is not in question in the editorialist's argument.

E. No. The argument does not mention setting aside funds for shortfalls in the future.

4. **C** [Strengthen]

The credited response for this help question will improve the argument. The scientist hypothesizes that the heating of a squirrel's tail probably plays a role in repelling snakes. The scientist supports the hypothesis by noting that squirrel's puff and wag tails to repel snakes and that their tails heat up at the same time. The scientist also notes that snakes have infrared sensors that can detect body heat. In making the hypothesis, the scientist assumes that two things that are correlated have a causal relationship, so the credited response will support the argument by addressing this causal flaw.

A. No. A rattlesnake's ability to heat its tail is not relevant to whether a squirrel's heating of its tail plays a role in repelling snakes.

B. No. This does not address whether the heat in a squirrel's tail is designed to repel snakes.

C. Yes. This would help the argument by providing additional evidence that the heat in a squirrel's tail repel snakes.

D. No. Other predators are irrelevant to the argument about whether heat in a squirrel's tail repels snakes. It is possible, for instance, that heat in the tail repels snakes as well as other beasts.

E. No. A mammal's ability to sense heat is not relevant to the argument about whether heat in the tail will repel a reptile.

5. **C** [Flaw]

This question asks you to describe a flaw in the argument. The critic argues that we should reject Fillmore's argument because Fillmore's conclusion is beneficial to Fillmore. The critic's argument is flawed because it assumes that a conclusion that is beneficial to its author is invalid without providing evidence for the conclusion's incorrectness. The credited response will describe this flaw.

A. No. The critic does not confuse necessary and sufficient clauses in the argument. The critic's argument is flawed because it does not provide evidence for the wrongness of Fillmore's argument.

B. No. The critic mentions that there is evidence that supports Fillmore's conclusion.

C. Yes. The only evidence the critic offers for Fillmore's wrongness is the fact that Fillmore's conclusion is self-beneficial.

D. No. The critic does not make appeals to another argument.

E. No. There are no inconsistent claims stated in the critic's argument.

6. **A** **Weaken**

The question asks you to weaken the conclusion so the credited response will hurt the argument. The argument concludes that the best approach to prescribing medicine would be to give patients a lower dose along with grapefruit juice. The author provides evidence that grapefruit juice has an effect on the absorption of medicine in which normal doses act like higher doses. This argument is flawed in that it assumes that grapefruit juice has no other effects on the drug's interaction with the body than to amplify the dose. The credited response will provide a reason that taking lower doses of some medicines with grapefruit juice is not the best medical approach.

A. Yes. This choice provides a reason not to take lower doses along with grapefruit juice. It weakens the argument by saying that the dose recommendation in the argument would be unreliable.

B. No. The cost of grapefruit juice is not relevant to the argument that the best medical approach is to take a lower dose of some medicines along with the juice.

C. No. The argument states that the chemical in grapefruit juice is the cause of the amplification of the drug absorption. The removal of the chemical from the juice is not relevant to the argument that the best medical approach is to take a lower dose of some medicines along with the juice.

D. No. The cause of the amplification of the drug absorption in grapefruit juice is not relevant to the question of the best medical approach of doses of some medicines along with the juice.

E. No. Doctor recommendations to avoid consuming grapefruit juice with some medications do not provide a medical reason that consuming grapefruit juice with a lower dose is not the best approach. To weaken the argument, an answer choice must provide a direct reason that the conclusion is wrong.

7. **E** **Principle Match**

The credited response should match the salesperson's argument as closely as possible. The salesperson advised that, given two equally priced options, the landlord should choose the option that was powerful enough rather than the option that was the most powerful option.

A. No. The advice in this choice does not match the salesperson's advice to choose the good enough option instead of the most powerful option.

B. No. This choice does not match the salesperson's advice because the two options in the argument are of equal price.

C. No. This choice does not match the salesperson's advice because the two options in the argument are of equal price.

D. No. This choice does not match the salesperson's advice because there is no mention of commission for the salesperson in the argument.

E. Yes. This choice matches the argument that suggests the good enough option over the most powerful option.

8. **A** **Necessary Assumption**

In this question, the credited response will help the argument by providing an assumption that is required by the argument. Use the Negation Test to confirm your answer choice. The argument concludes that focusing on the flaws of our leaders is a pointless distraction. The editorialist supports the conclusion by stating that the real question we should focus on is how our institutions and policies allow flawed leaders to get elected. There is a language shift between the "real question" in the evidence and "pointless distraction" in the conclusion. The credited response will connect these two things by stating directly that looking at the flaws of our leaders is not relevant to understanding how those leaders were elected.

A. Yes. This choice helps the argument by connecting the premises with the conclusion. Use the Negation Test. If examining the flaws of our leaders does reveal something about how institutions and procedures influence elections, then looking at these flaws is not a pointless distraction.

B. No. The relative rate of discussions of flawed leaders is not relevant to whether those discussions are pointless distractions.

C. No. This choice is not required by the argument. Use the Negation Test. If the procedures and institutions do not guarantee the election of flawed leaders, it may still be important to understand how they allow the election of flawed leaders.

D. No. Whether people have attempted to answer the real question is not relevant to whether looking at flawed leaders is a pointless distraction.

E. No. Satisfaction with the nation's leaders is not relevant to whether focusing on flawed leaders is a pointless distraction.

9. **E** Resolve/ Explain

In this question, the credited response will help the argument by providing an explanation for the seemingly disparate statements. The argument states that some doctors prescribe calcium supplements with lead despite the fact that lead is a dangerous substance even in small amounts.

A. No. The fact that lead is present in fruits and vegetables does not explain why doctors would prescribe calcium supplements that contain lead.

B. No. Removing lead from the body is not relevant to the fact that doctors sometimes prescribe calcium supplements with lead.

C. No. The fact that there are other potentially dangerous health concerns does not explain why doctors would prescribe calcium supplements with lead.

D. No. This choice does not explain the issue at hand. The fact that high calcium diets make small amounts of lead more dangerous makes the claim that doctors prescribe calcium supplements with lead even more contradictory.

E. Yes. This explains why some doctors would prescribe calcium supplements with lead over no supplement at all because the calcium supplements with lead may actually result in less lead in the bloodstream.

10. **E** Principle Strengthen

In this question, the credited response will help the argument by linking the principle to the conclusion in the application. The argument states that Matilde should not buy the vase for sale online because people should buy only antiques that can be authenticated and because the antique is intrinsically valuable. The credited response will show how this principle applies to Matilde specifically.

A. No. This choice does help because it does not state that Matilde finds the vase intrinsically valuable.

B. No. This choice does help because it does not state that Matilde finds the vase intrinsically valuable.

C. No. This choice is attractive, but it mistakes necessary and sufficient conditions. By addressing two factors that must be met in order to buy an antique, the principle does not actually address when someone should buy an antique. Instead, it points to two reasons that a buyer should not make a purchase.

D. No. This choice does not help because it does not state that Matilde has verified the authenticity of the vase.

E. Yes. Since Matilde cannot verify the authenticity of the vase, she should not buy it according to the principle.

11. **D** **Inference**

The credited response will be supported by information in the paragraph. The critic states that Waverly's textbook claims to be objective but that writing about art cannot be objective and that, in fact, Waverly writes better about art she likes than art she does not. The credited response will be supported by these facts.

A. No. The critic does not mention Waverly's views on art historians, so this is not supported by the text.

B. No. The critic does not mention that Waverly has strong opinions about the works in the textbook, so this is not supported by the text.

C. No. The critic states that Waverly intended to remain objective in writing her book.

D. Yes. The critic states that Waverly intended to remain objective in writing her book but that objectivity is impossible in writing about art. Therefore, Waverly failed to remain objective.

E. No. There is no evidence in the text that Waverly does not really believe she could be objective.

12. **E** **Sufficient Assumption**

The credited response will help the argument by proving that the conclusion is true based on the evidence. The argument concludes that the Sals did not smelt iron. This conclusion is based on evidence that there are smelting furnaces and tools for smelting copper and bronze and the Sals had words for copper and bronze but no words for iron. There is a language shift from the premises, which state that there are no words for iron, to a conclusion about not smelting iron.

A. No. This choice goes in the wrong direction. It states that having a word for something guarantees that it happened, but it does not help the argument that states that NOT having a word for something means it did not happen.

B. No. The familiarity of a culture with a metal is not relevant to the conclusion that the Sals did not smelt iron.

C. No. The link between words and actions for smelting copper and bronze is not directly connected to a link between not having a word for iron and the question of whether the Sals smelted iron.

D. No. The familiarity of a culture with a metal is not relevant to the conclusion that the Sals did not smelt iron.

E. Yes. This choice helps the argument by connecting the action of smelting a metal with having a word for that action.

13. **A**   Main Point

This question asks for the main conclusion of the argument so the credited response will match the conclusion stated in the argument. The argument concludes that community organizations that want to enhance support for programs should convince the public that these programs are beneficial to society. This is based on premises that state that it is easier to get public support for a program that is seen to be beneficial to society than a program that is not.

A. Yes. This matches the conclusion of the argument.

B. No. This is a premise.

C. No. This is a premise.

D. No. This is a premise.

E. No. The argument does not explicitly state that higher education is beneficial to society. It states that showing people that it is would increase public support.

14. **D**   Reasoning

The credited response will describe the role of the statement that the risk of satellites colliding will increase. The argument concludes that the risk of satellites colliding will increase in the future because a single collision will result in many fragments that will increase the risk of collision. The credited response will state that the claim in question is the conclusion.

A. No. The claim in question is the main conclusion of the argument. It does not support any other claims in the argument.

B. No. The claim in question is the main conclusion of the argument. It does not support any other claims in the argument.

C. No. The claim in question is the main conclusion of the argument. It does not support any other claims in the argument.

D. Yes.

E. No. The claim in question is the main conclusion of the argument. It does not support any other claims in the argument.

15. **E**   Resolve/ Explain

In this question, the credited response will help the argument by providing an explanation for the seemingly disparate statements. The paragraph states that young chicks given a new treatment for *Salmonella* had a lower incidence of infection than chicks not given the new treatment. However, the chicks given the new treatment did have a higher concentration of some bacteria than those that were not.

A.   No. If the treatment takes several weeks, this choice would not explain why the chicks had a lower incidence of infection.

B.   No. This choice does not explain why chicks given the treatment had a lower incidence of infection but higher concentrations of bacteria.

C.   No. The information about what happens in adulthood does not explain why young chicks had different concentrations of bacteria.

D.   No. This choice does not explain why chicks who received the treatment had a lower incidence of infection but a higher concentration of some bacteria.

E.   Yes. This choice explains why chicks who received treatment had a lower incidence of *Salmonella* and that this reduction in *Salmonella* bacteria simultaneously caused an increased concentration of other bacteria.

16.   **D**   **Flaw**

In this question, the credited response will hurt the respondent's argument by describing the problems with it. The respondent claims that the hierarchy present in lecturing is a strength based on premises that state that all teaching requires hierarchy. This argument is flawed in that it is based on a problematic comparison between hierarchy of information (arithmetic is simpler than calculus) and hierarchy of power (teacher is superior to student).

A.   No. The respondent does not concede to any of the debater's assumptions.

B.   No. The respondent does not mention teaching methods in any subject.

C.   No. The respondent's argument is about the strength of the hierarchy, so other potential weaknesses are not relevant to the conclusion.

D.   Yes. This choice points to the comparison flaw in the respondent's argument.

E.   No. The problem is not that the hierarchy of information mentioned in the respondent's argument is not present outside of math. The flaw is that the hierarchy of information is not the same as the hierarchy of power.

17.   **A**   **Strengthen**

In this question, the credited response will help the argument by improving the evidentiary support for the conclusion. The argument concludes that Han purple was probably discovered by accident. This is based on evidence that states that the process of synthesizing Han purple uses the same ingredients as the process of producing white glass during the period. The argument is flawed because it does not provide evidence of the happenstance creation of Han purple, so the credited response will likely provide some concrete link between the glass production and the finding of Han purple.

A.   Yes. This further links the creation of Han purple with the production of glass in the region.

B.   No. This choice shows how Han purple and glass are different, thereby hurting the conclusion.

C.   No. This choice shows how Han purple and glass are different, thereby hurting the conclusion.

D. No. While this information shows a similarity between Han purple and glass, it does not provide additional evidence that the two are related other than their similar ingredients.

E. No. The relative occurrence of Han purple and glass is not relevant to whether Han purple was discovered by accident during the creation of glass.

18. **A**   Flaw

In this question, the credited response will hurt the argument by describing the flaw in the argument. The medical researcher concludes that mild sleep deprivation is not unhealthy, but may instead bolster the body's defense systems. This is based on evidence from a survey that showed that people who get at least 8 hours of sleep have more illness than those that sleep significantly less. This argument is flawed in that the survey does not prove a causal relationship between sleep and illness. It also fails to show that those who get significantly less sleep suffer from "mild sleep deprivation."

A. Yes. This choice describes the causal flaw in the argument.

B. No. The medical researcher does not show that sleep is one of the factors in the frequency of illness.

C. No. There is no evidence that getting at least 8 hours of sleep is sufficient to cause illness.

D. No. This choice goes in the wrong direction.

E. No. Other negative impacts of getting at least 8 hours of sleep are not relevant to whether getting that amount of sleep causes a greater frequency of illness.

19. **A**   Parallel

In this question, the credited response will match the structure of the original argument. The argument concludes that temperatures did not drop below freezing last week based on the premises that state that if the temperatures had dropped below freezing last week, then the impatiens would have died and not continued to bloom. However, the impatiens did continue to bloom. The structure shows that A → B and B → C and given that ~C we can conclude ~A. The credited response will match this structure.

A. Yes. This argument follows the structure of the original argument.

B. No. This argument does not match because it states that A → B and B → C and given ~C we can conclude ~B.

C. No. The premises of this argument do not match the A → B and B → C structure of the premises in the original argument.

D. No. This argument concludes what should or should not be done rather than what is or is not true, so it does not match the original argument.

E. No. This argument concludes what should or should not be done rather than what is or is not true, so it does not match the original argument.

20. **E** Sufficient Assumption

In this question, the credited response will help the argument by proving its conclusion is true based on the premises. The argument concludes that building the new convention center will increase tax revenues because several large organizations will hold conferences in the new convention center. There is a shift from several national organizations holding conferences to the fact that several large conferences will take place at the convention center. The credited response will show that large organizations hold large conferences.

A. No. The argument does not discuss other ways to increase tax revenue.

B. No. The argument does not mention how increased numbers of visitors will increase tax revenue.

C. No. Other ways to increase tax revenues is not relevant to increase revenue due to the convention center.

D. No. The argument states that large conventions will cause increased numbers of visitors, so it does not need for current visitors to continue to visit in order to gain an increase in tax revenue.

E. Yes. This choice shows a link between national organizations and large conventions.

21. **B** Evaluate

The credited response will mention information that is missing from the argument that would help in evaluating the argument. The argument states that dogs have an aversion to being treated unfairly because the dog that did not receive a reward stopped obeying commands. The argument assumes that the dog stopped obeying due to unfair treatment, so it would be helpful to know why the dog stopped obeying commands.

A. No. The likelihood of obeying the initial command is not relevant to the discussion of dogs that stopped obeying the command after not receiving a reward.

B. Yes. This would provide additional information about why the dogs stopped obeying command by showing whether the unfair treatment has the same result as equally not giving rewards.

C. No. Differences outside of the trials are not relevant to why dogs in this trial stopped obeying commands.

D. No. Dogs that became more inclined to obey are not relevant to understanding why dogs stopped obeying commands.

E. No. The number of repetitions is not relevant to understanding why dogs stopped obeying commands.

22. **E** Inference

In this question, the credited response will be supported by the facts of the argument in the text. The argument states that a survey shows that people's satisfaction with income depends largely on how that income compares to their neighbors and not with the amount they make. The passage also states that people live in neighborhoods of people in the same economic class. The credited response will use this information.

A. No. This is not supported by the text, which states that people's satisfaction with their income is not strongly correlated with the amount they make.

B. No. This is not supported by the text since the text does not distinguish between age groups.

C. No. This is contradicted by the text, which states that people live in neighborhoods that are in their same economic class and that amount of income is not strongly correlated with satisfaction. Therefore, neighborhood should not strongly correlate to satisfaction.

D. No. The passage does not show the relative impact of satisfaction of income with satisfaction of life as a whole.

E. Yes. If satisfaction is correlated most strongly with income equality, increasing everyone's will not impact equality and will therefore not impact overall satisfaction.

23. **D**   Weaken

In this question, the credited response will hurt the conclusion by attacking the flaw in the argument. The geologist argues that people who argue against the dominant view of petroleum formation are incorrect because they are refuted by the presence of petroleum in biomarkers. The argument is flawed because it fails to link the presence of petroleum in biomarkers to proof that petroleum deposits were formed by fossilized remains instead of carbon deposits around at the formation of Earth.

A. No. The presence of biomarkers in fossils is not relevant to whether the presence of petroleum in biomarkers proves that petroleum came from living creatures and not carbon deposits.

B. No. The rise of living organisms is not relevant to whether the presence of petroleum in biomarkers proves that petroleum came from living creatures and not carbon deposits.

C. No. This fact does not address the argument against the dominant view of petroleum formation.

D. Yes. This would weaken the argument by linking the presence of petroleum in biomarkers to the presence of carbon deposits deep in the earth. This would show that the evidence does not weaken the argument put forth by people who go against the dominant view of petroleum formation.

E. No. This does not link the presence of petroleum in biomarkers to the view that petroleum was formed by carbon deposits deep in the earth.

24. **B**   Inference

In this question, the credited response will be an inference that is supported by the text in the argument. The passage states that drivers in accidents that cause personal injury or more than $500 in property damage must report the accident to the DMV unless they are incapable of doing so and that Ted was a driver in an accident who does not need to report the accident.

A. No. There is no evidence that Ted was injured or that his injury would be linked to a small amount of property damage.

B. Yes. If Ted's property was damaged more than $500, he would be required to report the accident unless he's incapable of doing so. Since the text says he does not need to report the accident, it must be true that any accident he is in that causes more than $500 in property damage also causes him to be incapable of reporting said accident.

C. No. There is no evidence that Ted's accident caused personal injury or more than $500 in property damage.

D. No. There is no evidence that a person must be incapable of reporting an accident due to injury.

E. No. There is no evidence that Ted is not incapable of reporting his accident to the DMV.

25. **D** **Parallel Flaw**

In this question, the credited response will match the flaw of the original argument. The student states that people who have an immunity to a microorganism will not have harmful symptoms from that microorganism and concludes based on this that a person who does not develop harmful symptoms must have an immunity. This argument confuses a sufficient condition (having an immunity leads to a certain situation) with a necessary condition (that a certain situation must be due to immunity). The credited response will also confuse a sufficient condition with a necessary condition.

A. No. This does not confuse necessary and sufficient conditions. The flaw in this choice is that the conclusion contradicts the original premise.

B. No. This argument has a comparison flaw. It assumes that two groups that are dissimilar in one way are dissimilar in another way.

C. No. This choice does not contain a flaw.

D. Yes. This choice confuses a sufficient condition (excessive taxation leads to decline in expansion) with a necessary condition (a decline in expansion must be caused by excessive taxation).

E. No. This does not confuse necessary and sufficient conditions. The flaw in this choice is that it assumes that because doctors are less likely to perform an activity that the activity does not impact health.

Section 2: Games

Questions 1–5

This is a 1D ordering game with range clues, so it a ranking game. The inventory consists of six musicians—G, K, P, S, T, and V—with 1-to-1 correspondence and no wildcards.

Clue 1. G ≠ 4

Clue 2. P—K

Clue 3. V—K—G

Clue 4. P—S—T or T—S—P

Combine clues 2, 3, and 4 to get two possible arrangements.

In one scenario, you know that P cannot be third, fourth, fifth, or sixth. G cannot be first, second, third, or fourth (rule 1), so it must be either fifth or sixth. You also know that S cannot be first or last, and since G must be fifth or sixth and T must be after S, that S cannot be fifth either. T cannot be first or second and K cannot be first, second, or fifth. V cannot be fourth or fifth. This means that P must be first or second, G must be fifth or sixth, and the sixth spot must be either T or G.

In the other scenario, K and G must be fifth and sixth, respectively, and V can be first, second, third, or fourth, so that means that T must be first or second, S must be second or third, and P must be third or fourth.

Here's the diagram.

G, K, P, S, T, V

Clue 1: G ≠ 4
Clue 2: P—K
Clue 3: V—K—G
Clue 4: P—S—T
         or
      T—S—P

1. **C** | Grab-a-Rule

    A. No. This violates rule 1 because G is fourth.

    B. No. This violates rule 4 because both T and P are before S.

    C. Yes. This choice does not violate any rules.

    D. No. This violates rule 2 because K is before P.

    E. No. This violates rule 2 because K is before P.

2. **D** | Specific

    Make a new line in your diagram and add the new information. If P is before S, then you need the first setup noted above.

    A. No. This is possible according to the first setup, but it doesn't have to be true. P could be first or second.

    B. No. This is possible according to the first setup, but it doesn't have to be true. P could be first or second.

    C. No. This is possible according to the first setup, but it doesn't have to be true. V could be before or after S.

    D. Yes. According to rule 4, P and T cannot both be before S, so since P is before S, T must be after S.

    E. No. This is possible according to the first setup, but it doesn't have to be true. S could be before or after K.

3. E General

Use the deductions, prior work, and trying the answers to determine which answer choice could be true.

    A.   No. K cannot be first (rule 2).

    B.   No. According to the deductions, G must be fifth or sixth.

    C.   No. According to the deductions, G must be fifth or sixth and S cannot be fifth or sixth, so S must be before G.

    D.   No. By combining the second and third rules, you can deduce that since P is before K and K is before G, then P must be before G.

    E.   Yes. In the first setup, K can be before S.

4. A General

This question asks for who cannot be third. Looking at the deductions, G can never be third, and that happens to be (A), the credited response.

5. E Specific

Make a new line in your diagram and add the new information. If the violinist is fourth, then both setups could apply. Fill in what you know. For the first setup, K and G would have to be fifth and sixth (rule 3) and P, S, and T would have to be first, second, and third, respectively. For the second setup, K and G would still have to be fifth and sixth, and T, S, and P would have to be first, second, and third, respectively. In either case, S must be second, V must be fourth, K must be fifth, and G must be fifth. The only things that could be false are that T and P are first or third. This makes (E) the credited response.

Questions 6–10

This is a 2D order game. There are four historians—F, G, H, and J—each giving a different one of four lectures—L, O, S, and W. Since order matters, put 1 through 4 on top of the diagram and make one row for the historians and one for the lectures. The clues are all range clues and there is one wildcard, S.

Clue 1. O—L

          W—L

Clue 2. F—O

Clue 3. H—G & H—J

From the first rule, note that L cannot be first or second and that both O and W cannot be fourth. From the second rule, note that F cannot be fourth, O cannot be first, and F cannot be with O. From the third rule, note that H cannot be third or fourth and that neither G nor J can be first. Combine the first and second rules to see that F—O—L so L cannot be second and F cannot be third. Since there are only four times, if H and F cannot be third or fourth, then they must both be either first or second, which means that G and J must be either third or fourth. Since L cannot be first or second, it must be third or fourth, and since the first lecture cannot be L or O, it must be S or W. Since the fourth lecture cannot be O or W, it must be L or S. This is actually a very restricted setup, and a little patience making deductions has a big payoff in being able to find the answers quickly.

Here's the diagram.

historian: F, G, H, J
lectures: L, O, S, W

	1	2	3	4
historian	~G ~J		~H ~F	~F ~H
lecture	~L ~O	~L		~O ~W

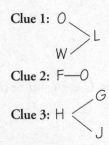

Clue 1: O、 W ＞ L

Clue 2: F—O

Clue 3: H ＜ G、 J

6. **E** [Grab-a-Rule]

   A. No. This violates rule 1 since both O and W are after L.

   B. No. This violates rule 3 since J is before H.

   C. No. This violates rule 3 since H is after G.

   D. No. This violates rule 2 since O is before F.

   E. Yes. This arrangement does not violate any of the rules.

7. **B** [General]

   Use the deductions, prior work, and trying the answers to determine what must be true.

   A. No. Since S can be first, F does not have to be earlier than S.

   B. Yes. From the deductions above, you know that H must be either first or second and that L must be either third or fourth. Thus, H must always be earlier than L.

   C. No. Since S can be fourth, it does not have to be earlier than G.

   D. No. Since S can be fourth, it does not have to be earlier than J.

   E. No. Since W can be third, it can be with G and does not have to be earlier than G.

8. E Specific

Make a new line in your diagram and fill in the information given. If W is third, then L must be fourth since L cannot be first or second (rule 1). Since O cannot be first (rule 2), that means it must be second, putting S first. Since F and H must be first and second, since O is second, that forces F into the first place (rule 2). That means H is second. J and G are interchangeable in the third and fourth spots. Cross off any answers that must be false since you are looking for what could be true. Choice (E) is the credited response.

9. A General

Use the deductions, prior work, and trying the answers to determine what must be false.

A. Yes. From the deductions above, you know that F must be either first or second and that L must be third or fourth, so they can never be at the same time. This must be false.

B. No. From the deductions above, you know that S can be fourth and so can G, so it could be true that S and G are at the same time. Question 10 also pairs G with S.

C. No. It was possible for G to be with W in question 8.

D. No. H was at the same time as O in question 8.

E. No. It was possible for J to be with W in question 8.

10. A Specific

Make a new line in your diagram and fill in the information given. If G and S are at the same time, then that must be either third or fourth. Since L must also be third or fourth (rule 1) and so must J (deduction), that means that G/S and L/W must fill the third and fourth times interchangeably. This leaves F, H, O, and W for the first and second times. Since F must be before O (rule 2), F and W are first and H and S are second. Eliminate answers that must be false.

A. Yes. If L is third, then S is fourth. This could be true.

B. No. O must be second so it cannot be third.

C. No. S is third or fourth with G. W must be first.

D. No. S is third or fourth with G. O must be second.

E. No. W must be first with F and O must be second with H.

Questions 11–16

This is a group game with fixed assignment. The diagram consists of three groups plus an out column. The inventory is six different colors, five of which are used in the three groups and one of which will be out. The clues are mainly spatial, conditional, and antiblock, and there are no wildcards.

Clue 1. W → W _ _ ; _ / _ _ → ~W

Clue 2. O → OP ; ~P → ~O

Clue 3. ~FT

Clue 4. ~PT

Clue 5. ~PY

The key to most grouping games is determining, if possible, how many spaces are in each group. Given that there are only five colors used over the three rugs, the number of colors per rug is limited to either: _ _|_ _|_ or _ _ _|_|_ . Don't forget, if W is used, it must go in group 3 (rule 1). In addition, any rug with O must have at least two colors due to rule 2. Combine rule 2 with rules 4 and 5 to deduce that T and O can never be together, and Y and O can never be together.

Make some deductions about each possible arrangement. For the _ _|_ _|_ arrangement, W is left out as per rule 1 and O and P make up one of the rugs with two colors. That leaves F, T, and Y to place. Since F and T can never be together (rule 3), one of them must be with Y in the other rug with two colors and the other must be alone. For the _ _ _|_|_ arrangement, either W is in the rug with three colors or W is out. If W is in, either O and P are with W, or O is out since it can't be alone (rule 2). This also means that with F, P, T, and Y left, then Y has to be with W as does one of F or T, and P must be a single-color rug. If W is out, then O and P have to be in the rug with three colors. Since O and P cannot be with T or Y, they must be with F, making T and Y the single-color rugs.

Here's the diagram.

Choose Five	1	2	3	unused
F, O, P, T, W, Y	(1) O P	F/T Y	T/F	W
	(2) _ _ _	_	_	_

Clue 1:   W → ⬚ W _ _

Clue 2:   O → ⬚ O P
          ~P → ~ O

Clue 3:   ⬚ F̷T

Clue 4:   ⬚ P̷T

Clue 5:   ⬚ P̷Y

11. **A**   **General**

This is almost a Grab-A-Rule question, but it is missing the color that is left out. That's not too hard to keep track of, though, so this question operates like a true Grab-A-Rule.

A. Yes. This does not violate any rules.

B. No. This violates rule 5 by putting P and Y in the same rug.

C. No. This violates rule 2 because O is in a rug without P.

D. No. This violates rule 3 because F and T are in the same rug.

E. No. This violates rule 1 by having W in a two-color rug.

12. **C**   General

Use the deductions, prior work, and trying the answers to determine which answer choice must be true.

A. No. This combination was used successfully in question 13. You also know from the deductions that F can be in a rug with W or with O and P, so it is possible.

B. No. This combination was used successfully in question 16, (B). You also know from deductions that F and T are somewhat interchangeable in the multicolored rugs with three colors.

C. Yes. If P is out, then O must be in, but O cannot be in without P (rule 2). This means that P must always be used.

D. No. Question 16, (C), worked with T not being used. If T is out, then W can be with O and P and the other two rugs can be F and Y.

E. No. It is possible for Y to be out. If Y is out, then W can be with O and P and the other two rugs can be F and T.

13. **E**   Specific

Make a new line in your diagram and fill in the information given. If P is a single-color rug, then O is out. That means that W must be in a three-color rug. According to the deductions, this is the WY F/T | T/F | O combination. This makes (E) the credited response.

14. **D**   Specific

Make a new line in your diagram and fill in the information given. With two solid rugs, then the third rug must have three colors. You are asked to determine which two colors cannot be the solid rugs. Prior work can cut down on your Process of Elimination time rather than trying out every answer.

A. No. F and P were used successfully as the two solid rugs in question 13.

B. No. If F and Y are the two solid rugs, then one possible combination is to have W with O and P in the multicolored rug and T out. This does not violate any rules.

C. No. P and T were used successfully as the two solid rugs in question 13.

D. Yes. If P and Y are the two solid rugs, F and T will be forced together in the same rug since O will have to be out (rule 2 and rule 3).

E. No. If T and Y are the two solid rugs, then one possible combination is to have W with O and P in the multicolored rug and F out.

15. **B** Specific

Make a new line in your diagram and fill in the information given. If F and P are in the same rug, then the OPF | T | Y | W (out) arrangement is in play. This makes (B) the credited response.

16. **A** Specific

Make a new line in your diagram and fill in the information given. If Y is a solid rug, then one of the _ _ _ | _ | _ arrangements must be used. This makes (A) the credited response since there cannot be exactly one solid rug.

Questions 17–23

This is a group game with fixed assignment since the inventory cannot be repeated. At least two of the six photographers available—F, G, H, K, L, and M—are assigned to one of two graduation ceremonies. Since not all the inventory has to be used, you also need an out column. The clues consist of a fixed choice clue and three conditional statements. There are no wildcards.

Clue 1. FH = in

Clue 2. L & M → ~LM

Clue 3. G = S → L = T; ~L = T → ~G = S

Clue 4. ~K = T → HM = T ; ~H = T or ~M = T → K = T

The key to most grouping games is determining, if possible, how many spaces are in each group. Since there must be at least two people assigned to each ceremony, the minimum number of the inventory used is four, leaving two to be either in or out. Since none of the clues force someone to be out, it is possible that all six people are used and that no one is out.

In addition, you can link together some of the clues. Clues 3 and 4 are both connected to clue 2. From clue 3, if G is in S, then L is in T. Now, take that to clue 2 to see that if L is in T, then M is either in S or out. Either way, K must then be in T (clue 4). The reverse of this is if K is not in T, then H, F, and M must all be in T (clues 4 and 1). Since M is in T, then L is either in S or out (clue 2), which means that G is either in T or out (clue 3).

Here's the diagram.

F, G, H, K, L, M

S	T	out
_ _	K/HM	_

Clue 1: [FH] = S/T
Clue 2: [LM]
Clue 3: G = S → L = T
         L ≠ T → G ≠ S
Clue 4: K ≠ T → [HM] = T
         H ≠ T or M ≠ T → K = T

17. **E**   Grab-a-Rule

A.   No. This violates the third rule by having G and L assigned to the same group.

B.   No. This violates rule 1 because F and H are not included.

C.   No. This violates rule 2 since L and M are in the same group.

D.   No. This violates rule 4 because K is not in T, which means M and H must be.

E.   Yes. This does not violate any of the rules.

18. **D**   Specific

Make a new line in your diagram and fill in the information given. If H is in the same group as L, then according to rule 1, F must also be in that group. From the deductions, the only way for H and L to be in the same group is in the first scenario. Be careful here—just because G in S guarantees that L is in T does not mean that L in T guarantees that G is in S. If L is in T, we know nothing about G—all we know is that M could be in S or be out and that K is in T. This makes (D) the credited response.

19. **B**   General

Use the deductions, prior work, and trying the answers to determine which answer choice could be everyone assigned at the same time to group S.

A.   No. According to the deductions, if G is in S then K is in T, and if K is in S, then G is either in T or out.

B.   Yes. With G in S, F and H must be together, but they can be in either S or T, so this works.

C.   No. According to the deductions, if G is in S then K is in T, and if K is in S, then G is either in T or out.

D.   No. This would violate the rule that H and F must be in the same group.

E.   No. This would violate the rule that if K is not in T, then both M and H must be in T.

20. **B**   General

Use the deductions, prior work, and trying the answers to determine which answer choice includes everyone that can never be in the out column. From the initial deductions you know that G, L, and M can be out, so eliminate (C), (D), and (E). The difference between (A) and (B) is K. What happens if you try to put K in the out column? Well, according to rule 4, then H and M must be in T, and F has to be in T as well (rule 1). M in T means L could be in S or be out, and if L is not in T, then G must be in T or be out. This means that at most L is in T, and the setup says that there must be at least two people in each group. That means (B) is the credited response.

21. **A**   Specific

Make a new line in your diagram and fill in the information given. If exactly four people are in, then two must be out. Since F and H must always be together in one of the groups, they must be there alone for this scenario. According to the deductions, if K is in S, then M, F, and H must all be in T. This won't work in this scenario, so K is in T, which means H and F are in S. Since the question asks for who must be in S, your work here is done; the credited response is (A).

22. **B** General

Use the deductions, prior work, and trying the answers to determine which answer choice contains a group of people who cannot be together in T.

A. No. This combination could work if K is in S based on the second scenario of the deductions.

B. Yes. This combination could never work. Since each group must have at least two people assigned, then with these four in T, G and L would be forced together in S, violating rule 3.

C. No. This combination worked in question 17.

D. No. This combination worked in questions 17 and 19.

E. No. This combination worked in question 19.

23. **C** Complex

This question asks you to replace a rule with another rule that will yield the same deductions. Since the initial rule is a conditional, look to see if any of the answers describes the contrapositive. The initial rule is ~KT → HT & MT so look for something that aligns with ~HT or ~MT → KT or even with the initial condition.

A. No. This symbolizes to KS → ~MS & ~HS. This does not match the original condition or its contrapositive.

B. No. This works out to KS → LS, which does not match the original condition or its contrapositive.

C. Yes. This becomes ~KT → HT & MT, which matches the original condition.

D. No. This becomes ~KT → ~ HL same, which does not match the original or its contrapositive.

E. No. This becomes ~HT & ~MT → KT. Be careful here! The initial "or" gets negated to "and" when you change "unless" to "if not." This does not match the original condition or its contrapositive.

Section 3: Reading Comprehension

Questions 1–8

The main point of the first paragraph is to question why great perfume isn't taken as seriously as other works of art. The second paragraph claims a parallel between perfume and other arts and details some of the characteristics of oil paintings. The main point of the third paragraph is to detail the characteristics of fine perfume that parallel the characteristics of fine oil paintings. The main point of the third paragraph is to discuss one possible reason that perfumes are not respected as art: that modern companies tamper with old formulas in a way that degrades quality. The Bottom Line of the passage as a whole is that fine perfume should be viewed as art and treated with similar respect.

1. **D**   Big Picture

    Use your Bottom Line of the passage to help you to evaluate the choices. The correct answer will describe the main idea of the passage.

    A. No. In the fourth paragraph, the author criticizes modern perfume companies for tampering with formulas.

    B. No. While this answer choice is supported by the passage, it is a premise that the author sets out in support of the main point.

    C. No. The author's discussion of the declining quality of perfume is limited to the last paragraph of the passage.

    D. Yes. This accurately matches the Bottom Line that fine perfume should be viewed as art and treated with similar respect.

    E. No. While this answer choice is supported by the passage, it is a premise that the author sets out in support of the main point.

2. **E**   RC Reasoning

    The question is asking for a situation that would be compatible with the author's views about changing perfume formulations. In the last paragraph, the author criticizes modern companies for altering classic formulas by substituting cheap chemical compounds, so the correct answer will respect the original formulas.

    A. No. While the author thinks that *Joy Parfum* is a masterpiece, he does not indicate that other perfumes should smells just like it.

    B. No. This is what the author criticizes in the fourth paragraph.

    C. No. While tempting, the author does not argue that natural chemical compounds are better than synthetic ones, he merely criticizes substitutions of chemical compounds (which could be natural or synthetic) for rarer, better ingredients.

    D. No. The author does not discuss popularity.

    E. Yes. The author criticizes changing perfumes from their original formulas so he or she would support undoing those changes.

3. **A**   Extract Infer

    The correct answer will be the statement that is best supported by evidence within the passage text. The passage says that the "noses" experiment with olfactory elements and produce sensations, so the correct answer should reflect that they are involved in the design and production of perfume.

    A. Yes. Perfumers are involved in the design and production of perfume.

    B. No. Collectors would not be producing sensations.

    C. No. Perfumes would not be experimenting.

    D. No. Marketing people would not be involved in experimenting with smells.

    E. No. Pricing people would not be involved in experimenting with smells.

4. **A** Extract
         Infer

The correct answer will be the statement about art that is best supported by evidence within the passage text.

A. Yes. At the end of the second paragraph, the author argues that a brilliant perfumer, like other artists, can call upon memories.

B. No. This answer choice is extreme. It is not supported that this combination can be detected in *any* work of art.

C. No. This answer choice is extreme. The author does not argue that aiming for commercial success *inevitably* results in failure.

D. No. This answer choice is extreme. The author discusses that the Old Masters used oil paints that causes changes in appearance over time, but there is no argument that they are the best.

E. No. The author does not argue the relative superiority of forms of art, only that perfume should be considered an art.

5. **B** Extract
         Infer

The correct answer will be the statement about *Joy Parfum* that is best supported by the evidence within the passage text.

A. No. There is no mention of increased appreciation of *Joy Parfum*, only a comment that colleagues do not eagerly seek it out.

B. Yes. The author describes it as a masterpiece in the first paragraph and spends the next two paragraphs detailing how perfume parallels other art.

C. No. This answer choice is extreme. While the author calls *Joy Parfum* a masterpiece, there is no support for the idea that it was the foremost accomplishment of its time.

D. No. There is no discussion of who appreciates it.

E. No. There is no discussion of how it compares to other perfumes of its era.

6. **B** RC Reasoning

The question is asking for analogous behavior to that of the "cynical bean counters." In the fourth paragraph, the author argues that the bean counters tamper with old formulas in order to reduce costs and presume customers won't notice the difference, so the correct answer should involve a reduction of costs without regard for quality.

A. No. This does not involve saving money.

B. Yes. This involves saving money without regard for how it will affect quality.

C. No. While this answer choice may be tempting due to the budget reduction, the second half of it does not match with the situation in the passage as there is no anticipation of declining revenue as a motivation for cost-cutting measures.

D. No. This does not involve curtailing costs.

E. No. While this answer choice may be tempting because it mentions slashing a budget, there is no favoritism of one project over another in the passage.

7. **B**   **Extract Infer**

The correct answer will be the statement that is best supported by the evidence within the passage text.

A. No. There is no discussion of consumer knowledge of perfume names.

B. Yes. The last paragraph discusses that corporations are substituting cheap chemical compounds that only approximate rarer, better ingredients in order to increase profits.

C. No. There is no discussion of what consumers want.

D. No. This answer is extreme. There is no support for the claim that perfume makers of the past would *never* tamper with a formula.

E. No. There is no discussion of which perfumes result in the highest profits.

8. **D**   **Structure**

The correct answer will correctly follow the organization of the passage. Use your notes on the main point of each paragraph to evaluate the answer choices.

A. No. While the first paragraph makes an observation that perfumes are not respected as art, the middle paragraphs do not elaborate on that idea; rather, they argue that perfume should be art. The explanation in the final paragraph is not an alternative.

B. No. The first paragraph does not offer a thesis, and the final paragraph does not reject a challenge.

C. No. While this answer choice may be tempting, the final paragraph describes a possible reason for the conventional wisdom rather than support for the idea that perfume should be treated as art.

D. Yes. The first paragraph asks why perfume isn't respected as art, the middle paragraphs discuss why perfume should be respected as art, and the final paragraph discusses one reason that perhaps perfume is not respected as art.

E. No. The first paragraph does not describe a problem, there are no consequences in the middle paragraph, and the final paragraph is focused on a possible explanation even though it makes mention of who's likely to blame.

Questions 9–16

The main point of the first paragraph is to introduce the idea of "stealing thunder"—revealing negative information in court before the other side uses it. The main point of the second paragraph is that lawyers' commonly held belief in the effectiveness of stealing thunder is supported by both simulated trials and by psychological experiments. The third paragraph provides another reason that stealing thunder may be effective and notes a limitation on its effectiveness. The Bottom Line of the passage as a whole is that stealing thunder is likely an effective trial strategy based on psychological research and experiments in simulated trials.

9. **C** Big Picture

Use your Bottom Line of the passage to help you to evaluate the choices. The correct answer will describe the main point of the passage.

A. No. The author notes that the effectiveness of stealing thunder has not been tested in actual trials.

B. No. While the author discusses a limitation of the strategy, the passage is not focused on unintended consequences of its use.

C. Yes. This accurately paraphrases the Bottom Line.

D. No. The focus of the passage is on the effectiveness of the technique rather than its risks.

E. No. The passage does not address the idea that the simulated trial experiments revealed limitations on the stealing thunder strategy.

10. **B** Extract Infer

The correct answer will be an example of stealing thunder that is best supported by the evidence within the passage text. The author describes stealing thunder as the defense attorney revealing negative information about his client before the opposing side has a chance to do so.

A. No. This describes information revealed about the wrong side.

B. Yes. This involved revealing negative information about the defendant before the other side brings it up.

C. No. The goal of stealing thunder is to bring the negative information up before the other side mentions it, not to respond to it.

D. No. The answer choice does not involve revealing negative information.

E. No. Mitigating circumstances are not negative information.

11. **D** Extract Fact

The question is asking for a factor that probably contributes to the success of the stealing thunder strategy. The correct answer will be explicitly supported by the passage.

A. No. The passage does not discuss the length of time between when the two sides discuss the negative information.

B. No. The passage does not discuss lawyers' skill.

C. No. The passage does not discuss how the negative information is revealed.

D. Yes. This is explicitly stated in lines 51–54.

E. No. The passage does not discuss juror screening.

12. **A** **Structure**

The question is asking why the author mentions the "cognitive framework" that jurors create. The passage states that a negative impression formed early in a trial can create a filter that jurors process additional information through as part of the discussion about why it's important that the negative information be framed positively.

A. Yes. This reflects the author's discussion of a filter that jurors may view additional information through.

B. No. The author does not discuss any preconceived notions that jurors may have.

C. No. The relative impact that a piece of information may have at various points in a trial is not discussed in the final paragraph.

D. No. The last paragraph focuses on the risk of a negative impression formed early on and not on the timing of the information relative to the other side.

E. No. The author does not contrast the benefits of positively framing negative information with gaining credibility; rather, both are components of successful stealing thunder.

13. **D** **Extract Infer**

The question is asking how the author feels about stealing thunder. The author argues that stealing thunder is likely a successful strategy based on the evidence, so the correct answer will reflect a positive view.

A. No. This answer choice is too negative, and the passage does not discuss how commonly used the technique is.

B. No. The author does not discuss precisely when the negative information should be revealed.

C. No. This answer choice is too negative, and there's no mention in the passage of crucial omitted evidence.

D. Yes. This answer agrees with the Bottom Line of the passage and is supported by the author's discussion of why stealing thunder works.

E. No. This answer choice is too negative, and there's no discussion of the experience of attorneys using the stealing thunder strategy.

14. **E** **Extract Fact**

The question is asking what support the author gives for his characterization of stealing thunder as a likely successful strategy. The correct answer will be explicitly supported by the passage.

A. No. The passage does not discuss client reactions.

B. No. The passage explicitly states that no studies have been done on actual trials.

C. No. The passage explicitly states that no studies have been done on actual trials.

D. No. The passage does not discuss analogous techniques.

E. Yes. The author discusses both simulated trials and psychological research in the second paragraph.

15. **A**   **Extract**
     Infer

This question is asking what the author means by suggesting that the stealing thunder technique is effective. The passage discusses that stealing thunder, when used appropriately, lessens the weight of negative information and can help jurors view subsequent information in a more favorable light.

A. Yes. Effective use of the technique would make jurors view the side using it more favorably than they otherwise would.

B. No. While there is some discussion of early positive framing in the passage, counterarguments are discussed as things that would potentially be formed by jurors, not introduced by attorneys.

C. No. This answer choice is extreme. While effective use of stealing thunder would aid the side using it, the passage does not support this idea of invariably favorable results.

D. No. The passage discusses the potential of the technique to make jurors think that negative evidence is less important.

E. No. While the negative information must be revealed prior to the opposition revealing it, it is intended to lessen the weight of the information and is not intended to be dramatic.

16. **D**   **Extract**
     Infer

The correct answer will be the statement that is best supported by the evidence within the passage text.

A. No. The author discusses the potential importance of framing the information positively for effectiveness, but does not mention it in the context of deciding whether to steal thunder.

B. No. The passage does not discuss jurors' outside knowledge.

C. No. The passage does not discuss reactions of opposing counsel.

D. Yes. The first paragraph of the passage discusses that there is no point in revealing negative information unknown to or unlikely to be used by the other side and that most lawyers believe in stealing thunder when the opposition would try to derive an advantage.

E. No. The passage discusses psychological research as a reason that stealing thunder might be effective, but it is not discussed in the context of a lawyer's decision to use the strategy.

Questions 17–21

Passage A

The first chunk introduces the idea that recent neuroscience findings change the way we think about the law, specifically that someone may be totally rational but not in control of his or her action. The second chunk argues that the criminal-justice system ought not to be justified based on retribution. The Bottom Line of passage A is that neuroscience findings mean that punishment should not be based on retribution because there is no preventative value. Passage A is persuasive in tone.

Passage B

The first paragraph argues that neuroscience fuels determinism, but determinism can coexist with free will. The second paragraph outlines the theory of "soft determinism" by distinguishing free actions and constrained actions. The third paragraph continues the discussion of free versus constrained. The Bottom Line of passage B is that actions from a disease-free brain are free actions unless they are constrained. Passage B is academic in tone.

17. B Big Picture

The correct answer will reflect the Bottom Line of each passage.

A. No. Passage B does not discuss punishment.

B. Yes. Both passages discuss how neuroscience findings impact views about free will.

C. No. Passage B does not discuss punishment.

D. No. Passage B does not discuss punishment.

E. No. Passage A does not discuss physical coercion.

18. A Extract Fact

The passage is asking for a concept that is mentioned in passage B but not mentioned in passage A.

A. Yes. Passage B mentions mental disorders in line 43 as an example of an external source that constrains actions.

B. No. Both passages discuss free choice or free will. Passage A discusses it in line 10 and passage B discusses it starting in lines 35–36.

C. No. Both passages discuss actions that are caused by forces beyond someone's control. Passage A discusses them starting in line 8 and passage B discusses them starting in line 39.

D. No. This is discussed in passage A, but it is not mentioned in passage B.

E. No. This is discussed in passage A, but it is not mentioned in passage B.

19. B Structure

The question is asking why the author of passage B mentioned David Hume. After claiming that it has long been argued that free will can coexist with determinism, the passage discusses that David Hume was a philosopher two centuries prior who argued that free actions can exist in a deterministic world, just as Ayer argued in the 1950s.

A. No. The author is bolstering Ayer's argument, not criticizing him.

B. Yes. The author is bolstering Ayer's theory of soft determinism by showing that it has been argued for a long time.

C. No. The author is arguing the theory's continued relevance.

D. No. There is no discussion of how long mechanistic descriptions of the brain have existed.

E. No. The author is supporting the claim that soft determinism has been argued for a long time.

20. **C** Big Picture

The question is asking about the relative tones of the passages. Use your Bottom Line of each passage.

A. This answer choice is reversed. Passage A is advocating a point of view, while passage B is presenting a theory.

B. No. Neither passage is negative in tone.

C. Yes. Passage A is advocating a point of view, while passage B is presenting a theory without passing judgment.

D. No. Neither passage uses irony.

E. No. Neither passage is negative in tone.

21. **C** RC Reasoning

The question is asking for an argument analogous to that in passage A. Passage A argues against the current punishment system because of new neuroscience findings. (Note: You can approach this question similarly to the way you would approach a Parallel the Reasoning Arguments question.)

A. No. Passage A does not discuss reducing features.

B. No. While this answer may be tempting because it mentions rationality, passage A does not discuss irrational actions.

C. Yes. As in passage A, this answer argues against a current system because of updated information about the brain.

D. No. Passage A rejects a justification based on new findings about the brain.

E. No. This answer choice does not discuss rejecting a current system.

Questions 22–27

The main point of the first paragraph is that while Mario Garcia's study of Mexican American activism succeeds on one level, it also suffers from two big flaws. The main point of the second paragraph is to discuss the first flaw: that Garcia inconsistently argues political diversity while also claiming underlying consensus among opposing groups. The main point of the third paragraph is to discuss the second flaw: that Garcia may be overstating the degree to which activists' views represent the people. The Bottom Line of the passage as a whole is that Garcia's study of Mexican American activism is undermined by two big flaws.

22. **E** Extract Fact

The question is asking for something that is true of the League of United Latin American Citizens that is not true of the Congress of Spanish-Speaking People. The author discusses that the League encouraged a strategy of assimilation, while the Congress advocated bilingualism and equal rights. The correct answer will be directly supported by the text of the passage.

A. No. The passage does not discuss what was popular with other citizens.

B. No. The passage states that the Congress was the organization that fought for equal rights.

C. No. The passage does not discuss these groups' positions on immigration.

D. No. The passage states that the League advocated assimilation.

E. Yes. In lines 21–22, the passage states that the League encouraged a strategy of assimilation into the United States political and cultural mainstream.

23. **A** **Extract Infer**

The question is asking for a statement about Garcia regarding the Mexican American political activists of the 1930s and 1940s that is best supported by the evidence within the passage text.

A. Yes. In the first paragraph, the passage states that Garcia gives persuasive evidence that activists of the 1930s and 1940s anticipated the reforms of the 1960s and 1970s.

B. No. The passage states that Garcia argues that earlier activists were more diverse than *historians* thought and does not compare the diversity of later activists.

C. No. The passage states that Garcia argues that the activists of the 1960s and 1970s were more militant.

D. No. This answer choice is extreme and unsupported. The passage does not discuss the proportion of activists who advocated bilingual education and equal rights.

E. No. This answer choice is extreme and unsupported. The second paragraph discusses that activist groups were centered on liberal reform, not revolution.

24. **B** **Extract Infer**

The question is asking for a statement about Garcia's view of Mexican Americans between 1930 and 1960 that is best supported by the evidence within the passage text.

A. No. In the third paragraph, the passage explicitly states that Garcia argued that the generation between 1930 and 1960 was more acculturated (assimilated to the dominant culture).

B. Yes. In the third paragraph, the passage explicitly states that Garcia argued that the generation between 1930 and 1960 was more acculturated (assimilated to the dominant culture) and hence more politically active.

C. No. In the third paragraph, the passage explicitly states that Garcia argued that the assimilation was a cause of increased political activity.

D. No. In the second paragraph, the passage discusses that politically active groups were focused on reform, not revolution.

E. No. This answer choice is extreme and unsupported. In the third paragraph, the passage explicitly states that the rhetoric of World War II was inclusive.

25. **B** `Extract Infer`

The question is asking for a statement about the author's view of Mexican American activists between 1930 and 1960 that is best supported by the evidence within the passage text.

A. No. While the passage mentions that the activists of the 1930s and 1940s were less militant than the Chicanos of the 1960s and 1970s, there is no support for the idea that this is because of a common goal.

B. Yes. In the second paragraph, the author argues that the groups were often diametrically opposed, yet their goals centered on liberal reform.

C. No. There is no support for the claim that the groups reached a consensus.

D. No. The passage does not discuss any relative numbers of those favoring assimilation versus cultural maintenance.

E. No. The passage does not discuss whether the activists' goals were achieved.

26. **D** `Extract Infer`

The correct answer will be the statement that is best supported by evidence within the passage text. Look for language that explicitly indicated uncertainty.

A. No. In the third paragraph, the author asserts that we cannot make such an assumption.

B. No. The author does not discuss any assumptions of earlier historians.

C. No. In the second paragraph, the author states that Mexican American activism in that period was characterized by intense and lively debate rather than consensus.

D. Yes. In the third paragraph, the author states that it is "not clear" how far the politically active outlook extended beyond activists.

E. No. In the second paragraph, the author states that these two organizations were often diametrically opposed to one another.

27. **E** `Extract Fact`

The correct answer will be the statement that is best supported by evidence within the passage text. Ethnic consciousness is mentioned at the end of the third paragraph.

A. No. At the end of the third paragraph, the passage discusses that rates of Mexican immigration and naturalization help to create variations in ethnic consciousness, but there is no claim of direct proportion.

B. No. The passage states that one cannot assume that an increase in Mexican Americans born in the United States necessarily increases activism and no correlation is made with ethnic consciousness.

C. No. The passage states that patterns of bilingualism are one factor that helps create variations in ethnic consciousness, but there is no discussion of assimilation in this portion of the paragraph.

D. No. The passage does not discuss the influence of Mexican American leaders.

E. Yes. This is explicitly stated in lines 55–57.

Section 4: Arguments 2

1. B

The question task could be rephrased as "What does Carol incorrectly believe Ming is saying?" or "How has Carol misinterpreted Ming?" The question asks you to determine what Ming's false belief about Carol is, which is an extract task. Ming concludes that it is "fortunate" that trans fats have been eliminated from many manufacturers' cookies, based on the premise that trans fat is particularly unhealthy. Carol responds by challenging Ming's conclusion, and she adds the premise that desserts are not healthy foods. From Carol's response, it needs to be true that she has assumed that Ming is endorsing desserts free of trans fat, or suggesting that they are healthy. Ming does no such thing.

A. No. Nothing in Carol's comments suggests that she is responding to this kind of a claim.

B. Yes. The evidence suggests that Carol believes that Ming is attributing health benefits to food without trans fat. This is supported by Carol's premise that "even without trans fats" desserts are not healthy.

C. No. Nothing in Carol's comments suggests that she is responding to this kind of a claim.

D. No. Nothing in Carol's comments suggests that she is responding to this kind of a claim, but Carol's response indicates that Carol would endorse this view.

E. No. Nothing in Carol's comments suggests that she is responding to this kind of a claim.

2. C

This questions asks you to find the main point of the argument. This is a Disagree argument, and not all Disagree arguments have the same conclusion. The author may argue that the theory with which he or she disagrees is false, that it may be false, or simply that it is not well supported. This author picks the third option, and states "no one should accept this explanation until historical evidence demonstrates that a change in values occurred prior to the Industrial Revolution." Like many Disagree arguments, this has four parts. The first sentence is a fact both the historian and the economist agree upon. The second sentence is a statement of the economist's theory. The third sentence states the author's conclusion as well as his or her primary premise, that facts are required to support explanations. Since this follows a pattern common to Disagree arguments, knowing the pattern helps you find the conclusion. The word "should" also helps tip you off that the third sentence contains the conclusion.

A. No. This is a fact that both the historian and the economist agree upon. Since it is taken as true from the start, it is a premise.

B. No. This is a fact that both the historian and the economist appear to agree upon. Since it is taken as true from the start, it is a premise, or a very safe inference based on one premise.

C. Yes. This correctly states the conclusion of this Disagree argument.

D. No. This states that the economist's argument is false, which is a distortion of that author's actual conclusion, that the economist's argument should not be accepted without facts. This answer choice goes too far outside the scope of the argument and does not match.

E.   No. The author states that in order to accept the economist's argument, we must have evidence that a change in values occurred before the Industrial Revolution. This answer choice, like some LSAT arguments, mistakes an absence of evidence for evidence of absence. The author never indicates that values did not spread, only that we need evidence that they did.

3.   **E**   Strengthen

First, find the conclusion for this Strengthen argument. The argument concludes that "the donated trees are probably consistent with the master plan." This is supported by one fact, that "most" of the plants sold by the nursery are native plants. "Probably" means something is more likely than not. Thus if "most," or more than half, of the plants sold by the nursery are consistent with the plan, then the plants from the nursery are "probably" consistent with the plan. But it is not proven by the premises that most of the plants sold by the nursery are consistent with the plan, only that they are native plants. Native plant are consistent with the plan only if they do not grow to be very large. The large-growing trees present an obstacle to the argument that needs to be ruled out. If the argument can prove that most of the nursery's plants are both native and not subject to growing large, then the author can prove the claim that the plants are "probably" in accord with the plan.

A.   No. This answer choice is has no relevance to the whether the donated trees are consistent with the plan.

B.   No. This answer choice does not help the argument. Since cottonwood trees are not consistent with the plan, the answer provides another a reason that the plants from Three Rivers Nursery might not be consistent. While this does not meaningfully weaken the argument, it goes in the wrong direction.

C.   No. Since the conclusion is only about trees, this answer about shrubs is not relevant to the conclusion.

D.   No. This answer choice is about tree species not native to the area, which is largely out of scope. The nursery sells mostly native plants, and the rarity of non-native plants does not give us any information about whether the plants from the nursery are consistent with the master plan.

E.   Yes. If the nursery sells mostly native plants, and no trees that grow to be very large, then the majority of the trees sold by the nursery necessarily conform to the master plan. So it is probable that the donated trees conform to the master plan. This answer choice rules out the possibility that the trees from the nursery, while probably native, are not consistent with the plan.

4.   **D**   Necessary Assumption

Find the argument's conclusion first: "*Diplodocus* must have fed on plants on or near the ground, or underwater." If you use the Why Test on this, it becomes clear that the author argues that this is the case because *Diplodocus*'s neck bones prevented it from raising its long neck to reach high growing vegetation. Just because one theorized means of reaching high vegetation does not automatically mean that *Diplodocus* never fed on high-growing vegetation. One way to look at this argument is that the author assumes that neck-raising is the only way to feed on high-growing vegetation. There is also language shift here between reaching high vegetation by raising its neck and reaching high vegetation at all. Necessary Assumption answers that are phrased in the negative lend themselves particularly well to the Negation Test. If you negate (D), you get "*Diplodocus* had some other way of accessing high-growing vegetation, such as by rising up on its hind legs." This utterly destroys the conclusion and confirms that it is the right answer.

A. No. What is true of modern animals is irrelevant to what *Diplodocus* fed on.

B. No. What *Diplodocus* could see is not necessarily relevant to what it ate. It may have used other senses to find food.

C. No. This answer gives another reason why *Diplodocus* could not lift its head, a fact already established in the premise. It does not directly relate to the conclusion.

D. Yes. This answer rules out the possibility that there might have been another way to reach high-growing foliage. The Negation Test makes this clear, as explained above.

E. No. This answer rules out other ways that *Diplodocus* could have eaten underwater vegetation, and it suggests that if *Diplodocus* ate underwater vegetation, it did so by lowering its head. However, it does not help at all to rule out high vegetation as a food source. If you negate it, you get "*Diplodocus* was able..." to get to underwater food sources, which is quite consistent with the conclusion.

5. **D** Principle
Strengthen

The question task asks you to find a principle that strengthens the conclusion. For most of these Principle-Strengthen questions, the right answer will be strong and prove the conclusion. Start by finding the conclusion: "The government should not assist them in rebuilding." This statement is a recommendation, and the word "should" tips you off that this is the conclusion. The most important premise is the last sentence, which indicates that the reason for following the conclusion is that landslides in the future could cause injury. Many Principle-Strengthen questions follow a pattern of giving you a specific fact (a premise) and a specific recommendation (the conclusion). The answer choices in these arguments are general recommendations; when you add the general recommendation in the answer to the specific fact in the premise, you guarantee the specific recommendation in the conclusion. Here, you need to look for an answer choice that connects the fact about landslides and future injury with the recommendation that the government not help, and remember that the right answer needs to take you from the premise to the conclusion.

A. No. This answer choice does not connect to the main premise about landslides. You can also diagram the unless statement this way: ~Government help → ~allowed to build. This statement leads away from the conclusion instead of toward it.

B. This answer ignores the main premise, which states that the reason the government should not help is the risk of landslides, so it is not relevant. Even if you ignore that, it would work against the conclusion and point toward recommending that the government help.

C. No. This answer ignores the main premise, which states that the reason the government should not help is the risk of landslides, so it is not relevant. Even if you ignore that, the answer would not be relevant here for another reason: These people are committed to their community.

D. Yes. This answer choice connects the government not helping with the risk of injury. Moreover, it goes the right direction. It guarantees that if there is the chance of serious injury, then there should be no government help.

E. No. This answer is irrelevant for at least two reasons: Discouraging residents is not clearly connected to withholding help, and second, there is no evidence in the argument that this area has an extensive history of landslides.

6. **B** **Necessary Assumption**

Look for the conclusion. The prediction about what's possible in the future is the conclusion here: "we can control future climate change…." Use the Why Test to confirm that this is the conclusion and find the key premise. Here the author would say that we can control future climate change *because* "human behavior is responsible for climate change." Since the question task asks you to find a necessary assumption, look for something that will connect the premise to the conclusion. Check your answer using the Negation Test. The right answer, when negated, will damage the conclusion.

A. No. A "purely natural cause" for climate change is not relevant to either the premise or the conclusion.

B. Yes. This connects the premise to the conclusion. Test it with the Negation Test: Human beings *cannot* control the aspects of their behavior that have an impact on climate change. When negated, the answer choice makes it impossible to control future climate change, which demolishes the conclusion.

C. No. This answer choice deals with the past, not the future, and is not relevant to the conclusion.

D. No. The danger to other species and the comparison between the danger to humans and to other species are not relevant to the conclusion.

E. No. The relative difficulty between recognizing behaviors and changing them is not relevant to the conclusion. Additionally, this answer choice goes in the wrong direction, giving more reason why it might be difficult to change behaviors, which works against the conclusion.

7. **A** **Inference**

This task, along with the phrase "reasonable to conclude," tells you that you need to find an inference. Consider whether any of the statements can be combined to get a conclusion. In this case, we know two things about the patients waiting for news: They are experiencing more stress than the other group, and they are feeling less pain. At least in this instance, there seems to be a demonstrated link between uncertainty, stress, and a lack of pain.

A. Yes. This is carefully worded ("sometimes") and is supported by the passage: Stress in these patients is clearly associated with less pain.

B. No. This is quite possible, but the argument gives you no evidence of whether the pain is beneficial, harmful, or neutral. This answer is unsupported.

C. No. This answer is fairly strongly worded ("usually") and while you know the lack of the information is associated with less pain, you have no information about the effect of the lack of information on the severity of the condition.

D. No. The passage gives no information about the cause and effect relationship between stress and reduced blood flow, so this answer is unsupported.

E. No. The passage gives no reason to think this; the proportion needing surgery could just as well be the same for both groups.

8. **B**   Flaw

This argument concludes that walking on hind legs is instinctive and not a learned behavior for these bears. Even though this argument does not use the words "cause" or "effect," this is an excellent example of a causal argument. One less-common causal assumption is that there can be only one cause for a particular result. This argument incorrectly rejects the possibility that the behavior is learned, simply because the shape of the bones shows that the behavior is natural. Since the question task asks for a description of the argument's flaw, the credited response will describe the problem with the argument, that one possible cause is rejected only because another possible cause exists. Look out for attractors that describe other common flaws on the test. These answer choices are both common and appealing.

A. No. This answer choice perfectly describes a sampling error. There is no evidence of a sampling in the argument, and you must accept the premise that standing and walking upright is natural for the bears.

B. Yes. This identifies the flaw in the argument. There is no evidence that the two causes for the behavior are mutually exclusive.

C. No. This is a perfect description of a shifting meanings argument, but there is no evidence in the argument that the meaning shifts.

D. No. The argument does presume that there are only two ways to explain the behavior, but it is a perfectly logical presumption. There is no other conceivable explanation for behaviors other than that they are learned or innate. The argument also fails to consider that both explanations could account for the behavior.

E. This is a perfect description of an appeal to authority, but there is no evidence of this. The scientists' determination is provided as a premise, and it relies on their research, not a general sense of respect for the scientists.

9. **B**   Resolve/ Explain

This argument establishes the premise that people are interested in and moved by "generally misleading" anecdotes. It also sets up an apparent paradox by establishing that people have fairly accurate beliefs about society. All of the facts presented are true, so you need to look for new information in the answer choice that allows the statements to be true at the same time. The only way to do this logically will be to establish that people do not base their whole belief system on these interesting and moving, but misleading anecdotes.

A. No. This answer may be appealing because it helps to explain why people are not interested in statistics. However, it does nothing to explain why people have accurate beliefs about society.

B. Yes. If people recognize the anecdotes to be unrepresentative, this shows how they can be interested and moved without the anecdotes shaping their views about society.

C. No. This may actually make the problem worse, since emotionally compelling anecdotes are misleading. This does nothing to explain why people's beliefs are surprisingly accurate.

D. No. This might explain why people like anecdotes, but since we know that most anecdotes are misleading, it does nothing to explain why people have fairly accurate beliefs.

74

E. No. This answer gives no explanation of why people hold fairly accurate beliefs. This answer makes the paradox worse, since we know the anecdotes cause an emotional response and are also misleading. This would give a reason why people would have inaccurate beliefs about society.

10. **C**   Evaluate

This argument concludes that Schweitzer's discovery helps to prove that dinosaurs are closely related to birds. Schweitzer's discovery is that *T. rex* and chickens have similar collagen proteins. Since the question task asks for an answer that is useful in evaluating the argument, look for a question whose answer would help to prove or disprove a key assumption. In this argument, the key assumption is that the similar collagen proteins shared by chickens and *T. rex* somehow mean they are related. The argument shows a language shift between "similar...proteins" and "closely related." So look for an answer that tells us whether similar proteins indicate that the animals are related.

A. No. This does not relate to the central assumption of the argument. The rarity of the find does nothing to prove or disprove the assumption that similar proteins indicate a close relationship.

B. No. This does not relate to the central assumption of the argument, and it does nothing to prove or disprove the assumption that similar proteins indicate a close relationship. Whether this evidence adds to the link between birds and dinosaurs is independent of whether there is any evidence against the link.

C. Yes. The answer to this question will prove or disprove the central assumption of the argument. If it is very unlikely for unrelated animals to have similar collagen protein, that indicates the argument is very strong, since similar collagen protein would then strongly indicate a relationship between birds and dinosaurs. If it is very likely for unrelated animals to have similar proteins, then Schweitzer's finding means very little, since the animals could have similar proteins but be unrelated.

D. No. This does not relate to the central assumption of the argument. Knowing whether this is possible or not does little to prove whether the similarity in collagen indicates a close relationship.

E. No. This does not relate to the central assumption of the argument. Whether the discovery was surprising has no bearing on whether similar collagen indicates a close relationship between the animals.

11. **A**   Inference

The passage establishes that the professor experienced serious subjective effects when she is sleep deprived, but that most students apparently noticed no objective changes in her when she is sleep deprived. Since the question task asks you to make an inference about the argument, the credited response will be provable using the information in the passage.

Avoid answer choices that rely on unsupported assumptions or make conclusions outside the scope of the argument.

A. Yes. While the professor experienced serious subjective effects when she is sleep deprived, most students apparently noticed no objective changes in her when she is sleep deprived. This comparison is provable using the information in the passage, since most students noticed nothing and the professor noticed several effects.

B. No. This answer choice is not true unless it is assumed that the subjective effects are the same as the overall effects. There is no evidence in the passage that the professor's assessment was more accurate than the students' assessment of her performance, only that it was different. This answer requires unsupported assumptions.

C. No. This answer is out of scope, since it compares professors' job performance to that of others. Since we have no information about the effect of sleep deprivation on others, this answer is unsupported.

D. No. This answer is out of scope, since it compares occasional sleep deprivation to extended sleep deprivation. Since we have no information about extended sleep deprivation, this answer is unsupported.

E. No. This answer is unsupported, since we cannot assume that the university students' assessment was accurate. Even if we had that information, the passage does not prove that there is a single other instance in which university students observed something astutely.

12. **D** **Resolve/ Explain**

Even though the answer choices are framed as principles here, the task is to "reconcile" the apparent conflict. The answer should do what every Resolve/Explain credited response does: add a new premise that shows how the other premises can be true at the same time. As with other Resolve/Explain questions, every statement is a premise, so take every statement as true and do not look for a conclusion. The "despite the fact" shows the contrast and helps you find the conflict. Look for an answer choice that tells us why our government should give priority to satisfying the needs of our people, even though it is not objectively more important to do so, and the people are equal in worth.

A. No. This answer choice makes the conflict worse. Since we know the satisfaction of our people's needs is no more objectively important than satisfying the needs of other people, this principle would suggest that the government not attempt to satisfy its people's needs. This answer choice gives a good reason why the two premises could not be true at the same time.

B. No. This answer choice makes the conflict worse. We know that other people are equally worthy, so if this principle is true, it gives us no reason why our government should give priority to our people. This answer choice gives a good reason why the two premises could not be true at the same time.

C. No. This answer does not solve the conflict, but makes the conflict worse. This answer choice identifies the second premise, about people's objective worth, as the primary premise in determining the first premise. Rather than presenting a new reason to prioritize our people's needs, it suggests that any new reason is relatively less important than the premise already given.

D. Yes. This answer agrees with the premises in the argument and shows how they can be true at the same time. This answer gives us a new principle that provides a reason why our government should satisfy the needs of its people despite the equal worth of all people. Everyone is equally worthy, but under this principle each government looks out for its own people.

E. No. This answer choice does not solve the conflict. There is no information in the argument or answer that allows us to determine whether there is some "other way" for the group's needs to be satisfied. So the principle about another way to satisfy needs is not clearly related to the conflict, and it is unclear what effect, if any, this principle has on the passage.

13. D Inference

This passage establishes that all neighborhoods will be swept once a month. Some neighborhoods will receive an extra sweeping in addition to the monthly sweeping. Consider whether any of the statements can be combined to get a conclusion. Two factors, taken together, are sufficient to guarantee at least one extra sweeping: The neighborhood is "qualified," and the neighborhood requests it. Try to predict what wrong answers might do. Beware of extreme quantity statements such as "all" or "no." Wrong answers in any inference question dealing with necessary or sufficient conditions may confuse necessary and sufficient or may play tricks by ignoring one of the conditions.

A. No. While excessive dirt from major construction is one circumstance that could result in a neighborhood becoming qualified, construction alone is not a factor that guarantees qualification. This is too strongly worded to be supported.

B. No. Two factors taken together are sufficient to guarantee that a neighborhood's streets will be swept more than once a month: The neighborhood is qualified, and the neighborhood requests a sweeping. Qualification alone does not guarantee an extra sweeping. This is too strongly worded to be supported.

C. No. This answer choice mistakes one part of a situation sufficient to guarantee more than one sweeping per month for a condition necessary to allow more than one sweeping. While any qualified neighborhood that requests a sweeping will be swept more than once a month, other neighborhoods might be swept more frequently for other reasons.

D. Yes. Since the city will satisfy all requests for interim sweepings immediately, and since every street will already be swept once a month, this must be true. Only the first and third sentences are needed to make this inference.

E. No. Qualified and requesting neighborhoods get an extra sweeping in addition to their regular monthly sweeping, but other neighborhoods might as well. "Qualified and Requesting → Extra Sweeping" does not mean "~Qualified → ~Extra Sweeping." This mistakes part of sufficient condition for a necessary condition.

14. A Reasoning

The question task asks for an answer that describes what the journalist is doing. These question tasks are match tasks, so you need to find an answer choice that matches what is going on in the passage. Start by identifying the argument's purpose. This argument is a Disagree argument, and the author disagrees with the view that journalists' withholding of information is "like lying...intentional deception and therefore unethical." The conclusion that the author disagrees with relies on a comparison between lying and withholding information. Understanding the common reasoning pattern helps here. The argument's author attempts to weaken this comparison in the most effective way of weakening a comparison, by pointing out a relevant difference between the two things being compared.

A. Yes. This answer choice matches perfectly. This describes most of what the author does and does not include anything that the author does not do.

B. No. This answer choice does not match. There is no evidence that the journalist considers the distinction between lying and withholding information to be controversial. Even more important, the author never provides a "clear instance."

C. No. This answer does not match. The author does define a concept: "to lie." But then the author's most important point is that it does not apply to all the cases under discussion. The equation of lying and withholding information is rejected.

D. No. This answer does not match. This argument is general in its approach, and it does not use examples or counterexamples.

E. No. This answer choice does not match. This argument is general in its approach, and it does not look at individual cases. The author never is quite consistent in the argument that lying is always wrong for journalists and that withholding information should not be considered lying.

15. **C**   Flaw

This argument concludes that "there is no reason to lower interest rates further." This is based on the premise that one reason to lower interest rates is invalid. One reason to lower interest rates is to stimulate the economy, and this stimulation is not needed. Focus on this gap: Just because one stated reason for a course of action is not valid, it is an error of logic to conclude that the course of action is unneeded. There might be many good reasons to lower interest rates that have nothing to do with stimulating economic growth.

A. No. This answer may be appealing because the argument involves experts, but this argument actually rejects the testimony of many economists. The economist making the argument rejects the colleagues' authority in favor of a different conclusion, based on a premise that no stimulation is needed.

B. No. It is clear that stimulation is the cause, and growth is the effect. The author correctly argues that since the particular effect of growth is already occurring, no stimulation is needed to achieve that result.

C. Yes. The argument jumps from proving that there is no need to stimulate economic growth to the overbroad conclusion that there is no need to lower interest rates, as explained above.

D. No. The author effectively rules out any need to stimulate economic growth, by showing that it is already happening. It does not matter whether there are other ways of stimulating growth, since none of them are needed, at least for the purpose of stimulating growth.

E. No, while the second part of this answer repeats a premise, the first part, involving further reductions and unsustainable growth, has no basis in the argument.

16. **E**   Sufficient Assumption

The argument concludes that Caravaggio's works do not fit the definition of Baroque painting, and it establishes one important fact in the premise: The definition of Baroque painting requires that it be opulent, heroic, and extravagant. We know from the premise that Caravaggio's works were realistic and showed a novel use of the interplay of light and shadow. The argument gives us no information about what those qualities mean with regards to the definition of Baroque, and no information about whether Caravaggio has the qualities necessary to be Baroque: "opulence, heroic sweep, and extravagance." We can represent this as "B → OHE" and "~OHE → ~B." Since the question tasks asks for a sufficient assumption, the credited response will clearly link Caravaggio with a lack of opulence, heroism, and extravagance, which will prove that his work does not fit the stated definition of Baroque.

A. No. This answer choice does not connect any parts of the argument or bridge any gaps. This answer choice is irrelevant.

B. No. This answer choice deals with only one premise, and it makes a statement that is already proven by that premise. Since Caravaggio had these two qualities, they can clearly exist together. This answer choice is irrelevant to the conclusion.

C. No. This answer choice deals with a prior time period and is therefore irrelevant.

D. No. This *appears* to bridge a gap in the argument, by linking realism with a lack of opulence, heroism, and extravagance. However, the language is weak, and even if a realist painting does not "usually" demonstrate these qualities, this answer does not prove that Caravaggio's paintings lacked heroism, opulence, and extravagance. So even if this were true, Caravaggio could still be considered Baroque.

E. Yes. If Caravaggio's work lacks *all* of the traits that are *required* by the definition of Baroque, this strongly worded answer proves that his work cannot fit this definition.

17. E   **Reasoning**

The author argues against the proponents of jury nullification by making the point that when juries are allowed to put jury nullification into practice, they often make mistakes. The author's only premise against jury nullification is the general statement that bad results often follow from this practice.

The question task here is a matching task. Watch out for appealing trap answers that describe a common pattern that does not match this argument, or other wrong answers that fail to describe the main thing this argument does.

A. No. This is a perfect description of an ad hominem or attack on the person making the argument. However, there is nothing in the argument above to indicate that the author is attacking the proponents of jury nullification rather than their arguments.

B. No. An argument with an inconsistency would have two premises that conflict with each other, and the proponents' arguments do not conflict with each other. This answer may be appealing because the word "but" appears and there is conflict in the paragraph. The conflict, however, is between the proponents' argument and the author's.

C. No. The author does not argue against any premise proposed by the proponents of jury nullification. Rather, the author brings in a new premise that shows a negative consequence of jury nullification.

D. No. This argument is very general, and the author never brings in an example. Rather, the author counters a general claim by bringing in a new general statement.

E. Yes. This is exactly what the author does, as explained above.

18. E   **Flaw**

This argument uses a premise about people 65–81 who suffer from insomnia, and it jumps to a conclusion that posits that people produce melatonin as they get older. In order to prove this, the argument would need a representative sample of younger people, a representative sample of older people, and evidence that the older people were deficient in melatonin. The evidence presented by the pharmacist does not provide any of these things. The sampling does not include younger people, and importantly includes only older people with insomnia. So perhaps it is the insomnia that is correlated with low melatonin, not advanced age. Perhaps insomnia occurs at the same rate in older and younger people, and any group with insomnia would respond well to melatonin supplements. No matter how large the sample the author has chosen, it could never be representative of the point the author is trying to make, since it samples only people with insomnia and does not allow us to make any comparison between younger and older people. As you read the answer choices, watch out for attractive wrong answers that describe common flaws that do not appear in this argument.

A.   No. This argument does infer a cause from a proven effect, but there is no discussion of intent. The author never states the intent behind giving people melatonin.

B.   No. This is an appealing answer, because the argument mentions manufacturers, who might be biased. But the argument never relies on these claims. Instead, it tries to use a factual premise to prove these claims.

C.   No. This perfectly describes an equivocation or shifting meanings flaw. But there is no term in the argument that is used in two different meanings.

D.   No. This answer is appealing, because the conclusion is a claim about cause, while the premise is about an effect. But the argument fails to prove that this purported cause and the purported effect are even related to each other, as explained above. So this answer fails to describe the main flaw.

E.   Yes. This answer describes the flaw: The argument uses a premise about people 65–81 who suffer from insomnia, and it jumps to a conclusion that compares younger people to older people. As explained above, this particular sample could never prove the author's conclusion, no matter how large it is.

19.   **C**   **Parallel**

Remember that "unless" is consistently the same thing as "if not." So that means that we can properly diagram the statement "it would sell out unless it was poorly promoted" this way: "~Poorly Promoted → Sell out." The contrapositive of this statement is "~Sell out → Poorly promoted." The author then points out that the concert did not sell out. So the contrapositive statement leads right from not selling out to the logically correct conclusion, the concert was "probably not properly promoted." The premise is not presented as absolute truth, but rather as the assessment of a knowledgeable individual, so this matches the carefully worded "probably" in the conclusion. The question task is to find an answer choice that follows the same logical pattern as the argument. The statements do not need to be in the same order as the argument, but you should look for an answer that has the same kind of conclusion as the original argument and follows the same logical steps to get there.

A.   No. One premise can be diagrammed as "Performed by highly skilled surgeon → patient probably survives," and the contrapositive would be "~patient probably survives → ~performed by a highly skilled surgeon." The argument establishes that the patient did not survive and then concludes that it was probably "not properly performed," a conclusion that has no basis in the premises. The "probably" in the premise also makes this argument unlike the original argument.

B.   No. This argument is superficially similar to the argument above. You can diagram the conditional statement as "Is labeled properly → contains organic compounds," and the contrapositive is "~contains organic compounds → is not labeled correctly." Then the argument establishes that the sample probably did not contain organic compounds, and it concludes that the sample is not labeled correctly. The crucial point of difference between this and the original article is the "probably" in the premise. The "probably" in the conclusion of the original argument makes the argument better, since the conclusion is easier to support. But the "probably" in the premise makes the argument weaker. Furthermore, the conditional statement appears to be based on the other premise in this answer choice, and not given directly by the expert, as it is in the original argument.

C. Yes. This can be diagrammed thus: "Properly repaired → ~noticeable," and the contrapositive is "noticeable → ~properly repaired." The argument establishes that the damage is noticeable, and it logically follows the arrow of the contrapositive to the correct conclusion, that the repair was probably not properly done. Just as in the argument above, the conclusion is hedged with the safe "probably," and the premise is presented as the assessment of a knowledgeable person.

D. No. The conditional statement can be diagrammed as "~damaged in a storm → ~roof requires repairs," and the contrapositive is "roof requires repairs → damaged in a storm." The argument establishes that the roof requires repairs, and if it were like the original argument, it would conclude that the roof was damaged in the storm. This answer choice, however, makes a conclusion totally unlike the original argument, that the builder was probably wrong.

E. No. The conditional statement can be diagrammed as "tests properly conducted → tests find lead in soil," and the contrapositive is "~tests find lead in soil → ~tests properly conducted." The argument then establishes that the tests did find lead in the soil, and it concludes that they were properly conducted. Unlike the original argument, this answer choice does not rely on the correct contrapositive. Instead, it assumes the unsupported conditional "Tests find lead in soil → tests properly conducted." Here the author has apparently flipped the conditions without negating them. So the conclusion is unsupported, and the argument is not parallel to the original argument.

20. D   Flaw

This Interpret argument puts forward the broad and fairly extreme conclusion that "global recessions can never be prevented." Statements about the future, especially statements using absolute quantity statements such as "never," are very difficult to support, no matter how strong the premises. The key premise here is that recessions can be prevented *only if* they are predictable, which can be diagrammed as "Prevented → predictable." This strong premise is followed by the weaker premise that economists, using the best techniques they have, in the past and present, consistently fail to predict recessions. So this argument would be quite strong if it were about the present. But since the conclusion leaps into the future and concludes that recessions *never* can be prevented, it is not supported. We would need a premise that economists could *never* predict a recession in order to support this extreme conclusion. So the flaw is the author's assumption that what is true of economists' ability to predict recessions will *always* be true.

A. No. This is a perfect description of a circular reasoning flaw, but there is no trace of circular reasoning in the argument.

B. No. The argument does not establish this, but whether economists claim to be able to predict or not is not relevant to the argument's validity.

C. No. This is a good description of a necessary and sufficient flaw. The argument does establish that predictability is necessary for prevention, which can be diagrammed as "Prevented → predictable." But the author never claims or assumes that predictability is sufficient for prevention, which would be diagrammed as "Predictable → prevented."

D. Yes. This perfectly matches the flaw as described above.

E. No. The argument does infer that something (prevention of recessions) will not occur. But this is not based just on the information that it is not predictable. It is based on two different things: information that economists do not seem to be able to predict it currently and a strong conditional statement that shows that prevention requires the ability to predict. This answer choice fails to describe the main components of the argument.

21. **A**   **Principle Match**

This argument concludes that the "newspaper exhibits an unjustified bias." The author of the letter offers the premise that Hanlon's statements were viewed skeptically by the newspaper, and that the newspaper's skepticism is unsupported by evidence. This question task is just a variant of a typical Principle-Match question, and you need to find the principle that is most in conflict with the argument. This is a Disagree argument in which the letter to the editor attacks the newspaper's behavior. Thus, any principle that matches the newspaper's approach is likely to conflict with the argument, so look for a principle that matches the newspaper's actions.

A. Yes. This principle matches the approach apparently taken by the newspaper, since the newspaper was skeptical about an extraordinary claim that was not supported by the evidence. The author of the letter appears to think the opposite, that such an extraordinary claim, unbacked by evidence, should be accepted without criticism. So this answer is in sharp contrast to the author's reasoning.

B. No. The issue of an "intermediary source" neither matches nor conflicts with the argument. It it irrelevant.

C. No. This principle fits with the author's conclusion, since the letter argues that Hanlon should not have been viewed skeptically by the newspaper.

D. No. This principle appears to relate to Hanlon's actions, not the newspaper's, so it is not in clear contrast or agreement with the author.

E. No. The author disagrees with the newspaper about the level of skepticism directed at Hanlon, not about whether the newspaper should publish an unconfirmed report. So this answer does not clearly match or conflict with anything in the argument.

22. **C**   **Flaw**

This argument establishes a premise that can be diagrammed thus:

Closely related → evolved only once;
~Evolved only once → ~closely related.

The argument then establishes that the species are not closely related and concludes that they evolved more than once. In order to reach this conclusion, the author needs to assume the following:

~Closely related → ~evolved only once.

This conditional statement is derived by negating both sides of the conditional in the premise, without flipping the conditions. So this is not a correctly derived contrapositive. The argument establishes that being closely related is sufficient to prove that this specialization evolved only once, but it incorrectly assumes that if a trait evolved only once, then all animals with that trait will necessarily be closely related.

A. No. This is a good description of a causal flaw, but it does not match the argument. There is a real causal relationship between evolving only once and being closely related, but the argument misunderstands this relationship.

B. No. This is a good description of an absence of evidence flaw, but it does not match the argument. The argument never points to unconfirmed evidence to claim that something is false.

C. Yes. This describes the flaw, as explained above.

D. No. The answer describes a confusion between probability and certainty, and it does not match the argument. The argument never establishes that the trait was even likely to have evolved more than once.

E. No. This answer simultaneously describes an appeal to authority flaw and a sampling error, but it does not match the argument. The argument is not based on the biologists' credentials, but rather on their argument, and there is nothing to indicate that they are unrepresentative.

23. **E** | Principle Match

This passage, like many Principle-Match questions, has no conclusion, but states two principles. Both deal with what the government of Country F must do whenever it sells a state-owned entity: First, it must seek out the highest price it can get on the market, and second, it must ensure that citizens of the country maintain a majority ownership of the company for no less than a year after the sale. This question task is just a variant of a typical Principle-Match question, and you need to find the answer that is most in conflict with the principles stated in the passage. The answer will need to match and be relevant to the principle in order to clearly conflict with it. So any answer choices that are not related to the principles stated above should be eliminated. The right answer will violate at least one principle, but the wrong answers need not match the principles at all. Note also that since the principles concern only what the government does, the right answer must present a situation in which the government actually plans the sale of a state-owned entity.

A. No. There is no part of this situation that violates a principle. The answer never shows non-citizens owning a majority share at any point in the first year.

B. No. There is no part of this situation that violates a principle. The location of sales and operations is not relevant to the principles.

C. No. There is no part of this situation that violates a principle. It is unclear whether anything about World Oil Company is relevant. If World Oil Company were majority owned by citizens of Country F, and it put in the highest bid, then the government would have violated its principles. But the answer proves neither of these things. It is unclear whether citizens own a majority share, unclear whether World Oil Company put in the highest bid, and unclear who the government is planning to sell to.

D. No. There is no part of this situation that violates a principle. The company with the highest bid is, from the information given, a company that could buy the utility in complete accord with the principles. The consortium with the second highest bid is not relevant, since there is no evidence that the government plans to sell the company to them in violation of the first principle.

E. Yes. This answer choice partially follows the second principle. It is unclear how long majority ownership will last, so it is not clear if the second principle is followed. But critically, this situation clearly violates the first principle, since the restrictions "reduce the price the government receives" and the first principle requires the government to sell the entity for the most it can get on the open market.

24. **D** | Weaken

The argument concludes that Activite must be effective, since the makers of the supplement offer a month's supply free as a promotion. The argument assumes that the only benefit the company could get out of this is the continued business from happy customers, and it assumes that the company does not benefit from the customers who take advantage of the offer and then choose not to buy Activite.

Although "since" usually marks a premise, it is important in this argument not to take the "since" statement as fact. On the extremely rare occasions when the test has presented something as support for the conclusion that is not meant to be taken as a factual premise, the word "would" has been used to show that the statement is meant to be part of the author's reasoning rather than a fact. If the since statement is taken as fact then you get the conditional "~effective → ~in company's best interest," and the contrapositive "In company's best interest → effective." But because this statement is meant to be taken as the author's reasoning rather than fact, there's a way it can be false. Look for an answer that shows how the offer can be in the company's best interest without the supplement being effective.

A. No. This shows that Activite is not a necessary source of these nutrients, but it does not show that Activite is not sufficient to provide the nutrients or that Activite is not effective. Activite can be effective without being the only way to increase energy and mental effectiveness.

B. No. This indicates that there are alternatives to Activite that are a better value, but it in no way diminishes the conclusion that Activite is effective. Activite can be overpriced and still have all the efficacy its makers advertise.

C. No. This does not give any reason why Activite might not be effective. If this promotion works even partially within a month, this gives only more reason to think that Activite is even more effective than people realize within that first month.

D. Yes. This adds an additional consideration to the argument. The author ignores the possibility that the makers of Activite might benefit from the promotion even when people are unhappy with the product. If the company makes a profit on the "free" supply by charging a premium for shipping and handling, the company can make a lot of money even if every customer hates their product.

E. No. While this proves that Activite is not guaranteed to be free of side effects, it does not prove that the supplement is not effective. Even if this answer were stronger and demonstrated a likelihood of side-effects, it would not weaken the conclusion, since even the most effective treatments can have serious side-effects.

25. **A**   Parallel Flaw

This argument concludes that Theresa probably approves of the prime minister. "Probably" is a quantity statement meaning "more likely than not" and is often a proxy for the concept of "most": If more than half of people in a group have brown hair, a random member of that group "probably" has brown hair. More than half of the people who disapprove of the prime minister overall disapprove of the prime minister's support for a tax increase. However, this is not the same thing as saying that more than half of the people who are in favor of the tax increase approve of the prime minister overall. It is possible that most or all of the people who approve of the tax increase disapprove of the prime minister overall because of an unrelated issue, such as ethics violations or social policy. Most A are B is a totally different statement from saying that most non-B are non-A, and the argument confuses these statements. Since the question task directs you to find a flaw similar to this flaw, look for this same pattern in the answer choices: The right answer will assume that "Most A are B" means that most non-B are non-A.

A. Yes. This argument matches the original argument piece by piece. The error is the same. Most of the people who support logging think it will reduce risk of fire, but there is no reason to think that because Andy does not think it will reduce the risk of fire means that he is likely to oppose logging. Like the original argument, the this answer assumes that the statement "most A are B" implies "most non-B are non-A."

B. No. This answer choice switches the conditions in the second sentence, relative to the original argument. In order for it to be similar, it would have to start by establishing that Bonita does not favor a new school. This makes a different error, assuming that since most A are B, most non-A are non-B.

C. No. This answer choice switches the conditions in the second sentence, relative to the original argument. In order for it to be similar, it would have to start by establishing that Chung does believe his situation has improved. This makes a different error, assuming that since most A are B, most non-A are non-B.

D. No. This answer choice is not in error; it assumes that since most A are B, a member of A is probably a member of B. This is not what the original argument does.

E. No. This answer choice is not in error; it assumes that since most A are B, a member of A is probably a member of B. This is not what the original argument does.

26. **B**   **Strengthen**

The argument concludes that a loss of nesting habitat probably caused a decrease in the mourning dove population in the area. A premise establishes that mourning doves nested in the nearby orchards, but a sprinkler system made the orchards inhospitable for the doves. This is a causal argument, and the purported effect is a premise: There was a decrease in the mourning dove population. The cause of this decrease is disputable. If the orchards make up a tiny percentage of the nesting habitat, this argument is weak. If the orchards make up most or all of the nesting habitat, then the argument is stronger. The argument requires, among other things, that the orchards make up a significant portion of the area's nesting habitat.

A. No. This answer choice provides another reason the mourning doves may be declining: People may be hunting them. This slightly weakens the argument.

B. Yes. This rules out any alternative places for the mourning doves to nest, indicating that the birds lost 100 percent of their habitat in the area. So even if the argument has not proven a causal relationship perfectly, it is clear that the doves lost all their local habitat and suffered a decrease in their population.

C. No. This answer is not clearly relevant to the conclusion. This shows that the mourning doves' aversion to sprinklers also applies to blue jays. But it does nothing to show that the cause for the decrease in mourning doves in the area is the loss of habitat. What happens to blue jays is not relevant to the mourning doves.

D. No. This answer choice is not relevant to the conclusion, which links a decline in mourning doves to a loss of habitat.

E. No. The argument already shows that the mourning doves in this area had nested in orchards. What mourning doves "often" do has no direct relevance to whether a loss of habitat caused a decline in local mourning doves.

Chapter 5
PrepTest 75:
Answers and
Explanations

ANSWER KEY: PREPTEST 75

Section 1:
Arguments 1

1. B
2. C
3. A
4. E
5. C
6. D
7. E
8. C
9. A
10. E
11. D
12. D
13. C
14. A
15. C
16. C
17. D
18. B
19. B
20. E
21. B
22. C
23. C
24. E
25. A

Section 2:
Reading
Comprehension

1. C
2. A
3. B
4. C
5. A
6. D
7. E
8. B
9. A
10. A
11. C
12. B
13. B
14. E
15. C
16. A
17. D
18. C
19. E
20. B
21. E
22. B
23. A
24. D
25. B
26. B
27. C

Section 3:
Arguments 2

1. C
2. B
3. C
4. D
5. A
6. B
7. B
8. C
9. E
10. C
11. E
12. B
13. C
14. D
15. E
16. A
17. B
18. E
19. C
20. D
21. E
22. A
23. A
24. B
25. A

Section 4:
Games

1. C
2. B
3. A
4. E
5. D
6. B
7. D
8. B
9. C
10. A
11. A
12. A
13. E
14. B
15. A
16. C
17. D
18. C
19. D
20. A
21. E
22. D
23. D

EXPLANATIONS

Section 1: Arguments 1

1. **B** **Necessary Assumption**

The pundit's argument makes the claim that the city made a mistake when it sold the rights to collect parking fees. This is supported by the fact that the parking company raised fees and reaped profits far greater than what the city gained in the sale of the property. The pundit then speculates that if the city had not sold the rights, then the city would have made that money. This argument makes a comparison between what the private company did and what the city could have done without first establishing that the city could in fact raise rates. The credited response will establish that the city's actions could be comparable to those of the private company.

A. No. This answer discusses other private companies, which are irrelevant to the conclusion that the city's actions were a mistake.

B. Yes. This answer establishes that the actions taken by the city could be the same as those taken by the private firm.

C. No. This answer choice claims that municipalities should always handle fees. This is too strong to be the assumption behind the argument about this specific incident.

D. No. This contradicts the argument. In the argument it was the private company, not the city, which raised the parking rates.

E. No. The efficiency at which rates are collected is irrelevant to the conclusion that the city made a mistake.

2. **C** **Principle Strengthen**

This argument claims that publications should give up trying to explain new developments in science to a wide audience. The proof offered for this solution is that metaphorical writing is necessary in order to reach a wide audience. However, metaphorical writings fail to convey the science accurately. The argument also states that if the writing is more rigorous, then the science is accurate but the wider audience is not reached. The argument assumes that since scientific rigor is lost, then the attempt to reach wide audiences should be given up. The credited response will state a general rule or principle that establishes that it is better not to reach a wide audience than to be inaccurate scientifically.

A. No. The argument claims that metaphorical writing should be given up, not balanced. This is irrelevant.

B. No. The issue in this argument is not how difficult it is to explain science, but that new developments should not be explained.

C. Yes. This answer choice clearly establishes a rationale for giving up attempting to explain science in a method that may be inaccurate.

D. No. This directly contradicts the conclusion.

E. No. The conclusion is about whether explanations should be given to a wide audience, not whether scientific writing can be free from metaphors.

3. **A** **Necessary Assumption**

This argument claims that rock music has almost nothing going for it. This is based upon the premises that it is musically bankrupt and socially destructive. The premises allow that the LPs from the 1960s and 1970s often had innovative art. Finally, the premises state that digital music production has almost ended the run of LPs. The argument assumes that since digital music is not the same as LPs, then it can have no features in common with LPs. The credited response will establish that there are not many similarities between LPs and digital music.

A.   Yes. This answer choice eliminates the possibility of digital music including the same feature that made rock LPs worthwhile.

B.   No. The conclusion allows for the possibility that some rock LPs might still exist because it states that rock music has almost nothing going for it.

C.   No. The conclusion is focused on rock music today, not that of the 1960s and 1970s.

D.   No. The premises and conclusions allow for some LPs to still have innovative cover art. This is not the assumption in the argument.

E.   No. The argument establishes a contrast between the art of LPs and digital music. Whether rock music has become more destructive is not the assumption in the argument.

4. **E** **Reasoning**

This argument claims that babbling is a linguistic task. This is established by explaining the method used by researchers. Babies open their mouths wider on the right. In nonlinguistic studies, people open their mouths wider on the left. The argument proceeds by establishing two alternatives: nonlinguistic and linguistic. It then provides evidence for what nonlinguistic vocalization looks like to establish that babies' communication is different. The credited response will outline this.

A.   No. There is no counterargument.

B.   No. This argument does not weaken a general principle. Instead, it establishes a contrast.

C.   No. The test outlined is not described as a potential test, but something that was actually performed. Also, the argument never claims that this is the only method by which a hypothesis is tested.

D.   No. The argument never refutes the possibility that the interpretation about babies' vocalization might be incorrect.

E.   Yes. It outlines the two alternative explanations provided and that one is preferred to the other.

5. **C** **Weaken**

This argument claims that planting a large number of trees will help fulfill a commitment to reducing carbon dioxide emissions. This is based upon the claim that trees absorb carbon dioxide. The argument assumes that there are no other factors to consider when enacting this plan. The credited response will introduce another consideration that will cast doubt upon the success of the plan to plant large numbers of trees.

A. No. The argument is focused on what the country will do to reduce carbon dioxide emissions. Whether or not private land owners must be paid to participate is irrelevant to the conclusion that planting trees will help the country fulfill its commitment.

B. No. The amount of deforestation is irrelevant to the conclusion about planting more trees.

C. Yes. This answer choice provides a reason to doubt that planting trees will reduce carbon dioxide emissions since more will be produced than consumed.

D. No. What climate researchers believe is irrelevant to whether the proposal will be successful.

E. No. Gases other than carbon dioxide are not relevant to this argument.

6. **D** `Resolve/ Explain`

This argument establishes that SUVs are safer for their occupants when involved in crashes than are smaller vehicles. The argument then establishes a paradox by stating that despite this fact, many safety analysts are alarmed at the trend of the increasing number of SUVs. The credited response will provide a reason for the analysts to be concerned about the safety of SUVs in collisions despite the fact that their occupants are less likely to be injured.

A. No. This answer choice makes the problem worse.

B. No. Be careful not to make assumptions: SUVs having a larger fuel capacity does not provide sufficient reason for safety analysts to be concerned about their use.

C. No. Be careful not to make assumptions. Regardless of whether they have more passengers, the argument still states that those passengers are safer.

D. Yes. This answer choice shows that passengers in smaller vehicles may be less safe even though the passengers in SUVs are safer.

E. No. This does not explain why analysts are concerned about the growing number of SUVs.

7. **E** `Flaw`

This argument claims that in order to break the cycle of higher taxes, then Sherwood should not be reelected to the city council. This is based upon the fact that despite Sherwood's claims to be an opponent of high taxes, during his tenure on the city council during the last 10 years taxes consistently increased year after year. This argument assumes that what is true of the council's votes as a whole must also be true of this particular individual. The credited response will identify this flaw.

A. No. While there is a generalization made about Sherwood, we are not presented with any sample of his voting record.

B. No. This is irrelevant to the argument.

C. No. There are no sufficient or necessary conditions about Sherwood's bid for reelection.

D. No. Sherwood is not attacked personally.

E. Yes. This describes the flaw that what is true of the city council as a whole is not necessarily true of Sherwood the individual.

75

8. **C** **Main Point**

This argument claims that the owners of the catering company should reconsider their decision to raise their rates. The argument opens by establishing the position that the catering company is raising their rates to cover hiring and training costs. The argument then states a contrasting stance as the conclusion. This is followed by the premise that the mission of the company is low-cost gourmet catering, which will be jeopardized by this action. The credited response will correctly identify the conclusion.

A. No. This is a premise of the argument establishing the company's position.

B. No. This is a premise of the argument establishing the company's position.

C. Yes. This is the claim that the client is making.

D. No. This is a premise in support of the claim that the company should not raise its rates.

E. No. This is a premise in support of the claim that the company should not raise its rates.

9. **A** **Strengthen**

This argument claims that the red admiral's flight style evolved as a means of avoiding predators. This is supported by the premise that they fly in an inefficient manner. The argument also notes that predators avoid poisonous butterflies, but the red admiral has to have other means of predator evasion. The argument assumes that there are no other causes for the erratic flight pattern of these butterflies. The credited response will provide additional evidence for predator evasion or will eliminate alternative reasons for the butterflies to have this flight pattern.

A. Yes. This answer choice precludes the possibility that the erratic flight style of red admirals is shared by poisonous butterflies that already have means of evading predators.

B. No. Whether or not predation is the most common cause of death is irrelevant to the claim that red admirals develop their flight pattern to evade attack.

C. No. This answer choice does not limit the erratic flight pattern to nonpoisonous butterflies.

D. No. The inefficiency of other insects is irrelevant to the claim about why red admiral butterflies have this flight pattern.

E. No. What other butterflies' predators may eat is irrelevant to the claim that red admirals evolved this flight pattern.

10. **E** **Principle Strengthen**

This argument establishes the position that copyright statuses benefit society through their protection of original works. The argument then contrasts this protection with the cost to society through the creation of monopolies since the protection in many countries extends decades past the life of the author. The argument concludes this time frame is too long since the benefits of protection are offset by societal costs. The argument assumes that the costs of protection must not outweigh the benefits. The credited response will establish a general rule under which the benefits of a rule are not overshadowed by the costs of that same rule.

A. No. The consistency of a statute is not relevant to the claims that copyright protection is too long.

B. No. Repealing statutes is not at issue in this argument. This is irrelevant to the conclusion.

C. No. This contradicts the conclusion that copyright protection is already too long in many countries.

D. No. This argument is about the benefits and costs of copyright law to society. Limiting rights is irrelevant to this argument.

E. Yes. This answer choice stipulates that benefits of a law should exceed that law's costs.

11. **D** Weaken

This argument claims that the policing strategy is the cause of the crime rate falling by 20 percent. The argument assumes that the only relevant cause to the crime rate falling is the policing strategies. The credited response will introduce another consideration that may have also contributed to a lower crime rate.

A. No. The fact that the chief's city still has a higher crime rate does not weaken his claim that his strategy was the cause of the decrease.

B. No. The crime rate several decades before this time is irrelevant to the claim that the strategies were the cause of the decrease in crime during the police chief's tenure.

C. No. Just because the crime rate leveled off does not weaken the claim that the police chief's strategies were the cause of the decrease.

D. Yes. This answer choice suggests that the decrease in crime rate in the chief's city may have been part of a larger pattern in that country that would not have been affected by city-specific policies.

E. No. The variation of rates within the city is not relevant to the claim that it was the chief's policing strategy that caused the decrease.

12. **D** Flaw

This argument concludes that concern for the well-being of the people is a necessary condition for the successful government of Acredia. This argument opens with the conditional statement by the Duke of Acredia that concern for the welfare of the people is a necessary condition for the successful ruling of that country. The argument then establishes that if a government of Acredia has fallen, then that ruler disregarded the welfare of the people. The argument assumes that since rulers who did not focus on the people's welfare were not successful, then focusing on their welfare is a necessary condition to their rule. This confuses something that is sufficient to maintain a successful rule as necessary for that rule. The credited response will identify this flaw.

A. No. The changes in people's needs over time is irrelevant to the conclusion that concern for well-being is a necessary feature of a ruler in that country.

B. No. This reverses the premise. The absence of concern has been a feature of rulers who fell, but it is not established as always being present.

C. No. There is no appeal to a biased source.

D. Yes. This answer choice describes how the argument assumes that since a lack of concern was a feature of deposed governments that all governments in that country must be concerned for the people in order to be successful.

E. No. The argument does not assess the character of past rulers.

13. **C** Inference

This argument establishes that Professor Burns notes that the recent observations fail to confirm a previous finding of a comet reservoir. Burns is cited as using this as definitive proof that the earlier hypothesis is incorrect. The argument then states that the data Burns used were obtained under poor conditions. The credited response will be a statement that is supported by these three facts.

A. No. This answer choice makes a speculation beyond the facts mentioned. This is an unsupported prediction.

B. No. This answer choice goes beyond the fact mentioned. All that is known of the recent observations is that they were obtained in poor conditions.

C. Yes. Professor Burns's interpretation of the data is likely flawed since the data were less than optimal.

D. No. This answer choice makes a speculation beyond the facts mentioned. This is an unsupported prediction.

E. No. The data were obtained in poor conditions, but this does not necessarily mean that the data are totally worthless. This answer choice is too strong.

14. **A** Reasoning

This argument concludes that society would not be better off if the government passed laws forcing people to be polite. This is based upon the premise that such laws would create more problems than politeness does. This is in spite of the fact that if people refrained from being impolite then society would be improved. The credited response will correctly identify the role played by the statement that society would not be better off with laws enforcing politeness. In this case, this statement is the conclusion.

A. Yes. The statement in question is conclusion of the argument.

B. No. The statement in question is not used as evidence for something else in the argument.

C. No. The statement in question is not used as evidence for something else in the argument.

D. No. The statement in question is not an illustration of a premise. It is the conclusion.

E. No. The statement in question does not describe a phenomenon. It is the conclusion of the argument.

15. **C** Strengthen

This argument concludes that some of the planets in oval orbits obtained those orbits by interacting with other planets in orbit around the same star. This is supported by the premise that many of the planets in our solar system have circular orbits, while comets in our solar system have ovate orbits. The argument assumes that nothing else could cause a planet around a distant star to have an oval orbit. Additionally, the argument assumes that the comparison between our solar system and a distant plant is valid. The credited response will provide additional evidence in support of the claim that another planet caused the ovate orbit or it will remove obstacles to the conclusion being true.

A. No. The size of the affected planet is not relevant to the conclusion that the oval orbits were caused by other planets around that star.

B. No. What failed to happen in our solar system is not necessarily relevant to what happened in another system. If anything, this choice would weaken the conclusion by demonstrating at least one example of when planets were not affected by other planets.

C. Yes. This removes an obstacle to the conclusion since the argument never established that stars whose planets had ovate orbits also had more than one planet in orbit.

D. No. How comets in our system obtained their oval orbits is not relevant to the claim that planets in another system got their oval orbits.

E. No. If each of these known planets had no other known planets, then the conclusion is implausible. This would weaken the conclusion.

16. **C** [Reasoning]

This argument concludes that saltwater irrigation would be cheaper than other irrigation if undertaken near the ocean. This is based upon the premises that the water would not have to be pumped far and that pumping water is the single greatest cost of irrigation. The credited response will correctly identify the claim that pumping is the greatest cost of irrigation as a premise in support of the conclusion that saltwater irrigation is cheaper than other types of irrigation.

A. No. This claim is not disproved in the argument.

B. No. This is a stated fact in the argument, not a hypothesis.

C. Yes. The claim is a premise in support of the conclusion.

D. No. This is a premise and not the conclusion.

E. No. This is a premise in support of the conclusion, but no evidence is provided for this statement.

17. **D** [Inference]

This argument establish that critics worry that pessimistic news reports will harm the economy by causing people to lose faith. The argument establishes that everyone has direct experience with the economy every day. Journalists contend that they cannot worry about the effects of their work. Finally, the argument establishes that people defer to journalists only when they have no direct experience in something. The credited response will be a statement that is supported by a statement or combination of these statements.

A. No. The statements above do not support the claim that the critics are in fact wrong. This is too strong.

B. No. Foreign policy is not mentioned by the argument. This is unsupported information.

C. No. This is the opposite of what the argument suggests. Since people have direct experience with the economy, they are not likely to defer to journalists. Thus, the journalists' pessimistic reports will not likely have an effect.

D. Yes. Since people have direct experience with the economy, they do not defer to journalists. Thus, the opinions of the journalists are not likely to affect people's opinion of the economy.

E. No. Just because journalists cannot worry about the effects of their reports in order to do their jobs well does not mean that they should not worry. This is unsupported.

18. **B** **Flaw**

This argument claims that the recent accusations of graft in the precinct are unfounded. This is based upon the definition of graft as gifts of cash or objects valued at greater than $100. The police captain then states that no officer in that precinct has accepted such gifts. The argument assumes that the definition of graft is all encompassing and that no other forms of graft or bribery exist. The credited response will identify this flaw.

A. No. The captain makes a claim about the officers in his precinct based upon knowledge of those officers. This is not a limited sample.

B. Yes. This correctly describes the assumption that since no officer has accepted a specific form of graft that no graft has occurred.

C. No. The statement is about the actions of the police officers and not an appeal to their characters.

D. No. This answer choice describes other forms of corruption that are irrelevant to the conclusion, which is focused specifically on graft.

E. No. The premise does not contradict the conclusion.

19. **B** **Resolve/ Explain**

This argument establishes that hourly wages vary greatly in different regions, but average hourly wages for full-time jobs in each region increased. The paradox is that despite the average in each region increasing, the country's overall hourly wage decreased. The paradox is predicated upon how averages function. The credited response will indicate a way that overall wages could go down despite the regional increases.

A. No. A decrease nationally for the past three years does not explain why the average in each region was higher.

B. Yes. If employees moved to regions with lower average wages, they may have seen their personal wages decrease while the average wage within that region might still have increased.

C. No. People who are unemployed would not have wages that are part of the full-time job wage average.

D. No. This is an established fact in the argument and does not resolve the paradox.

E. No. This does not resolve the paradox since the ratio of full-time manufacturing and service jobs is unknown.

20. E Inference

This argument establishes the fact the 35 percent of people with schizophrenia had damage to the subplate in their brains. People without schizophrenia lacked this damage. The argument then establishes that damage to the subplate must have occurred prior to the second fetal trimester. The credited response will be an answer choice that is supported by one or a combination of these statements.

A. No. Just because 35 percent of people with schizophrenia also had this type of damage does not mean that the damage in fact caused schizophrenia. This is too strongly worded.

B. No. The treatment of schizophrenia is not mentioned in this argument. This is unsupported.

C. No. Schizophrenia and damage were found together. This does not prove that the damage caused the schizophrenia. This is too strongly worded.

D. No. The facts do not establish a genetic cause for the damage to the subplate. This is unsupported.

E. Yes. This answer choice takes the correlation between the damage and the schizophrenia as a potential cause.

21. B Strengthen

This argument concludes that ranchers will purchase a global positioning device for their cattle at the current cost. This claim is made despite the fact that outfitting a herd of cattle with this device is far more expensive than other means of keeping cattle in their pastures. The argument assumes that there is some reason that the device will be purchased. The credited response will introduce a consideration that makes the purchase of the device a reasonable alternative to fencing.

A. No. This contradicts the conclusion, which states that ranchers will purchase the device at its current price.

B. Yes. If cattle follow the same few animals, then ranchers would not need to purchase a device for each member of their herd. They would need to purchase only a few for these cattle who lead.

C. No. The stress caused to the cattle is irrelevant to the claim that ranchers will purchase the device at its current price.

D. No. Since the device is only as effective as fences cannot explain why ranchers will purchase this device rather than just installing fences, which are established as cheaper.

E. Yes. This contradicts the conclusion, which states that ranchers will purchase the device at its current price.

22. C Parallel Flaw

This argument claims that it is more economical to shop at a food co-op than at a supermarket. The premise is that a food co-op is a type of consumer cooperative and that consumer cooperatives offer the same products as stores at a cheaper price. The structure of this argument is that a specific thing (food co-ops) is part of a larger group (consumer cooperatives) that has a feature that can be compared with another thing (stores). The flaw in this argument is a part to whole comparison. The argument assumes that what is true of consumer cooperatives in general is also true of food co-ops specifically. The credited response will contain a response that has this same pattern and flaw, but it will not necessarily be in the same order as the original argument.

A. No. This answer claims that sports cars use more gasoline since they burn more gas per mile than other cars. This is a comparison between two categories, not between parts and wholes.

B. No. This answer claims that it is better to purchase frozen vegetables and provides two reasons to do so. This argument is flawed, but it does not focus on part to whole relationships.

C. Yes. This answer claims that bikes belong to a larger category of private means of transportation. Since private means of transport produce more pollution than public transportation, this answer claims that bikes produce more pollution than buses. This is the same pattern and flaw as the original argument.

D. No. This answer is based on a claim about where people shop based upon the types of food they prefer. While this argument is flawed, it does not make a comparison between parts and wholes.

E. No. This answer claims that the best way to lose weight is to increase consumption of artificial sweetener. While this argument is flawed, this does not focus on the part to whole relationship between sweeteners.

23. **C** **Sufficient Assumption**

This argument concludes that it is a mistake to claim that accidents are partly the fault of railway companies when adults ignore warning signs. This is supported via an analogy about how adults are responsible for protecting small children from injury, but licensed drivers should know better. The argument assumes that knowing how to avoid danger is sufficient to prevent a railway company from being liable for any injury caused to that adult. The credited response will explicitly link the premise to the conclusion and will force the conclusion to be true.

A. No. Stating that some drivers may ignore larger gates does not force the claim that railway companies are not responsible for those injuries.

B. No. This answer choice is a necessary assumption to the claim that railways are not responsible, but it is not in and of itself sufficient for forcing the conclusion.

C. Yes. This answer choice places the responsibility fully upon capable adults who ignore warnings.

D. No. Whether or not small children are harmed when drivers go around railway gates would not force railway companies to not be at fault.

E. No. The issue in the conclusion is whether railway companies are partially at fault when adults ignore warning signs. The limits of a company's responsibility are irrelevant to this conclusion.

24. **E** **Flaw**

This argument claims that if a survey is well-constructed, then survey respondents' desire to fulfill the surveyor's expectations of them will not affect the results of that survey. This is based upon the premise that people provide answers that they perceive are desired, but that well-constructed questions preclude the possibility of indicating a desired answer. This argument assumes that the only cause for respondent bias is to be found in the questions themselves. The credited response will identify an alternative cause for respondents to provide answers that they perceive the interviewer desires.

A. No. The conclusion is focused solely on how crafting questions will prevent people from responding the way they perceive the surveyors wants them to. Other types of survey flaws are irrelevant to this argument.

B.   No. This answer cites an exception to the first premise and is not a flaw in the argument.

C.   No. The issue is not whether surveyors have expectations of an answer, but whether the respondents perceive that this is so. This is irrelevant to the conclusion.

D.   No. This answer choice cites an exception to the first premise and is not a flaw in the argument.

E.   Yes. This answer choice provides an alternative cause for respondents to provide answers they think the surveyor wants despite having well-crafted questions.

25.   **A**   **Parallel**

This argument claims that the availability of television reduces the amount of reading that children do. This is supported by two premises, which establish that when TV is unavailable, children read more and that when TV becomes available again, they read less. The structure of this argument is that two items are correlated. The correlation holds in two different patterns. The conclusion assumes a causal relationship between the two items. The credited response will have this same pattern.

A.   Yes. The two items are interest rates and money supply. When the availability of money fluctuates, so does the interest rate. When the money supply is stable, so are interest rates. This matches the premises of the original argument. The conclusion in this answer also assumes that because the availability of one thing leads to changes in the occurrence of another, then that thing must cause those changes.

B.   No. This argument claims that candy consumption disrupts appetite. This claim is based on the unrelated premise that a lack of candy consumption causes hunger. This does not match the pattern in the original argument.

C.   No. This is a causal argument; however, this argument has three linked causes. This does not match the correlation as causation pattern above.

D.   No. This argument claims that voting behavior is influenced by things other than the candidates' records. The argument provides some proof for that claim. This does not follow the correlation as causation pattern in the original argument.

E.   No. The argument must match the structure of the original argument as closely as possible. The original argument discusses the availability of an alternative, but it never claims that the children or adults were watching TV. This answer choice goes beyond the structure of the original argument by claiming that adults are performing other activities, which in turn leads to a decrease in reading.

Section 2: Reading Comprehension

Questions 1–7

The main point of the first paragraph is to present the question of whether the use of video by indigenous peoples has impacted indigenous culture. The second paragraph introduces the Weiner view, that the use of video technology negatively impacts indigenous cultures. The third paragraph explains the contrasting view, held by Ginsburg that video technology not only doesn't harm indigenous culture, but also can help preserve it. The final paragraph discusses evidence from Turner consistent with the Ginsburg position. The Bottom Line of the passage as a whole is that there is debate over how video technology impacts indigenous cultures and that there is some evidence to indicate that it can help preserve culture.

1. **C**   **Big Picture**

   Use your Bottom Line of the passage to help you to evaluate the choices. The correct answer will describe the main idea of the passage.

   A. No. While this answer choice is supported by the passage, it captures the point of view in the second paragraph only and is too narrow.

   B. No. This answer choice is too extreme. The passage discusses that video technology can help preserve culture, but it does not go so far as to say the "colonial gaze" has been eliminated.

   C. Yes. This accurately matches the Bottom Line that there is a debate over the impact of video technology and some evidence to support the idea that it can help preserve culture.

   D. No. The passage doesn't mention long-term impact.

   E. No. While this answer choice is supported by the passage, it captures only the fourth paragraph and is too narrow.

2. **A**   **Extract Infer**

   The question is asking for Ginsburg's attitude towards Weiner's point of view. The correct answer will reflect that she disagrees with his position.

   A. Yes. Ginsburg argues that video technology can strengthen indigenous culture, in direct opposition to Weiner's view.

   B. No. While Ginsburg disagrees with Weiner, she does not scold him and "censure" is too extreme.

   C. No. Ginsburg's point of view is in direct opposition to Weiner's, so "mild" does not accurately reflect her position.

   D. No. Ginsburg disagrees with Weiner.

   E. No. Ginsburg disagrees with Weiner.

3. **B**   **RC Reasoning**

   The question is asking for a situation analogous to the Kayapo's use of video. As discussed in the fourth paragraph, the Kayapo's use of video aesthetically mirrors their cultural practices. The correct answer should describe the incorporation of something new while preserving the characteristics of the original.

A. No. This answer choice involves altering the characteristics of the original.

B. Yes. New ideas are incorporated in, but the tradition remains.

C. No. This answer choice involves altering the characteristics of the original.

D. No. This choice does not involve the incorporation of something new.

E. No. This choice does not involve the incorporation of something new.

4. C **Extract Fact**

The correct response will be directly supported by the discussion of Weiner in the passage.

A. No. This is not discussed in the passage.

B. No. This is not discussed in the passage.

C. Yes. This is supported by line 22.

D. No. While this term is mentioned in the passage, it is not part of Weiner's point of view.

E. No. This is not discussed in the passage.

5. A **Extract Infer**

The correct answer will be the question that is most directly related to evidence within the passage text.

A. Yes. The passage discusses that the Kayapo are primarily an oral society and use video to document transactions.

B. No. While the term "noble savage" is mentioned, the passage does not discuss its origin.

C. No. The passage gives an example of only one culture that has adopted video technology.

D. No. The passage does not discuss specific technologies in the fifteenth century.

E. No. The passage mentions that video equipment is inexpensive, but it does not discuss why.

6. D **Extract Infer**

The question is asking about the relationship between Turner and Weiner's points of view. The correct answer will be consistent with the discussion of Turner and will reflect that Turner's research undermines Weiner's point of view.

A. No. Turner does not discuss diverse practices; he discusses only what he has found with the Kayapo.

B. No. Turner does not discuss the availability of video technology.

C. No. Weiner is concerned with the preservation of traditional practices, he just doesn't think that video is the best way to do it.

D. Yes. This is consistent with Turner's findings and addresses Weiner's claim that video changes cultural values.

E. No. Turner does not discuss other technologies.

7. **E** | **Structure**

The question is asking what the author means by "technological determinism." The correct answer will be directly supported by the author's discussion in the third paragraph.

A. No. There is no discussion of an exchange of technology.

B. No. The passage discusses use of technology by indigenous peoples rather than by anthropologists.

C. No. The passage does not argue that there is a dependence on technology.

D. No. The passage does not discuss ethical values.

E. Yes. Ginsburg argues that technology does not shape culture, which is unlike Weiner's view.

Questions 8–14

The first paragraph discusses the current approach for dealing with disqualification and recusal of judges. The second paragraph sets out issues with the current approach. The third paragraph proposes a course of action to solve the problem of biased judges. The final paragraph rebuts potential objections to the author's proposal. The Bottom Line of the passage is that the current system for the disqualification and recusal of judges is inadequate and could be improved by requiring judges to explain the reasoning for their judgments.

8. **B** | **Extract Fact**

The question is asking for a direct statement from the passage critiquing the current rules.

A. No. The passage mentions that bias might interfere with judges' reasoning, but it does not argue that the rules do.

B. Yes. This is explicitly supported by line 15.

C. No. This answer contradicts the author's argument that transparency in judicial reasoning is important.

D. No. This is untrue. The passage states that some jurisdictions allow parties to court proceedings to request disqualification.

E. No. This is untrue. The passage states that the current rules focus on both impropriety and the appearance of impropriety.

9. **A** | **Structure**

The question is asking for the point of the second paragraph. The correct answer should capture the author's critique of the current approach.

A. Yes. This accurately describes that the second paragraph is critiquing the current approach.

B. No. This answer choice confuses the order of the passage. The solution is presented in the third paragraph.

C. No. There are no concrete examples in the second paragraph.

D. No. The second paragraph does not discuss history.

E. No. The rest of the passage focuses on a solution, not a defense of the author's critique.

10. **A**   Extract
            Infer

The correct answer will be supported by the author's discussion of the principle in the fourth paragraph.

A. Yes. The author introduces the principle with "under the law."

B. No. The author is not providing a definition.

C. No. The author cites the principle as rationale for his or her proposal and as a response to potential critiques of the proposal.

D. No. The author concurs with the principle and thinks it should be applied.

E. No. The principle relates to the author's proposal to change the means of addressing judicial bias.

11. **C**   Extract
            Infer

The correct answer will be consistent with the author's critique of the current system.

A. No. In the second paragraph, the author argues that the current rules are vague.

B. No. The current statutes are not incompatible. Additional requirements for the disclosure of legal reasoning could be added to the current rules.

C. Yes. This answer is supported by lines 22–24.

D. No. These statutes work in tandem with rules that require judges to recuse themselves.

E. No. The author does not discuss a need for a guarantee.

12. **B**   Extract
            Infer

The answer will be consistent with the author's proposal to require judicial reasoning in the third and fourth paragraphs.

A. No. The author concedes that this new plan may not eliminate all bias, but it will eliminate the harm caused by bias.

B. Yes. The author argues that such a proposal would eliminate harm.

C. No. This answer choice is extreme. While the author concedes that such explanations may not always reveal the judge's actual reasoning, that is not enough to support the word "usually."

D. No. The author does not discuss changes in public perception.

E. No. The author does not discuss any impact on judges recusing themselves as a result of having to reveal their reasoning.

13. **C**   RC Reasoning

The question is asking for an answer that is consistent with the author's description of "real reasoning," which is contrasted with the judge's stated reasoning.

A. No. The author is discussing the reasoning behind a judge's disposition in a case, not the reasoning about recusal.

B. No. This is outside the scope of what is discussed in the passage.

C. Yes. This would be reasoning that a judge would not likely articulate.

D. No. This would be the judge's stated reasoning.

E. No. This would be the judge's stated reasoning.

14. **E**   Extract Infer

The correct answer will be supported by the author's critique of the current approach that the current rules are vague and focus on the appearance of bias.

A. No. The author does not discuss assurances to the general public.

B. No. The author does not discuss how judges feel about the current rules.

C. No. The author does not discuss the frequency of removal for bias.

D. No. The author does not discuss the frequency of removal for bias.

E. Yes. The author discusses that the current rules focus on appearance of bias and therefore may cause actual instances of bias to be overlooked.

75

Questions 15–20

Passage A

The first chunk discusses that there may be some justification for lying to liars because liars forfeit their right to honesty. The second chunk discusses the moral questions that arise and concludes that while a liar has no right to the truth, that is not sufficient justification for someone to lie to a liar. The Bottom Line of passage A is that someone's dishonesty is not sufficient justification to lie to that person.

Passage B

The first paragraph introduces Kantian morality. The second paragraph applies Kant's principles to the question of whether liars have a right to honesty and concludes that they don't because by making the rational decision to lie, they are authorizing people to lie to them. The Bottom Line of passage B is that lying authorizes other people to lie to you, but it does not compel them to lie to you.

15. **C** `Big Picture`

The correct answer will reflect the Bottom Line of each passage. The Bottom Line of passage A is that someone's dishonesty is not sufficient justification to lie to that person. The Bottom Line of passage B is that lying authorizes other people to lie to you, but it does not compel them to lie to you.

A. No. Passage B does not discuss harm.

B. No. Neither passage discusses criminal wrongs.

C. Yes. The Bottom Line of each passage answers this question.

D. No. Passage A does not discuss duties.

E. No. Passage A does not discuss rational beings.

16. **A** `Extract Fact`

The correct answer will be explicitly supported by passage A, but it will not appear in passage B.

A. Yes, Passage A discusses harm as a reason not to lie to liars, whereas passage B does not mention harm.

B. No. This is not mentioned in passage A.

C. No. This is not mentioned in passage A.

D. No. This is mentioned in passage B.

E. No. No specific instances are mentioned in passage A.

17. **D** `Structure`

The correct answer will describe the logic of each passage. Both passages discuss the implications of the view that it's acceptable for liars to be lied to.

A. No. Passage A does not refute any objections.

B. No. Passage B does not use an analogy.

C. No. Neither passage uses a specific example.

D. Yes. Passage A points out the harm to society that results from lying, and passage B argues that an assertion of a duty to punish would be excessive.

E. No. Neither passage defines a term.

18. **C** `Extract Infer`

The correct answer will be best supported by the text of passage A.

A. No. Passage A does not discuss rationality; it is discussed by passage B.

B. No. Passage A does not discuss moral duties; they are discussed in passage B.

C. Yes. This answer is explicitly supported in lines 24–27 of passage A.

D. No. This answer choice is extreme. The passage states merely that a person's characteristic as a liar is not sufficient to justify lying.

E. No. Passage A does not discuss innocent persons.

19. **E** **Extract Infer**

The correct answer will reflect passage A's discussion of rights that are forfeited, based on behavior and passage B's discussion of someone obtaining the right to lie because someone else has lied.

A. No. There is no discussion of legal rights in passage A.

B. No. There is no discussion of an individual in a position of authority in passage B.

C. No. There is no discussion of groups in passage A.

D. No. Passage A discusses rights that can be forfeited.

E. Yes. This accurately captures the discussion of rights in each passage.

20. **B** **RC Reasoning**

The question is asking for something that would reconcile passage A giving an instance in which lying would not create a right to lie even though passage B says that lying is a rational act that creates a right to lie. The correct answer will be consistent with both positions.

A. No. Lying in response to a pathological lie would not be pathological.

B. Yes. If the pathological lie is not rational behavior, then according to passage B it does not create the right to lie.

C. No. Passage B would still find sufficient reason to lie in this case.

D. No. This is inconsistent with the argument in passage A that a right to lie is not created in this case.

E. No. The lowering of standards is not relevant to passage B.

Questions 21–27

The first paragraph introduces the persistent, faulty belief that glass flows and offers a potential explanation for this mistaken belief. The second paragraph introduces evidence that debunks the belief. The third paragraph goes into further detail about the evidence. The fourth paragraph gives the actual reason that glass in old windows is thicker at the bottom. The Bottom Line of the passage is that despite the beliefs of many, glass in windows does not actually flow and this is supported by evidence.

21. **E** **Big Picture**

Use your Bottom Line of the passage to help you to evaluate the choices. The correct answer will describe the main point of the passage that despite the beliefs of many, glass in windows does not actually flow and this is supported by evidence.

A. No. While this is true based on the passage, it is a detail and too narrow in scope for a main point question.

75

B. No. While this is true based on the passage, it is a detail and too narrow in scope for a main point question.

C. No. There is no discussion of how Zanotto calculated the time needed for glass to flow by a noticeable amount.

D. No. This is not supported by the passage. The author argues that the movement of glass did not contribute to noticeable differences in thickness.

E. Yes. This accurately paraphrases the Bottom Line.

22. **B** Extract Infer

The correct answer will be best supported by the passage text.

A. No. The passage discusses the differences in pre- and post-nineteenth-century techniques, but it does not address differences between the seventeenth century and medieval times.

B. Yes. This is explicitly addressed in the fourth paragraph.

C. No. This is outside the scope of the passage. There is no mention of the existence or lack of windows before medieval times.

D. No. This answer choice pulls language from multiple parts of the passage, but there is no discussion of the type of glass used in uneven windowpanes.

E. No. The passage mentions that there were impurities in older glass, but it does not discuss how they got there.

23. **A** Extract Infer

The question is asking the author's attitude toward Zanotto's study results. The author uses the study to support his point, so the correct answer should reflect a favorable attitude.

A. Yes. This is an accurate description of the study results and reflects the author's positive view.

B. No. The passage does not indicate that there has been any additional research.

C. No. The passage does not indicate that there has been any additional research.

D. No. The results debunk only one view.

E. No. The results debunk only one view.

24. **D** Extract Infer

The correct answer will be supported by something the passage says about the atomic structure of glass. The passage notes that glass does not have a fixed atomic structure.

A. No. This is contradicted by the passage. At the end of the first paragraph, the author asserts that glass will behave as a solid.

B. No. This is contradicted by the passage. In the second paragraph, the author discusses Zanotto's study results showing that it would take far more than a few millennia for glass to move in a noticeable way.

C. No. The passage states that glass behaves as a solid when it's cooled below the transition temperature.

D. Yes. In the third paragraph, the passage states that glass could have the ability to flow when raised to over 350 degrees Celsius.

E. No. This is contradicted by the passage. In the first paragraph, the author discusses that glass does not have a fixed crystalline structure, but still behaves as a solid.

25. B **Extract Infer**

The question is asking about the reason that the author gives for people believing that glass flows noticeably downward. In the first paragraph, the author states that the mistaken belief is likely due to a misunderstanding about glass's lack of crystalline structure.

A. No. While the confusion is related to the lack of crystalline structure, it arises out of a knowledge that there is no crystalline structure and misunderstanding about the consequences of that fact.

B. Yes. The author states that the cause is likely a misunderstanding of the consequences of a lack of crystalline structure.

C. No. The author does not discuss glassmaking methods in the first paragraph.

D. No. The author's discussion of transition temperatures is in a different part of the passage and is unrelated to the mistaken belief people held.

E. No. The language in this answer choice is tempting, but the author argues that the misunderstanding stems from an assumption that liquid and solid glasses are similar rather than dissimilar.

26. B **RC Reasoning**

The question is asking for a situation similar to the mistaken belief about glass. The persistent mistaken belief was based on a misunderstanding of the structure of glass, while the real cause of thicker glass at the base of windows was the manufacturing process. The correct answer will match this logic.

A. No. This does not match the passage. The passage does not discuss correction as an issue in the misunderstanding.

B. Yes. This matches the mistaken attribution of an effect to the glass itself rather than the manufacturing process.

C. No. This does not match the passage. The passage makes no mention of a shortened life span.

D. No. This does not match the passage. The passage does not discuss quality in relation to the mistaken belief.

E. No. This does not match the passage. The passage does not discuss durability.

27. C **Extract Infer**

The correct answer will be the statement best supported by the passage's discussion of the transition temperature of glass. The passage states that this is a range of a few hundred degrees Celsius, below which glass behaves as a solid.

A. No. The passage does not provide relative transition temperatures.

75

B. No. The passage does not indicate that Zanotto calculated the temperature precisely, merely that he has calculated the time needed for a noticeable flow.

C. Yes. The passage states that glass would need to be heated to at least 350 degrees for any sort of noticeable flow, and given that the range is a few hundred degrees, the top end of the range would need to be a few hundred degrees above 350.

D. No. This is unsupported by the passage. Glass within the transition temperature range would be able to flow downward.

E. No. This is contradicted by the passage. The passage states that it is a range of a few hundred degrees, not a specific temperature.

Section 3: Arguments 2

1. **C** Main Point

In this question, the credited response will fill in the blank an answer choice that is supported by the premises stated in the argument. The argument states that individuals who have skills and knowledge to apply new technology will prosper and those that do not may lose jobs. Similarly, firms that do not resist technology will overcome those firms that do resist innovation. The credited response will match these premises and make a point that combines the facts presented.

A. No. There is no information presented in the argument about dislocating workers, so this does not match the argument.

B. No. The argument presents information pointing out that companies who resist technological innovation will lose jobs to those firms that do not resist such innovation.

C. Yes. The argument presents information pointing out that companies who resist technological innovation will lose jobs to those firms that do not resist such innovation.

D. No. The argument presents information pointing out that companies who resist technological innovation will lose jobs to those firms that do not resist such innovation.

E. No. There is no information presented in the argument about prioritizing new technology over new industries.

2. **B** Necessary Assumption

This question asks you to help the argument. Identify the conclusion and premises; then look for a language shift or gap between them. The argument concludes that the Hydro can likely attribute its success to customers who want to appear environmentally conscious. The argument bases this conclusion on premises that state that sales of the Hydro are rising and that the Hydro is comparable in price and fuel efficiency to its competitors. In order to attribute the success of the Hydro to the appearance of being environmentally conscious, the author must assume that the Hydro appears to be uniquely environmentally conscious among its competition.

A. No. The argument seeks to explain the reason for the Hydro's increased sales based on it appearing to be environmentally conscious. The author makes no argument about its popularity.

B. Yes. In order to attribute the success of the Hydro to the appearance of being environmentally conscious, the author must assume that the Hydro appears to be uniquely environmentally conscious among its competition.

C. No. The safety record of the Hydro is irrelevant to the argument about it appearing to be environmentally conscious.

D. No. The author states that buyers of the Hydro want to appear environmentally conscious to their neighbors but makes no assumption that the neighbors are also buyers of the Hydro.

E. No. The actual interest of Hydro buyers in environmental causes is not relevant to the argument about whether they want to appear environmentally conscious.

3. **C** Principle Strengthen

The argument concludes that it would be unfair for McBride's complaint to be dismissed simply because she was given an incorrect form to file the complaint. The credited response will be a principle that proves this conclusion based on the facts presented in the argument.

A. No. A rule requiring information for those wishing to file complaints would not address the conclusion that dismissing the complaint would be unfair.

B. No. There is no information presented in the argument that Form 283 or Form 5 are unduly burdensome, so this does not address the conclusion that dismissing the complaint would be unfair.

C. Yes. This would prove the conclusion is true based on the premises stated in the passage.

D. No. There is no evidence that the agency gave McBride the incorrect form because the process is too complex, so this choice does not address the conclusion that dismissing the complaint would be unfair.

E. No. There is no evidence presented to indicate whether the business in this situation could defend itself, so this choice does not address the conclusion that dismissing the complaint would be unfair.

4. **D** Inference

In this question, the credited response will be supported by the text. The passage states that the size of a bird's spleen is an indicator of that bird's health. The passage also states that birds killed accidentally have larger spleens than those killed by predators.

A. No. The passage does indicate that predators tend to kill sickly birds, but there is no information to suggest that predators are unable to kill healthy birds.

B. No. This choice is the reverse of what is stated in the passage. It is possible that most sickly birds are not killed by predators.

C. No. The passage does indicate that predators tend to kill sickly birds, but it does not state why or how they do so.

D. Yes. The passage does indicate that predators tend to kill sickly birds since sickly birds have smaller spleens and the birds killed by predators have smaller spleens.

E. No. The passage indicates that spleen size is an indicator of health but provides no evidence that spleen size causes poor health.

5. A Resolve/
Explain

The credited response to this question will make sense of the seeming contradiction in the passage. The conflict as described is that on one hand, home ownership is an indicator of financial prosperity. On the other hand, home ownership correlates with high levels of unemployment.

A. Yes. This explains one reason that homeowners may have a high level of unemployment since relocating to a place with a job is more challenging if one is a homeowner.

B. No. This would make the conflict worse by showing that jobs are more readily available near homeowners.

C. No. This choice shows that the correlation between home ownership and unemployment is ubiquitous but does not explain why such a correlation exists.

D. No. This would make the conflict worse by showing that homeowners have a greater support network helping them find jobs.

E. No. This cannot explain the correlation between home ownership and unemployment because there is no link between economic security and unemployment.

6. B Strengthen

The credited response to this question will help the hypothesis that when hornworms' first meal is from a nightshade, they enjoy the chemical in nightshade and nothing else tastes as good. The scientists base this hypothesis on the fact that hornworms that feed first on nightshade will not eat other plants later in life, but those that feed first on other plants will eat other plants later in life.

A. No. The preference for specific varieties of nightshade plant is irrelevant to whether the hornworm becomes habituated to indioside D.

B. Yes. If removing the taste receptors makes hornworms feed on other plants, then the taste receptors must be responsible for the preference to nightshade. This would support the hypothesis that the taste receptors are habituated to indioside D present in nightshade plants.

C. No. The location of eggs is not explicitly relevant to the appetites of hornworms.

D. No. This would weaken the hypothesis by pointing out an alternative reason for the food preferences of hornworms.

E. No. This choice is not strong enough to help the argument. There is no evidence that the taste receptors have reactions to chemicals in plants.

7. B Flaw

This question asks for a description of the flaw in the employee's argument. The employee argues that her boss is incorrect in stating that her presentation should have included detailed profit projections. The employees bases this conclusion on the premise that people's attention wanders when they get too much detail. The argument is flawed in that it assumes more detailed profit projections would provide too much detail to the audience.

A. No. The argument makes no assumptions about the boss's previous assertions about the employee's presentations.

B.   Yes. The argument assumes more detailed profit projections would provide too much detail to the audience.

C.   No. Other reasons an audience's attention may wander during a presentation are not relevant to whether providing more detailed profit projections would cause the audience's attention to wander.

D.   No. The conclusion is about a single case and bases it on information about that case that may fit a generalization.

E.   No. The employee is consistent in her use of the term "detail."

8.   **C**   `Main Point`

The conclusion states that the local media shows too much deference toward public officials. This is based on premises that the local media believe Clemens is an honest politician, that Clemens was caught up in a scandal, and that the reporters failed to expose the scandal sooner. The credited response will match the conclusion of the argument.

A.   No. This is a premise.

B.   No. The author states that the media were wrong about Clemens being an honest politician and this is offered as a premise.

C.   Yes. This matches the conclusion and the other statements in the argument support it as the main point.

D.   No. This is a premise.

E.   No. This is an assumption made by the author in making the point that the local media show too much deference toward public officials.

9.   **E**   `Parallel`

The original argument concludes that there has never been life on the Moon. This is based on premises that state that if life existed on the Moon, there would be signs of life there and numerous trips to the Moon have occurred without noticing any of these signs. The credited response will offer a similar argument that bases a conclusion on an absence of evidence to the contrary despite numerous attempts to collect the evidence.

A.   No. This argument does not base its conclusion on an absence of evidence despite an opportunity to collect the evidence.

B.   No. The original argument concludes something that is certain, "there has never been life on the Moon," while this argument concludes the likelihood of something being true.

C.   No. This argument concludes that voters will go with Hendricks because Hendricks is tough on crime, but it does so by pointing to one factor (out of many possibilities) that would lead to Hendricks's winning of the election. It assumes that since there is one pathway to winning the election that the pathway must be true.

75

D.   No. This argument assumes that evidence of rodents in the warehouse is an indication of causation. There is no premise about the lack of evidence.

E.   Yes. This argument concludes that the army is not planning an attack because if it were planning an attack there would be evidence and reports do not show the evidence.

10.   **C**   **Flaw**

This question asks for a description of the flaw in the television host's argument. The host claims that there must be evidence the defendant is not completely innocent despite the fact that there was a strong alibi and exculpatory evidence and a jury found the defendant not guilty. The host bases the conclusion on the premise that the prosecutor wouldn't have brought charges unless the defendant was at least partially guilty. This argument assumes that the prosecutor has such expertise or authority that all other evidence to the contrary must be wrong. The credited response will describe this flaw.

A.   No. The host provides ample evidence for the view that the defendant is not guilty but nonetheless believes the contrary because an individual believes it to be so.

B.   No. This argument is not circular. The host's conclusion is based on the premise that a prosecutor must have thought the defendant was guilty and that therefore the defendant must be guilty.

C.   Yes. This argument assumes that the prosecutor has such expertise or authority that all other evidence to the contrary must be wrong.

D.   No. The host does not confuse two definitions of the term "guilt."

E.   No. The host does not believe the jury was wrong because of the quick verdict. The host's conclusion is based on the premise that a prosecutor must have thought the defendant was guilty and that therefore the defendant must be guilty.

11.   **E**   **Reasoning**

Describe the professor's reasoning to answer this question. The professor states that the evidence against Sauk is that Sauk is more imitator than innovator and had opposing viewpoints to Providence and concludes that this evidence is insufficient to attack the writings of Sauk because it is not relevant to Sauk's writing. The critics' conclusion should therefore be rejected. The credited response will match this argument.

A.   No. The professor does not take issue with the validity of the critics' premises.

B.   No. The professor does not put forth any new evidence that Sauk's writing has aesthetic merit.

C.   No. The professor does not mention the viewpoints of the critics.

D.   No. The professor does not take issue with the validity of the critics' premises.

E.   Yes. The professor states this evidence is insufficient to attack the writings of Sauk because it is not relevant to Sauk's writing.

12.   **B**   **Principle Strengthen**

This question asks for a principle that will validate the application in the passage. The policy states that the safety inspector shouldn't approve a process that has not been used safely for more than a year or if it does not increase factory safety. The author states that the safety inspector shouldn't approve a welding process because it does not increase factory safety. The credited response should fill in the missing component of the principle about a process being used safely in another factory.

A. No. This choice does not specify whether a factory has used the new process safely for the last year.

B. Yes. This choice speaks to the missing component of the principle about a process being used safely in another factory.

C. No. The principle does not require a comparison of the safety of various processes.

D. No. This choice does not specify a time frame, so it does not apply to the principle in question.

E. No. This choice does not specify whether a factory has used the new process safely for the last year.

13. **C** **Weaken**

This question asks for an answer choice that will weaken the administrator's claim. The administrator argues that graduate students are incorrect in their holding that teaching assistants are employees. The administrator bases this conclusion on the premises that even though assistants get paid for teaching classes, they are getting paid in order to fund their own education and would not be teaching if they could fund their own education using other funding. The administrator assumes that because they are funding their education, they should not be counted as employees and the credited response will attack this assumption.

A. No. The additional costs of granting employee benefits is not relevant to the logic of the administrator's argument.

B. No. This choice does not address the nature of the argument because there is no mention of whether adjuncts are funding an education.

C. Yes. This would weaken the argument by showing that the teaching posts have another reason for existing other than helping teaching assistants fund their education.

D. No. The fact that teaching assistants can make more money than necessary to fund their education does not address the fact that they are funding their education with money from their teaching post.

E. No. The amount or vigor of work completed by teaching assistants is not relevant to the argument about whether their funding an education prevents them from being employees.

14. **D** **Parallel Flaw**

The credited response will have a similar flaw to the main argument. Branson states that if people were to move from major cities to rural areas that the country's pollution would be reduced. This is based on the premise that the largest pollution comes from large cities and that these cities would pollute less with a smaller population. Branson's argument is flawed in that it assumes that pollution caused by population wouldn't disperse at the same level into rural areas at the same time it decreases in cities.

A. No. This argument assumes that Monique pays a larger housing cost because she lives in a city with high average housing costs. This is a type of comparison flaw and does not match the original argument's flaw.

B. No. This argument assumes that Karen's family would have more space in a single-family home than in an apartment because single-family homes are typically larger. This is a type of comparison flaw and does not match the original argument's flaw.

C. No. This argument assumes that because other fields are now planted with corn, that Ward's fields are planted with corn. This is a type of comparison flaw and does not match the original argument's flaw.

D. Yes. This argument concludes that Javier should eat smaller portions at meals with the largest calories and eat the remaining portions as snacks. This assumes that the calorie savings from the three meals wouldn't disperse into the snacks at the same time, as it reduces the calories of the three meals.

E. No. This argument does not contain a flaw and does not match the original argument's flaw.

15. **E** Sufficient Assumption

Identify the conclusion and premises, and then find an answer choice that validates the claim. The conclusion states that buyers were wrong in stating that safety was an important concern. This conclusion is based on premises that state that ninety percent of buyers stated that safety was an important concern, but only half of them referred to objective sources of safety, while the others referred to ads and promotional materials. The author assumes that ads and promotional materials are not valid sources and that people who think they are learning about safety do not care about safety.

A. No. The relative priorities of safety and other purchasing factors are not relevant to whether people who said safety was important were correct.

B. No. This does not prove the conclusion because it does not link incomplete safety information with whether buyers truly value safety as an important concern.

C. No. This is a necessary but not sufficient assumption since it does not speak to whether buyers who do not consult objective sources truly value safety as an important concern.

D. No. This does not prove the conclusion because it does not link knowledge of objective sources of safety information with whether buyers truly value safety as an important concern.

E. Yes. If this is true, it validates the argument by showing that half of the people who say safety is important were wrong by not consulting objective sources.

16. **A** Flaw

This question asks for a choice that hurts the conclusion by describing its flaw. The theorist argues that an organism incapable of planned movement does not have a central nervous system. This conclusion is based on premises that state that for an organism to have planned movement, it must be able to represent its environment and send messages to its muscles via a central nervous system. The argument is flawed in that it assumes one of two necessary components of planned locomotion is sufficient for planned locomotion.

A. Yes. The theorist states that a central nervous system is a necessary component in the premises, and the conclusion assumes it is a sufficient component.

B. No. The theorist states that an organism must be able to represent its environment in order to have planned locomotion.

C. No. The theorist states that the ability to represent its environment is necessary for planned locomotion but does not assume that the ability serves no other purpose.

D. No. Adaptations are not relevant to the theorist's argument.

E. No. The theorist does not make or assume a connection between the ability to represent an environment and a nervous system.

17. **B** Necessary Assumption

Help this argument by finding a necessary assumption. The author concludes that rocket engines must have both short and long nozzles to work most effectively throughout their ascents. This is based on premises that state that rocket engines are most effective when the pressures of exhaust gasses and the atmosphere are equal and that a short nozzle achieves this equalization at lower altitudes and a longer nozzle achieves this equalization at higher altitudes. The author assumes that having both nozzles is a way to be most effective and that it is the only way to be most effective.

A. No. The difficulty of equipping nozzles onto a rocket is not relevant to the argument about the way to make a rocket engine the most effective.

B. Yes. The author assumes that all rockets pass through both low and high altitudes. If this is not true, that rockets do not pass through the upper atmosphere, then rockets do not need long nozzles to be most effective.

C. No. The argument does not state that a rocket engine must be most effective in order to accomplish its goal of reaching higher altitudes.

D. No. The argument indicates the author believes that the pressure should change from one stage of ascent to the next.

E. No. The author argues that rockets must have both long and short nozzles, but it does not indicate that at least one engine must have both. It might be possible, for instance, that a rocket have two engines one with a short nozzle and one with a long nozzle.

18. **E** Flaw

Hurt the argument by describing a flaw. The consumer advocate argues that manufacturers of children's toys shouldn't overstate the dangers of their products. The advocate bases this conclusion on premises that state that a company should overstate the dangers posed by their products only if it reduces injuries but that toy companies overstate the dangers for the purpose of protecting themselves from lawsuits. The argument assumes that because companies overstate the dangers for that purpose that it doesn't also have the benefit of reducing injuries.

A. No. The author does not state necessary or sufficient reasons for actually reducing injuries caused by a product.

B. No. The argument is not about the results of overstating dangers but what reasons would justify their use.

C.   No. There is no sample mentioned in the argument.

D.   No. The argument does not assume that overstating a danger always fails to prevent injuries. The author states that preventing injuries is the only reason a manufacturer should overstate a danger.

E.   Yes. The argument assumes that because companies overstate the dangers for that purpose that it doesn't also have the benefit of reducing injuries.

19.   **C**   Necessary Assumption

Help the argument by finding a necessary assumption. The argument concludes that drinking tea boosted immune systems of people in the study. This is based on premises that state that participants who drank tea and no coffee responded to germs faster than those who drank coffee but no tea. The author assumes that there is no other factor responsible for the expedited response than the consumption of tea.

A.   No. The author does not assume that there are not other participants who drank both tea and coffee.

B.   No. Other health benefits of coffee are not relevant to the conclusion about whether drinking tea boosted immune systems.

C.   Yes. If this were true, then tea doesn't benefit immune systems because the reason tea drinkers' response was faster than that of coffee drinkers is because coffee had a detrimental effect on the immune systems. In that case, tea does not have a benefit.

D.   No. This answer choice does not explicitly address the participants in the study.

E.   No. Other health benefits of coffee and tea are not relevant to the conclusion about whether drinking tea boosted immune systems.

20.   **D**   Reasoning

Match the description of the reasoning to the argument. The engineer concludes that semiplaning monohulls will probably be profitable. This is based on premises that state that the semiplaning monohull, such as the airplane, offers greater speed and reliability over traditional ships. The sentence in question is premise that the author seeks to overcome by showing the similar advantages of semiplaning monohulls and jet airplanes.

A.   No. This part of the analogy does not support the conclusion that semiplaning monohulls will be profitable.

B.   No. The comparison between semiplaning monohulls and conventional ships is not rejected by the analogy between jet airplanes and other planes.

C.   No. This part of the analogy does not support the conclusion that semiplaning monohulls will be profitable.

D.   Yes. The sentence in question is a premise that the author seeks to overcome by showing the similar advantages of semiplaning monohulls and jet airplanes.

E.   No. The argument's main conclusion is does not contain an analogy between types of airplanes.

75

21. **E** **Strengthen**

Help the argument by providing additional evidence to support the conclusion. The argument claims that Paraguay is the place where maté originated. This is based on premises that state that maté is used more widely and found in more varieties in Paraguay than anywhere else. The argument assumes that because of the variety and wide use, that it must have originated in Paraguay.

A.   No. This choice supports the notion only that maté has been in Paraguay for a long time, not that it originated there.

B.   No. This would weaken the argument by showing a reason that maté may have come to Paraguay with migrants from another location.

C.   No. The location of the best maté in the world is not relevant to the argument about where maté originated.

D.   No. That maté is not found many places outside of South America does not address the exact country of its origin.

E.   Yes. This draws a link between wide use and length of time in a certain area. Therefore, if it is more widely used in Paraguay than anywhere else, it has been there longest and is likely to have originated there.

22. **A** **Resolve/ Explain**

The credited response will be the one choice that does not hurt the argument that mismanagement of the economy caused that average family income to decrease over an eight-year period.

A.   Yes. The fact that there was a rise in family income in 1996 does not change the fact that over the eight years following 1996, the average family income dropped 10 percent. Since this does not hurt the argument, it is the answer.

B.   No. This weakens the argument by showing a noneconomic reason for the drop in family income over the eight-year period in question.

C.   No. This weakens the argument by showing a noneconomic reason for the drop in family income over the eight-year period in question.

D.   No. This weakens the argument by showing that family incomes dropped due to a generational shift in the workforce, not due to economic mismanagement.

E.   No. This weakens the argument by showing that policies enacted by the previous ruling party are responsible for the decline in family income.

23. **A** **Necessary Assumption**

Help this argument by finding a necessary assumption. The author concludes that gardeners who plant using the phases of the moon are less likely to lose those plants to frost. This is based on premises that state that gardeners who plant using the phases of the moon tend to get better results than those that do not, and those that do not, typically plant during the first warm spell of the spring, which leaves them vulnerable to late frosts.

A. Yes. This choice links planting with the phases of the moon and the likelihood of frost destroying plants. If this were not true, then gardeners who plant using the phases of the moon would not be less likely to lose plants to frost.

B. No. If the phases of the moon affect this part of weather, then gardeners who plant during the first warm spell would not always be less successful than those that plant using the phases of the moon.

C. No. The types of plants used by each type of gardener are not relevant to the timing of a late frost.

D. No. The reason that using phases of the moon works is not relevant to whether it works.

E. No. Professional gardeners are not relevant to the argument about amateur gardeners.

24. **B** `Inference`

The columnist states that, on average, a significant amount of money from tourism in developing countries goes to foreign owners of businesses and that this goes up as tourism becomes more established. The columnist goes on to show that tourists can spend money at local business to counteract money going to foreign businesses. The credited response will be a true statement based on the facts presented by the columnist.

A. No. The columnist does not make a recommendation about where tourists should spend their money.

B. Yes. This must be true if on average 70 percent or more of tourism dollars go to foreign business owners.

C. No. There is no evidence that this is true of any country.

D. No. There is no evidence tying money that goes to foreign business owners to an increase in poverty of local citizens.

E. No. There is no evidence that obtaining accommodations and other services from local people has no effect on foreign business owners. It is possible that these people still increase profits for those businesses indirectly.

25. **A** `Necessary Assumption`

Help this argument by finding a necessary assumption. The argument concludes that it is impossible to know whether industrial pollution caused the recent decline in populations of amphibians. This is based on premises that state that populations of amphibians vary from year to year based on weather. The credited response will explain why variations based on weather make it impossible to understand the cause of a decline in these populations.

A. Yes. If this is not true, then the argument fails logically. If the species that are affected by industrial pollution are not the same ones that vary greatly due to weather, then that cannot be used as a premise.

B. No. The author does not assume that the population declines are different in making the claim that weather-related declines make knowing about pollution-related declines impossible.

C. No. The author does not assume any cause for the decline in the population in making the argument that the possibility of weather-related declines make knowing about pollution-related declines impossible.

D. No. The author does not make an assumption about a future state in which pollution either increases or declines.

E. No. The author makes no connection between pollution and weather.

Section 4: Games

Questions 1–6

This is a grouping game with fixed assignment (each item in the inventory is used once). The inventory consists of seven employees who each get either a $1,000 bonus, a $3,000 bonus, or a $5,000 bonus. The bonuses go on top of your diagram. Four of the employees—K, L, M, and P—work in Finance and the other three employees—V, X, and Z—work in Graphics. Since you know what department each employee works for you should represent this information with subscripts. There are no wildcards.

Clue 1. VG, XG, and ZG ≠ $1,000

Clue 2. E → ~E – E

Clue 3. E = LF, MF, and XG

Deductions: There are some major deductions here. First, note that LF, MF, and XG cannot be in the $1,000 group. So, the only employees who can get $1,000 bonuses are KF and PF. Next, since neither VG nor ZG can be in the $1,000 group, and XG must get a higher bonus than both of them, you know that VG and ZG both go in the $3,000 group and XG must be in the $5,000 group. Since LF and MF must get higher bonuses than KF and PF, they cannot be in the $1,000 group and must be in either the $3,000 or $5,000 groups. This means that KF and PF cannot be in the $5,000 group and must be in either the $1,000 or $3,000 groups.

Here's the diagram.

K L M P V X Z
F F F F g g g

	~L ~M		~K ~P
1K	3K	5K
	V Z	X
	g g	g

Clue 1: $\frac{V \; X \; Z}{g, g, g}$ ≠ 1K

Clue 2: ~ HE—HE

Clue 3: L, M, X, = HE

Combine 2 & 3: K, P—L, M
V, Z—X

1. **C**   Grab-a-Rule

Use POE to eliminate answer choices that cannot be true.

A. No. This violates rules 2 and 3 because XG is in the $3,000 group.

B. No. This violates rule 1 because ZG is in the $1,000 group.

C. Yes. This choice does not violate any rules.

D. No. This violates rules 2 and 3 because KF is in the same bonus group as MF.

E. No. This violates rule 1 because VG is in the $1,000 group.

2. **B**   Specific

Make a new line in your diagram and add the new information. If LF and MF do not get the same bonus, then one of them is in the $3,000 group and one is in the $5,000 group (rules 2 and 3). This means that both KF and PF must be in the $1,000 group (rule 2). Since LF could get either the $3,000 or the $5,000 bonus, (B) is the credited response.

3. **A**   Specific

Make a new line in your diagram and add the new information. If only one employee can be in the $1,000 group, then it must be either KF or PF (rule 2). The other will have to be in the $3,000 group, forcing LF and MF into the $5,000 group (rules 2 and 3), making (A) the credited response.

4. **E**   General

Use prior work and your deductions to determine which answer must be true.

A. No. While it could be true that only one employee receives a $1,000 bonus, both KF and PF could be in the $3,000 group, forcing LF and MF into the $5,000 group (rules 2 and 3).

B. No. If both KF and PF are in the $1,000 group and LF and MF are in the $5,000 group, then only VG and ZG are in the $3,000 group.

C. No. Since KF and PF or LF and MF can be in the $3,000 group and VG and ZG are already there (rules 1, 2, and 3), that means there can be up to four employees in the $3,000 group.

D. No. If LF and MF are in the $3,000 group, then XG is the only employee in the $5,000 group (see deductions).

E. Yes. From the deductions, only LF, MF, and XG can be in the $5,000 group since they are the Highly Effective employees and must get larger bonuses than the other employees.

5. **D**   Specific

Make a new line in your diagram and add the new information. If only two employees can be in the $5,000 group, then one of LF or MF must be in the $3,000 group since XG is already in the $5,000 group. This will force both KF and PF into the $1,000 group (rule 2), making (D) the credited response.

6. **B**   General

Use prior work and your deductions to determine which answer must be false.

A. No. As seen in question 4 (B), if both KF and PF are in the $1,000 group and LF and MF are in the $5,000 group, then only VG and ZG are in the $3,000 group. This could be true.

B. Yes. The maximum number of employees who could receive $1,000 bonuses is two—KF and PF. Since VG and ZG are already in the $3,000 group, and it is possible to add even more employees to this group, there is no way for there to be more employees in the $1,000 group than in the $3,000 group.

C. No. If KF and PF are both in the $1,000 group and only one of LF or MF is in the $3,000 group, then the other must be in the $5,000 group with XG, meaning that there could be the same number of employees receiving $1,000 bonuses as there are receiving $5,000 bonuses.

D. No. If LF and MF are in the $3,000 group, then both KF and PF are in the $1,000 group and XG is the only employee in the $5,000 group (see deductions). So it is possible to have more employees receive $1,000 bonuses than $5,000 bonuses.

E. No. It is possible for more employees to receive $3,000 bonuses than receive $5,000 bonuses. See question 2 (B).

Questions 7–11

This is a grouping game with fixed assignment. There are three groups—1, 2, and 3—and seven trees—H, L, M, O, P, S, and W—in the inventory. There are two wildcards.

Clue 1: HO_

Clue 2: ~MW

Clue 3: L/W = 1

Clue 4: M/O = 2

Clue 5: 3 > 1

Notice how every clue has an element that is in another clue. That means you can make deductions. Since the key to working with games with grouping is to try to narrow down the number of items that can be in each group, you should start with the HO_ block to see how it will fit in the diagram. If you try to put that block into group 1, then according to clue 5, group 3 has to have at least 4 trees. This would use all seven trees and leave none for group 2, but since you know that M/O must be in group 2 (clue 4), then HO_ cannot be in group 1. Try to put this block into group 2. Since O is in group 2, that will force M to be in a different group (clue 4). Since there are now three items in group 2, and only four items left, then only one can be in group 1 and the other three must be in group 3 (clue 5). So M must be in group 3 (clue 3). If L is in group 1, then W is in group 2 and P and S are in group 3. If W is in group 1, then L, P, and S are interchangeable in the remaining spaces.

Next, put HO_ in group 3. Since O is not in group 2, then M is (clue 4). With the block there, group 3 has exactly three items in it (clue 1), so group 1 can have one or two items. If it has one, then the remaining two items must be in group 2. If group 1 has two items, then the single remaining item must be in group 2. If L is in group 1, then W must be in group 3 because M is in group 2 (clue 2) and S and P are in group 2 with M or one is with L in group 1 and the other is with M in group 2. If W is in group 1, then L, S, and P are interchangeable in the remaining spaces, noting that L cannot be in group 1 with W.

Here's the diagram.

H, L, M, O, P, S, W

Clue 1: $\boxed{HO\ \_\_}$

Clue 2: $\boxed{M\ \cancel{W}}$

Clue 3: $\frac{L}{W} = 1$

Clue 4: $\frac{M}{O} = 2$

Clue 5: $3 > 1$

	1	2	3
(1)	__	__ __ __	__ __
(2)	__ __	M __	H O __

7. D — Grab-a-Rule

A. No. This violates the first rule.

B. No. This violates the fifth rule.

C. No. This violates the third rule.

D. Yes. This doesn't violate any rules.

E. No. This violates the fourth rule.

8. B — Specific

Make a new line in your diagram and add the new information. If H is in group 2, then you are using the first scenario. In either case in the first scenario, M must be in group 3, making (B) the credited response.

9. C — General

Use prior work and your deductions to determine which answer is a list of any tree that can be in group 1 at any time.

A. No. H cannot be in group 1 (deductions).

B. No. H cannot be in group 1 (deductions).

C. Yes. One of L or W must be in group 1 (rule 3) and S and P are wildcards with no restrictions. See question 10 (A).

D. No. S needs to be on this list. See question 10 (A).

E. No. This violates rule 3, which says that L or W must be in group 1, so L and W need to be on this list.

10. A Specific

Make a new line in your diagram and add the new information. If W is in group 3, then according to the deductions, you are using the second scenario. So, W is in group 3 with H and O, L is in group 1, and M is in group 2. One of S or P can be in group 1 with L and the other in group 2 with M, or both S and P can be in group 2 with M. This makes (A) the credited response.

11. A General

This question is asking which tree, if in group 2, completely determines where all the other trees are.

A. Yes. If W is in group 2, then it is with H and O (deductions), which forces M into group 3 with P and S so that group 3 has more trees than group 1, and that leaves L for group 1.

B. No. If S is in group 2, you cannot determine where any of the other trees must be.

C. No. If P is in group 2, you cannot determine where any of the other trees must be.

D. No. If M is in group 2, then O and H are in group 3, but you cannot determine where L, W, S, or P must go.

E. No. If L is in group 2, then W must be in group 1, but you cannot determine where O, H, M, S, or P must go.

Questions 12–18

This is a 1D order game with ranking. The inventory consists of seven librarians—F, G, H, K, L, M, and Z—which are being scheduled Monday through Saturday. There is one librarian assigned each day Monday through Friday and two librarians assigned on Saturday. The days go across the top of the diagram. There are no wildcards.

Clue 1: H—L

Clue 2: H—G & M—G

Clue 3: F—K & M

Clue 4: K—Z

Clue 5: ~ L on Sat → L—F ; F – L → L on Sat

Combine the clues to get two possible arrangements.

There are lots of deductions here. From one scenario, you know that H, L, and F must be on Monday, Tuesday, and Wednesday, respectively. M and K can be on Wednesday or Thursday, and G and Z must be on Saturday together.

For the second scenario, L is on Saturday according to clue 5, so F must be on Monday or Tuesday, and H could be any day Monday through Friday, but not Saturday. M and K could be any day Monday through Friday, and one of G or Z can be on Saturday with L, but the other could be earlier in the week. G cannot be Monday, Tuesday, or Wednesday, and Z cannot be Monday or Tuesday.

Here's the diagram.

F, G, H, K, L, M, Z

Clue 1: H—L

Clue 2: H ⟍ ⟋ G (M)

Clue 3: F ⟨ K , M

Clue 4: K—Z

Clue 5: L ≠ Sat → L—F
F—L → L = Sat

	M	T	W	Th	F	S
	$\frac{G}{Z}$	$\frac{G}{Z}$	$\_G$		$\_F \mid F$	$\frac{H}{M}$
(1)	H	L	F	M/K	K/M	G Z
(2)	—	—	—	—	—	L $\frac{G}{Z}$

---

12. **A** Grab-a-Rule

A. Yes. This does not violate any rules.

B. No. This violates rule 5 because L is after F and is not on Saturday.

C. No. This violates rule 3 because K and M are before F.

D. No. This violates rule 4 because K is after Z.

E. No. This violates rule 1 because L is before H.

13. **E** General

Use your deductions to determine who cannot be on Tuesday.

A. No. In the second setup, F could be on Tuesday.

B. No. In the second setup, H could be on Tuesday.

C. No. In the second setup, K could be on Tuesday.

D. No. In the second setup, M could be on Tuesday.

E. Yes. In the first setup, Z must be on Saturday; in the second setup, Z must be on either Friday or Saturday, so Z cannot be on Tuesday.

14. **B** Specific

If K is earlier than M, then you end up with two scenarios in which M is before G. That means that K must also be before G, making (B) the credited response.

15. **A**   Specific

Make a new line in your diagram and add the new information. If Z is on Thursday, then you are working with the second setup. This will force G into Saturday with L, since only Z or G can be on Saturday with L. So F must be earlier in the week than L, making (A) the credited response.

16. **C**   Specific

Make a new line in your diagram and add the new information. If M is on Tuesday, then F must be on Monday (rule 3), so L must be on Saturday (rule 5), making (C) the credited response.

17. **D**   Specific

If F is before H, L must be on Saturday (rule 5) with either G or Z. F is on Monday, and K, M, and H round out the rest of the week. This makes (D) the credited response, since M must be on a day earlier than Saturday.

18. **C**   Complex

This question wants you to substitute a new rule for rule 3 that gets you the same deductions. Rule 3 has F before both K and M, so you need an answer that is going to make F come before both K and M.

A. No. If F can't be on Monday, Tuesday, or Wednesday, then you do not have the same deductions.

B. No. Limiting F or H to Monday may seem helpful, but if H is on Monday, then both K and M can be after F.

C. Yes. If only H and L can be earlier than F, then K and M must come after F, giving you the same deductions you had originally.

D. No. This puts F earlier than K, but M could still be before.

E. No. This puts F earlier than M, but K could still be before.

Questions 19–23

This is a variation on an ordering game in which not all the elements are used necessitating an out column. The inventory consists of four types of features—F, M, I, and T—which can not only be left out but also repeated. At least three features (note that they do not have to be different features) have to take up three or more of the five slots available in a newsletter. If there is no feature in a slot, then there is a graphic in that slot. There is one wildcard.

Clue 1. _ _+ for 1 → consecutive

Clue 2. F or T → F1 or T1 ; ~F1 & ~T1 → ~F & ~T

Clue 3. one I or ~I

There's really not much to work with here. It's worth noting that if there isn't F or T in slot 1, then both F and T are out, which means the features are made up of I and M. You might think it would be worth trying to figure out all the possible combinations of features, but there are many since you can have three or more features, and graphics besides. So, you are starting off with a blank diagram.

Here's the diagram.

F, M, I, T, g

	1	2	3	4	5	out

Clue 1: feat > 1 →
        consecutive

Clue 2: F or T → FI or TI

    ~FI & ~ TI → ~F & ~ T

Clue 3: exactly one I
    or ~ I

19. **D**   Grab-a-Rule

A. No. This violates rule 3 since I is used twice.

B. No. This violates rule 2 since F or T is not in the first slot and there is another T.

C. No. This violates rule 2 since I is in the first slot and F is in a later slot.

D. Yes. This doesn't violate any rules.

E. No. This violates rule 1 since there is one T split up in non-consecutive slots.

20. **A**   Specific

Make a new line in your diagram and fill in the information given. If T is out, and F is in slots 4 and 5, then there must be another F in slot 1 (rule 2). This makes (A) the credited response.

21. **E**   General

Use the deductions, prior work, and trying the answers to determine what must be false.

A. No. This could be true. If I is in slot 1, then T and F are out, but there can be two or more M's.

B. No. This could be true. If there is one F in slot 2, then there must be T in slot 1 (rule 2). There are no other restrictions on the number or type of features.

C. No. This could be true. If there is one T in slot 3, then there is at least an F in slot 1. There are no other restrictions on the number or type of features.

D. No. This could be true. If all the features are M or T except slot 1, then as long as T is in slot 1 then this could work.

E. Yes. This must be false. If the features in the first four slots are either I or M, and there is a feature in slot 5, it cannot be T or F since that would violate rule 2.

22. **D** **Specific**

Make a new line in your diagram and fill in the information given. If I is in slot 1, then T and F must be out (rule 2) and there must be at least two M features. Even if one of the M's is in slot 5, the other would have to be in one of slots 2, 3, or 4, making (D) the credited response.

23. **D** **General**

Use the deductions, prior work, and trying the answers to determine what must be false.

A. No. This could be true. As long as the remaining features were all T and either the F or one of the T's is in slot 1.

B. No. This could be true. As long as there is a T in slot 1, then both F and M can be out.

C. No. This could be true. This is just exchanging an F for the T in (B). As long as there is an F in slot 1, this works.

D. Yes. This must be false. If both F and T are out and there is only 1 M, then there will not be enough features to meet the minimum requirement of three. According to rule 3, there can be only one I.

E. No. This could be true. As long as there is an F in slot 1, then both I and T can be out.

Chapter 6
PrepTest 76:
Answers and
Explanations

ANSWER KEY: PREPTEST 76

Section 1: Reading Comprehension		Section 2: Arguments 1		Section 3: Games		Section 4: Arguments 2	
1.	C	1.	B	1.	D	1.	C
2.	B	2.	B	2.	C	2.	B
3.	D	3.	C	3.	D	3.	D
4.	A	4.	C	4.	B	4.	B
5.	D	5.	C	5.	A	5.	C
6.	A	6.	D	6.	B	6.	D
7.	D	7.	E	7.	B	7.	C
8.	B	8.	E	8.	C	8.	E
9.	B	9.	B	9.	D	9.	C
10.	C	10.	B	10.	A	10.	E
11.	B	11.	A	11.	C	11.	B
12.	D	12.	B	12.	E	12.	B
13.	D	13.	D	13.	C	13.	D
14.	B	14.	E	14.	A	14.	B
15.	E	15.	A	15.	C	15.	D
16.	C	16.	C	16.	B	16.	B
17.	C	17.	D	17.	E	17.	A
18.	B	18.	B	18.	B	18.	E
19.	E	19.	C	19.	E	19.	A
20.	C	20.	E	20.	C	20.	C
21.	C	21.	B	21.	B	21.	C
22.	C	22.	A	22.	A	22.	A
23.	D	23.	E	23.	B	23.	D
24.	B	24.	D			24.	D
25.	A	25.	D			25.	C
26.	B	26.	E				
27.	E						

EXPLANATIONS

Section 1: Reading Comprehension

Questions 1–6

The first paragraph offers a negative opinion about a piece of music. The main point of the second paragraph is that the quote refers to a Beethoven piece, but it could also characterize Schoenberg's work. The main point of the third paragraph is to show that the music of both Beethoven and Schoenberg caused controversy and that it took time for Beethoven's music to be accepted, alluding to the idea that it may take time for Schoenberg's music to be accepted. The point of the fourth paragraph is to describe the first of Schoenberg's three evolving styles. The point of the fifth paragraph is to describe the second style, which lacked tonal basis. The point of the six paragraph is to discuss the third style, which incorporated the 12-tone technique and was difficult to follow, though technically masterful. The main point of the seventh paragraph is that Schoenberg's music is most important because it captures emotions not captured before. The Bottom Line of the passage as a whole is that Schoenberg's music, while sometimes difficult to listen to, shares commonalities with other composers and moved through three phases, culminating in a style that is important because of how it captures emotions.

1. **C**   **Big Picture**

Use your Bottom Line of the passage to help you to evaluate the choices. The correct answer will describe the main idea of the passage.

A. No. While this is a true statement based on the passage, it is too narrow and does not capture how important Schoenberg's music is.

B. No. Though the author notes some similarities with Beethoven, the author does not claim that Schoenberg should be as highly regarded.

C. Yes. This is a paraphrase of the predicted Bottom Line and fully captures the main idea of the passage.

D. No. The passage states that it is Schoenberg's delineation of emotional states that makes his music essential.

E. No. The passage does not focus on Schoenberg's acceptance.

2. **B**   **RC Reasoning**

The question is asking for a situation that parallels the way that Schoenberg's work is disturbing. The passage states that Schoenberg's work is disturbing because it unflinchingly faces difficult truths.

A. No. This would be more similar to the incoherent, shrill, and ear-splitting characteristics that the author claims are not what make it disturbing.

B. Yes. This is unflinchingly facing difficult truths.

C. No. The author states that Schoenberg was the first to capture these emotional states.

D. No. This would be more similar to the incoherent, shrill, and ear-splitting characteristics that the author claims are not what make it disturbing.

E. No. The author does not discuss unfamiliarity in this portion of the passage.

3. **D** `Structure`

The question is asking why the author employs the quote from Kotzebue. The author's discussion of the quote draws a connection between Schoenberg and Beethoven.

A. No. This answer does not connect to Schoenberg.

B. No. The quote referred to Beethoven.

C. No. The author is not trying to impugn Beethoven.

D. Yes. The discussion of the quote in the next two paragraphs indicates that Beethoven's popularity grew in time.

E. No. The author does not discuss general critical consensus.

4. **A** `Extract Infer`

The correct answer will be the statement that is not supported by evidence within the passage text. The four incorrect answers will be supported by evidence in the passage.

A. Yes. Only Schoenberg began in the late-Romantic manner.

B. No. The quote in the first paragraph was written about Beethoven's work, but the author says that it is also an accurate description of Schoenberg's work.

C. No. In the second paragraph, the author states that both Beethoven and Schoenberg stirred controversy.

D. No. In the third paragraph, the author states that both Beethoven and Schoenberg worked in constantly changing and evolving musical styles.

E. No. In the third paragraph, the author states that both Beethoven and Schoenberg altered the language and extended the expressive range of music.

5. **D** `Extract Infer`

The correct answer will be the statement that is best supported by evidence within the passage text. In the seventh paragraph, the author argues that Schoenberg's work is essential because he captured emotions that had not previously been captured.

A. No. While the author acknowledges that Schoenberg had an awe-inspiring level of technical mastery, that's not what the author says makes Schoenberg's music essential.

B. No. The author does not state an opinion about this aspect of Schoenberg's work.

C. No. While this is an accomplishment that the author acknowledges, it is not what the author says makes Schoenberg's work essential.

D. Yes. In lines 50–53, the author states that this is what makes Schoenberg's work essential.

E. No. The author does not state an opinion about this aspect of Schoenberg's work.

6.   A   **Extract Infer**

The correct answer will be the statement that is best supported by evidence within the passage text. In the fourth paragraph, the author discusses that each style acknowledged tradition and lit the way for progress.

A. Yes. This is supported by the author's claim that each style lit the way for progress.

B. No. This answer is extreme. The author never claims that any of the styles are an inexplicable departure from the previous style.

C. No. This answer is extreme. The author never claims that any of the styles are an inexplicable departure from the previous style.

D. No. This answer is extreme. The author never claims that any of the styles are an inexplicable departure from the previous style.

E. No. This answer is extreme. The author never claims that any of the styles are an inexplicable departure from the previous style.

Questions 7–13

The main point of the first paragraph is to introduce the issue: that biotechnology patents may hurt basic research. The main point of the second paragraph is to discuss why researchers think that patents might hinder their research. The point of the third paragraph is to address the concerns raised about patents and argue that patents are not likely to be enforced when it comes to noncommercial research and that they create an incentive to innovate. The Bottom Line of the passage as a whole is that biotechnology patenting is not likely hindering basic research.

7.   D   **Big Picture**

Use your Bottom Line of the passage to help you to evaluate the choices. The correct answer will describe the main idea of the passage.

A. No. This is the threat that the author explores, but he or she ultimately concludes that patents don't threaten progress.

B. No. The author acknowledges the shift but does not indicate that it is controversial.

C. No. This answer choice is too negative and does not capture the main idea. At the end of the passage, the author discusses that patents have a positive impact.

D. Yes. This accurately paraphrases the Bottom Line that concerns about biotechnology patterns are not valid.

E. No. While this is mentioned in the passage, this answer is too narrow and it is not the main idea of the passage.

76

8. **B**   Extract
           Infer

The correct answer will be the statement that is best supported by evidence within the passage text. The researchers in lines 30–31 are those who oppose biotechnology patents and fear that there will be prohibitively high fees to use patented materials.

A. No. Market conditions would allow the prohibitively high fees that these researchers fear.

B. Yes. Since they fear prohibitively high fees, they would favor a system without fees.

C. No. The fees that they oppose would be a measure to prevent access.

D. No. This portion of the passage discusses only corporate patent holders.

E. No. This portion of the passage does not discuss funding for research projects.

9. **B**   Extract
           Fact

The correct answer will be directly supported by the passage text. The first paragraph discusses that university researchers rely on research funding that is conditional on the patentability of results.

A. No. The passage does not discuss academic advancement.

B. Yes. This is directly supported by lines 4–7.

C. No. The first paragraph does not discuss access to basic research.

D. No. The passage does not discuss exploitation of researchers.

E. No. The passage does not discuss whether researchers would prefer a competitive or communal model.

10. **C**   Extract
            Infer

The correct answer will be the statement that is best supported by evidence within the passage text.

A. No. The passage mentioned that inventors took steps to protect their discoveries before patents were available.

B. No. This is a fear of researchers, but the passage does not argue that it actually happens.

C. Yes. This is discussed in the third paragraph. Litigation is usually undertaken only to protect market position.

D. No. The author mentioned that researchers rely on such funding but does not pass judgment on that reliance.

E. No. The passage does not discuss the innovativeness of the researchers who oppose patenting.

11. **B**   Structure

The question is asking why the author brings up the early days of biotechnology. The passage discusses that even in the days before patents, researchers took measures to protect their work.

A. No. The passage does not provide such an account.

B. Yes. The context of this reference is that even in the days before patents, researchers took measures to protect their work.

C. No. The passage does not argue that biotechnology was untainted by commercial motives even at its inception.

D. No. There is no discussion of sophistication in this portion of the passage.

E. No. This reference is used to counter the idea that patenting biotechnological discoveries will not necessarily hinder progress.

12. **D** Extract Infer

The correct answer will be the statement that is best supported by evidence within the passage text.

A. No. The passage does not discuss policy makers, so we cannot infer what they are likely or unlikely to do.

B. No. This answer choice is extreme and unsupported. There is no discussion of what patent holders believe about the pursuit of basic research, only that they would be likely to sue only when market position is threatened.

C. No. This answer choice is extreme and unsupported. There is no support for a claim about whether researchers are generally unable to obtain funding.

D. Yes. The second paragraph discusses that patent holders might charge fees to use their materials for research.

E. No. This answer choice is extreme and unsupported. There is no discussion of the quantity of biologists willing to teach in academia.

13. **D** Extract Infer

The question is asking what the author thinks will happen with basic, noncommercial research involving patented materials. Lines 45–48 state that the author thinks that whether the patent could or would be enforced in this situation is questionable.

A. No. This is presented as a fear of some researchers, not as the author's opinion.

B. No. The author states that patent litigation is usually initiated only to protect a market position, which would not be threatened by basic noncommercial research.

C. No. The passage does not discuss whether universities restrict research due to patent concerns.

D. Yes. In the third paragraph, the author states that there has been a judicial tradition to respect a completely noncommercial research exception to patent infringement.

E. No. The passage does not discuss such offers.

Questions 14–19

The main point of the first paragraph is that wampum was used for political purposes, though it became a medium of exchange due to misinterpretations by Europeans. The second paragraph describes the two types of wampum and what they represented. The third paragraph describes wampum belts and how they were used within the Haudenosaune Confederacy to frame and enforce its laws. The Bottom Line of the passage as a whole is that the wampum symbol system evolved from religious significance into a powerful and effective political tool for the Haudenosaune group of nations.

14. **B**   Big Picture

Use your Bottom Line of the passage to help you to evaluate the choices. The correct answer will describe the main idea of the passage.

A. No. This answer is untrue. The passage states that loose beads were the simplest and oldest form of wampum.

B. Yes. This accurately paraphrases the Bottom Line.

C. No. This answer is extreme and untrue. While the Europeans used wampum solely for commercial exchange, its use within the Haudenosaune was spiritual and political.

D. No. Wampum was used to communicate prior to the Haudenosaune Confederacy.

E. No. While this is suggested by the first paragraph of the passage, it is not the main idea.

15. **E**   Structure

The question is asking why the author mentions the fishing practice in the second paragraph. The passage describes the use of wampum to communicate with the spirits thought to have created fish as an example of how the beads were used.

A. No. The beads were thrown into the water in this example, which would not pass on knowledge.

B. No. There is no discussion of whether this practice changed after contact with the Europeans.

C. No. The fishing practice is an example of an early religious use of wampum that came before the more formal use in the Haudenosaune Confederacy.

D. No. The author does not argue that this practice was learned of by studying wampum.

E. Yes. The author is discussing the simplest use of wampum to represent basic ideas such as the sky-yearning or earth-loving spirits who created fish.

16. **C**   Structure

The correct answer will paraphrase the main point of the last paragraph, which describes wampum belts and how they were used within the Haudenosaune Confederacy to frame and enforce its laws.

A. No. While the passage mentions that wampum belts combined string wampum, the focus of the paragraph is on the symbolism and usage of the belts.

B. No. The focus of the paragraph is on wampum belts and their symbolism and usage.

C. Yes. This accurately describes the contents of the final paragraph.

D. No. The passage does not detail the contents of the Haudenosaune Confederacy's constitution.

E. No. While the passage claims that the wampum symbol system was effective, there was no evidence given.

17. **C** **Extract Infer**

The correct answer will be the statement that is best supported by evidence within the passage text.

A. No. This answer is unsupported. The passage does not discuss an alternate reality.

B. No. The author discusses the use of color prior to the Haudenosaune Confederacy.

C. Yes. In the third paragraph, the passage discusses combining string wampum to form stylized symbols.

D. No. The passage does not argue that the color associations shifted over time, only that the arrangements of the colors directed interpretation of symbols.

E. No. This answer is unsupported. The passage does not discuss what would have happened if the Europeans had had different information.

18. **B** **Extract Infer**

The correct answer will be the statement that is best supported by evidence within the passage text.

A. No. The passage does not discuss the use of wampum for commercial purposes prior to contact with the Europeans.

B. Yes. The third paragraph states that the formation of the Haudenosaune Confederacy was the major impetus for a more deliberate system of use of wampum.

C. No. The passage does not discuss recodification of the laws of the Haudenosaune Confederacy.

D. No. The passage does not provide a timeline of whether contact with Europeans came before or after the use of wampum to codify the laws of the Haudenosaune Confederacy.

E. No. The passage does not discuss any changing of the wampum bead colors.

19. **E** **Extract Infer**

The correct answer will be the statement that is best supported by evidence within the passage text.

A. No. The passage does not discuss other peoples.

B. No. This answer choice is extreme and unsupported. The passage does not mention whether Europeans were aware of wampum's true significance.

C. No. The first paragraph states that Europeans used wampum solely to purchase goods.

D. No. The passage states that the peoples who made up the Haudenosaune Confederacy had been warring tribes.

E. Yes. The passage uses language such as "possibly indicating" in the third paragraph.

Questions 20–27

Passage A

The main point of the first paragraph is that Karl Popper is hyper focused on negative evidence and that theories are scientific only if they can be tested with a search for negative evidence. The main point of the second paragraph is that theories can fail for various reasons and the negative evidence is not necessarily conclusive. The Bottom Line of passage A is that Popper's obsession with negative evidence goes too far.

Passage B

The main point of the first paragraph is that an incorrect auxiliary assumption about the orbit of Uranus led to an incorrect prediction, but Newton's laws were not thought to be incorrect. The main point of the second paragraph is that Newton's theory was rejected when Einstein's new theory provided accurate results. The Bottom Line of passage B is that a prediction can be wrong either because of an incorrect auxiliary assumption or because of an incorrect theory.

20. **C** [Big Picture]

The correct answer will be supported by the Bottom Lines of both passages.

A. No. While this is mentioned in passage A, it is not mentioned in passage B.

B. No. Passage A does not mention planetary orbits.

C. Yes. Passage A discusses the extent to which negative evidence is conclusive and passage B uses negative evidence (the actual orbits of Uranus and Mercury) to help determine the validity of auxiliary assumptions and predictive theories.

D. No. Neither passage argues for a specific technique for confirming a theory.

E. No. This answer choice is extreme. Neither passage claims that experimentation is irrelevant.

21. **C** [Extract Fact]

The correct answer will be mentioned in passage A and there will be an example of it in passage B.

A. No. Passage B uses results to repudiate theories or assumptions, not the other way around.

B. No. Passage A does not mention revising a theory.

C. Yes. Passage A discusses using negative evidence to disprove a theory and passage B gives the example of Mercury's orbit that was used to disprove Newton's theory.

D. No. Passage A does not mention planetary orbits.

E. No. Passage A does not mention non-testable theories.

22. **C** [Extract Infer]

Passage A mentions a disturbing force as something that would need to be lacking for a theory's prediction to come true. The correct answer will be something in passage B that reflects this description.

A. No. Uranus was the subject of the prediction, not an outside force.

B. No. The sun was the subject of an auxiliary assumption, not an outside force.

C. Yes. Neptune was an outside factor that was not included in the prediction's original assumptions.

D. No. Mercury was the subject of a prediction, not an outside force.

E. No. Passage B never mentions the moon.

23. **D** `Extract Infer`

The question is asking what the author thinks about Popper. The author accuses Popper of believing that positive evidence has no value as evidence and that negative evidence is disproof. The correct answer will be the statement that is best supported by evidence within the passage text.

A. No. The author is arguing that Popper's idea is too extreme because the reality is more complicated than Popper treats it.

B. No. The author is arguing that Popper overestimates the value of negative evidence.

C. No. The author is not arguing that the idea fails in all cases, just that Popper takes it to the extreme.

D. Yes. The author is accusing Popper of being too extreme.

E. No. The author's criticism is that the idea is too extreme, not that it doesn't fit one particular theory.

24. **B** `Structure`

The question is asking for a result from passage B that would serve as evidence for the claim that negative evidence is rarely conclusive.

A. No. Passage B does not discuss the discovery of Uranus, only the difficulty predicting its orbit.

B. Yes. Newton's laws accurately predicted the orbit of Neptune and it was the assumption that Neptune didn't exist that made the prediction about Uranus inaccurate.

C. No. This would be an effective use of negative evidence.

D. No. Failure to find something is not negative evidence. Negative evidence is finding something that goes against a theory.

E. No. The successful use of a theory is positive evidence, not negative evidence.

25. **A** `RC Reasoning`

The question is asking for an astronomical body that serves as negative evidence like the black swan did in passage A.

A. Yes. The observed orbit of Mercury did not match Newton's prediction, serving as evidence that Newton's theory was incorrect.

B. No. The assumption that there were no other nearby planets caused the prediction to fail, not Newton's theory.

C. No. The existence of Neptune negated an auxiliary assumption, not Newton's theory. Newton's theory accurately predicted the orbit of Neptune.

D. No. Passage B does not mention Venus.

E. No. The sun was the subject of an auxiliary assumption and did not negatively impact the validity of Newton's theory.

26. **B** **Extract Infer**

The question is asking for a point of disagreement between passage A and passage B. The correct answer will be best supported by the text of passage B.

A. No. Passage B does not express an opinion about Popper.

B. Yes. Passage B discusses that Newton's theory was ultimately rejected even though it had accurately predicted the orbit of Neptune and other planets.

C. No. Passage B discusses the importance of auxiliary assumptions and the role they played in evaluating Newton's theory.

D. No. Passage B does not express an opinion about the logical asymmetry between positive and negative experience.

E. No. Passage B discusses one bold theory, but it does not opine on what scientific research involves.

27. **E** **RC Reasoning**

The question is asking for a scenario analogous to the discovery of Neptune. The author of passage B discusses that Neptune was discovered when scientists reconsidered their assumptions that there was no other planet near Uranus after incorrectly predicting the orbit of Uranus rather than rejecting Newton's law. The orbit of Neptune was consistent with the predictions of Newton's theory. The correct answer will involve the discovery of something that was previously assumed not to exist, but its discovery is consistent with the theory at hand.

A. No. The discovery of the second high tide is not consistent with the theory.

B. No. The discovery of Neptune did not settle a debate.

C. No. This answer does not involve the discovery of something that was previously assumed not to exist.

D. No. This answer does not involve the discovery of something that was previously assumed not to exist.

E. Yes. The third undetected particle is similar to Neptune in that it was not previously assumed to exist, but then the discovery of it was consistent with the law of conservation of energy.

Section 2: Arguments 1

1. **B**   **Flaw**

The argument concludes that industrial by-products have entered the swamp's ecosystem. This conclusion is based on the facts that industrial by-products cause elevated hormone activity, that abnormal development of certain body parts in reptiles occurs only with elevated hormone activity, and that several alligators with developmental abnormalities were discovered in the swamp. The argument mistakes a sufficient condition for a necessary condition: It assumes that nothing but industrial by-products could have caused the elevated hormone activity. The credited response will identify this flaw.

A. No. The argument is concerned only with developmental abnormalities that do result from elevated hormone activity, so other abnormalities are irrelevant.

B. Yes. This answer choice describes the flaw of mistaking a sufficient condition for a necessary condition.

C. No. Even if we knew that the industrial by-products were in food instead of or in addition to being in the swamp, the argument would still contain the flaw of assuming that the by-products are the only cause of elevated hormone activity.

D. No. The argument does not require more reptiles to have developmental abnormalities.

E. No. The argument is limited to a particular swamp, so the sample does not have to be representative of alligators in general.

2. **B**   **Main Point**

The fill-in-the-blank space is preceded by the logical indicator "So," signaling that the credited response will be the main point of the argument. The government official states that residents who are foreign citizens cannot serve as cabinet secretaries because they cannot perform all of the duties of the position. He also states that cabinet undersecretaries are expected to serve as cabinet secretaries when the actual secretary is unavailable. The implication is that foreign citizens should not serve as cabinet undersecretaries either for the same reason: They would not be able to perform all of the duties of the cabinet secretary if they had to step in to serve when the actual secretary was unavailable. The credited response will indicate that foreign citizens should not serve as cabinet undersecretaries.

A. No. The argument is not structured to lead to a prescriptive remedy for the problem of foreign citizens' being unable to perform all of the duties of a cabinet secretary.

B. Yes. This answer choice correctly describes the conclusion that the argument is structured to lead to.

C. No. The argument does not imply that prior experience as a cabinet undersecretary is required to be a cabinet secretary.

D. No. This answer choice contradicts the argument: The argument states that the rule against appointing foreign citizens as cabinet secretaries is wise.

E. No. This answer choice contradicts the argument: We know that cabinet undersecretaries are expected to stand in for cabinet secretaries, and nothing in the argument suggests that this practice should change.

76

3. C **Point at Issue**

Doris concludes that we should encourage students to become involved in student government if the goal is to make students more outspoken. Her conclusion is based on her observation that all members of the student government are outspoken. She assumes that joining the student government caused the students to become outspoken. Zack concludes that encouraging students to join the student government will not make them more outspoken. His conclusion is based on his assertion that students who join the student government are outspoken before they join. Doris and Zack disagree about whether joining the student government makes students more outspoken. The credited response will identify this point of disagreement.

A. No. Neither Doris nor Zack states what should be the case regarding outspokenness.

B. No. While Doris would agree with this statement, Zack does not take a position on whether students should be encouraged to become more involved in student government.

C. Yes. Doris would agree with this statement, while Zack would disagree with it.

D. No. Doris and Zack both agree with this statement.

E. No. Neither Doris nor Zack states or implies that becoming involved in student government is a necessary condition for outspokenness.

4. C **Flaw**

The biologist concludes that critics of a behavioral study on chameleons should not doubt its results despite its small sample size. His conclusion is based on an appeal to the study author's professional standing and past record of strong research. He assumes that the study author's credentials are sufficient to prove the value of this particular study; he fails to consider that this study may be flawed despite the study author's credentials. The credited response will identify this flaw.

A. No. This answer choice describes a flaw of the study itself but not of the biologist's argument.

B. No. The mechanism of vitamin D production regulation is irrelevant.

C. Yes. This answer choice describes the flaw that the biologist focuses on the study author's reputation rather than on the study itself.

D. No. The biologist focuses on the study author while ignoring the critics' valid doubts.

E. No. The biologist defers to the study author's past record of strong research; if anything, he holds the critics to a higher standard than the study author.

5. C **Necessary Assumption**

The political scientist concludes that the government does not support freedom of popular expression, disagreeing with those who claim that the government's acceptance of the recent protest indicates that the government does support freedom of expression. He supports his conclusion by indicating that supporting freedom of expression requires accepting ideas that the government both opposes and approves of. He states that the government supported the message of the recent protest. The argument assumes that the government would not have accepted the recent protest if it had not supported the message of the protest. The credited response will establish this fact.

A. No. The government's involvement in organizing the protest rally is irrelevant.

B. No. The message of the protest rally is irrelevant.

C. Yes. This answer choice provides the sufficient side of the contrapositive of the conditional stated in the argument: If the government would not have accepted the protest rally whose message it opposed, then the government cannot be said to support freedom of popular expression.

D. No. That some groups fear a government response does not prove that the government would actually oppose the group's ideas.

E. No. Whether the government fears a backlash has no bearing on whether the government accepts or opposes an idea.

6. **D**   **Principle Strengthen**

The lawyer concludes that the victim surcharge used to fund services for victims of violent crimes is unfair to nonviolent criminals. His conclusion is based on the fact that the surcharge applies to all crimes rather than just to violent crimes. He assumes that services for victims of violent crimes should be funded by surcharges collected only from violent criminals. The credited response will state a general rule or principle that establishes that services for victims of violent crimes should be funded by surcharges collected only from violent criminals.

A. No. The argument is not about deterrence.

B. No. The argument is not about the relative size of the penalties but rather about how those penalties are used.

C. No. This answer choice is a premise booster, but it does not comment on the fairness of using surcharges collected from nonviolent criminals to fund services for victims of violent criminal.

D. Yes. This answer choice establishes that surcharges collected from nonviolent criminals cannot be used to fund services for victims of more serious crimes.

E. No. The argument is not about the amount of the fine but rather about how the amount collected should be used.

7. **C**   **Resolve/ Explain**

The economist concludes that, as his country has increasingly become a service economy, in which manufacturing makes up a smaller proportion of the workforce, the country has engaged in less international trade. The credited response will explain the connection between an increasing service economy and a decrease in international trade.

A. No. This answer choice makes the situation more puzzling.

B. No. This answer choice does not explain why an increasing service economy has led to a decrease in international trade.

C. Yes. This answer choice explains that most services cannot be traded internationally because they are delivered locally only.

D. No. This answer choice has no connection to international trade.

E. No. This answer choice makes the situation more puzzling.

8. **E**   Reasoning

Merton concludes that elevated rates of heart disease are caused by air pollution from automobile exhaust. His conclusion is based on a study that showed that people who live on very busy streets have higher than average rates of heart disease. He assumes that living on such streets causes an increase in the rates of heart disease; he fails to consider other causes or relevant considerations. Ortiz suggests that Merton has failed to consider other causes, indicating that other lifestyle factors could contribute to heart disease. The credited response will describe how Ortiz responds.

A.   No. Ortiz does not dispute the accuracy of the study Merton cites but rather implies that Merton has not considered all of the relevant evidence.

B.   No. Ortiz does not mention other effects of air pollution.

C.   No. Ortiz does not dispute the accuracy of the study Merton cites.

D.   No. Ortiz does not bring up a counterexample because Merton does not state a general rule or principle.

E.   Yes. Ortiz brings up other lifestyle factors as potential causes of heart disease and indicates that Merton needs to rule them out.

9. **B**   Weaken

The argument concludes that the fishing ban at Quapaw Lake is likely responsible for the recovery of its fish population. The conclusion is based on a comparison between Quapaw Lake and Highwater Lake. Both lakes were experiencing declines in fish populations ten years ago. A moratorium on fishing was imposed at Quapaw Lake, and the fish population subsequently recovered. No such moratorium was imposed at Highwater Lake, and the fish population has continued to decline. The argument assumes that the ban caused the recovery of the fish population; it fails to consider alternate causes or relevant considerations. One such consideration is whether any fishing actually took place prior to the official ban: The argument assumes that the ban led to a change in the amount of fishing at Quapaw Lake. The credited response will introduce new evidence that undermines the conclusion or point out a relevant consideration that the argument missed.

A.   No. This answer choice might explain why the fish population has continued to decline at Highwater Lake, but it is unclear how it affects the fish population at Quapaw Lake.

B.   Yes. This answer choice establishes that the fishing ban did not actually change the amount of fishing at Quapaw Lake, thus suggesting that something else must have been responsible for the recovery of the fish population.

C.   No. The relative size of the lakes is irrelevant.

D.   No. This answer choice is too vague to weaken because we do not know whether such lakes are similar to Quapaw Lake and Highwater Lake in regards to fish population decline and fishing bans.

E.   No. The argument is about the fish population only, so the variety of fish is irrelevant.

10. **B** Sufficient Assumption

The argument concludes that Asian elephants do not run. The conclusion is supported by the fact that Asian elephants always have at least two feet on the ground. The argument assumes that the Asian elephant cannot run with two or more feet on the ground. The credited response will explicitly link the premise to the conclusion and force the conclusion to be true.

A. No. A premise states that the Asian elephant can accelerate, so this answer choice does not help us determine whether it can run.

B. Yes. A premise states that the Asian elephant does not have all of its feet off the ground at once, so added to the conditional statement of this answer choice, the conclusion that the Asian elephant cannot run is proved.

C. No. That the Asian elephant can walk as fast as some animals run does not confirm whether the elephant itself can run.

D. No. This answer choice does not discuss running.

E. No. This answer choice does not discuss running.

11. **A** Resolve/Explain

The passage explains that, last week, Styron hammers slightly outsold Maxlast hammers. This surprising result happened despite the fact that the Maxlast hammers were on sale and displayed in a prominent position in the store while the Styron hammers were at their usual price and in their usual place in the store. The passage indicates that both brands usually have roughly equal sales figures. The credited response will explain why the Maxlast hammers were outsold despite the supposed advantages of being on sale and being in a more visible display.

A. Yes. This answer choice explains that customers did not actually notice the Maxlast hammers (or, presumably, that they were on sale) even though they were placed in an ostensibly prominent position in the store.

B. No. This answer choice does not explain why the sales figures changed.

C. No. The reason customers bought the Maxlast hammers is irrelevant to why the sales figures changed.

D. No. This answer choice makes the result more surprising.

E. No. This answer choice does not explain why the sales figures changed.

12. **B** Weaken

The argument concludes that ginkgo may not have directly enhanced the memory of mice that consumed ginkgo in a study of maze navigation. The conclusion is based on the results of a comparative study that showed that mice whose diet included ginkgo were more likely to remember how to navigate a maze than mice that had a normal diet. The premises also indicate that other studies have found that ginkgo reduces stress in mice and that lowering very high stress levels is known to improve recall. The argument assumes that the mice that consumed ginkgo were actually highly stressed and that the consumption therefore reduced their high stress levels. The credited response will provide new evidence that undermines the conclusion or point out a relevant consideration that the argument missed.

A. No. Higher doses of ginkgo might still reduce stress in mice, but this answer choice does not confirm whether the mice were stressed.

B. Yes. This answer choice points out that the mice were not actually highly stressed, so the ginkgo could not have lowered very high stress levels.

C. No. This answer choice does not confirm whether the mice were stressed.

D. No. The mechanism by which ginkgo reduces stress is irrelevant to whether it actually does so. Furthermore, this answer choice does not confirm whether the mice were stressed.

E. No. The argument concerns recall, not the initial learning.

13. **D** Inference

The passage presents a single statement: Some politicians who strongly supported free trade among Canada, the United States, and Mexico now refuse to publicly support extending free trade to other Latin American countries. The credited response will be an answer choice that is supported by this statement.

A. No. The passage does not tell us anything about politicians who do support extending free trade to other Latin American countries.

B. No. The passage does not tell us anything about politicians who do support extending free trade to other Latin American countries.

C. No. The passage concerns two different instances of establishing free trade. Changing their position would mean that the politicians who supported free trade among Canada, the United States, and Mexico later decided that they are against free trade among those countries. Extending free trade to other Latin American countries is a separate issue.

D. Yes. That some politicians supported the initial free trade agreement but do not support the extension of that agreement implies that not all politicians who supported the initial free trade agreement now support the extension of that agreement.

E. No. The phrase "[refuse] to support publicly" in the passage is not synonymous with the phrase "publicly oppose" in this answer choice. Some politicians could simply remain silent on the issue, neither supporting nor opposing the idea of extending free trade.

14. **E** Principle Match

The passage presents a principle and its application, and the question stems suggests that the application is unsupported. The principle can be diagrammed as a conditional: If a person or business knowingly aids someone in infringing on a copyright, then that person or business is also guilty of copyright infringement. The contrapositive is that if a person or business is not guilty of copyright infringement, then that person or business did not knowingly aid someone in infringing on a copyright. The application of the principle indicates that the Grandview Department Store is guilty of copyright infringement. To properly make this conclusion, we need to know that the Grandview Department Store knowingly aided someone in infringing on a copyright, but the application tells us only that the store contains a self-service kiosk that a customer used to print copyrighted wedding photos. The credited response will link the idea of providing the kiosk to knowingly aiding in copyright infringement.

A. No. This answer choice does not explain how providing a kiosk constitutes knowingly aiding someone in infringing on a copyright. A comparison between self-service and full-service facilities is irrelevant.

B. No. This answer choice does not explain how providing a kiosk constitutes knowingly aiding someone in infringing on a copyright. The obligation to report illegal activity is irrelevant to the store's guilt.

C. No. This answer choice does not explain how providing a kiosk constitutes knowingly aiding someone in infringing on a copyright. Such a notice would not necessarily exonerate the store, nor do we know whether this store even posted such a notice.

D. No. This answer choice does not explain how providing a kiosk constitutes knowingly aiding someone in infringing on a copyright. Monitoring the facilities would not necessarily exonerate the store, nor do we know whether this store did in fact monitor its facilities.

E. Yes. This answer choice explains how providing a kiosk constitutes knowingly aiding someone in infringing on a copyright.

15. **A** | Main Point

The fill-in-the-blank space is preceded by the logical indicator "then," signaling that the credited response will be the main point of the argument. The argument states that, although journalism's purpose is to inform people about matters relevant to the choices they must make, newspapers and television news programs often contain sensationalistic gossip that is of little relevance to people's lives. The implication is that such gossip is included for reasons unrelated to the purpose of journalism. The credited response will indicate that gossip is included in newspapers and television news programs for nonjournalistic reasons.

A. Yes. This answer choice completes the conclusion that gossip is included in newspapers and television news programs for nonjournalistic reasons.

B. No. News media might still achieve their purpose even if they contain elements that do not contribute to that purpose.

C. No. A premise states that gossip is of little relevance to people's lives, and no statements imply that such relevance has changed over the years.

D. No. The idea of keeping an audience entertained is not discussed.

E. No. People who are interested in journalism can nevertheless be interested in sensationalistic gossip as well.

16. **C** | Flaw

The argument concludes that most citizens would prefer a legislature that is 40 percent Conservative, 20 percent Moderate, and 40 percent Liberal. This conclusion is based on the results of a survey that demonstrated that 40 percent of respondents would prefer a Conservative legislature, 20 percent a Moderate legislature, and 40 percent a Liberal legislature. The argument confuses the whole and the part: It assumes that the preferences of the surveyed group are also the preferences of most of the individual persons surveyed. The credited response will identify this flaw.

A. No. The conclusion does not prescribe a certain course of action but rather interprets the survey's results.

B. No. The argument does not use circular reasoning.

C. Yes. This answer choice describes the flaw of assuming that the preferences of a group represent the preferences of most individual members of that group.

D. No. The potential bias of the researchers does not affect the misinterpretation of the survey's results.

E. No. Both the premises and the conclusion refer to percentages.

17. **D** Inference

The city leader presents facts about the city's spending options. Adopting the new tourism plan would increase tourist revenues by at least $2 billion and create as many jobs as a new automobile manufacturing plant while costing less than building a new automobile manufacturing plant. Spending the money necessary to convince an automobile manufacturer to build a plant in the city would be a reasonable expenditure. The credited response will be an answer choice that is supported by a single statement or by a combination of statements from the passage.

A. No. The term "should" is unsupported, and the term "least expensive" is too strong: The passage does not imply which option should be pursued, nor do we know what the least expensive option would be because there may be other job-creation measures that are not discussed in the passage.

B. No. The term "in general" is too strong: The passage discusses a particular instance, but we cannot extend the reasoning to most instances.

C. No. The term "cannot" is too strong: The passage does not imply that the city can afford only one of the options.

D. Yes. If it would be reasonable to spend the money to convince an automobile manufacturer to build a plant in the city, and adopting the new tourism plan would cost less, then it is likely that spending the money to adopt the new tourism plan would also be a reasonable expenditure.

E. No. The term "only" is too strong: The passage states that building a new automobile manufacturing plant would also create jobs.

18. **B** Necessary Assumption

The argument concludes that one should not trust the anecdotal evidence that purportedly shows that many medical patients can predict sudden changes in their medical status. The premises rely on an appeal to an apparently analogous case that has been disproved: the claim that a disproportionately high number of babies are born during full moons. This claim has been disproved by pointing out that maternity room staff are simply more likely to remember full-moon births. The argument assumes that medical staff are likewise more likely to remember when their patients correctly predict changes to their medical status than when such predictions are incorrect. The credited response will confirm that the analogy can be extended in this way.

A. No. The argument does not require the article to be empirically disproved soon.

B. Yes. This answer choice confirms that the analogy with full-moon births can be extended to patients' predictions.

C. No. The sincerity of the patients' predictions is irrelevant to whether those predictions prove an instinctual ability to predict changes to their medical status.

D. No. The argument does not require full-moon births to be uncommon but rather requires them to be less common than they are believed to be.

E. No. The argument can be made regardless of how widely held the belief is.

19. **C**   Flaw

The politician concludes that legislators should reject the argument that increases in multinational control of manufacturing have shifted labor to nations without strong worker protections and thus decreased workers' average wages. He bases his conclusion on the fact that the argument comes from union leaders, who have an interest in seeing wages remain high. He assumes that the union leaders' self-interest cannot coincide with a valid justification for opposing multinational control; he attacks the union leaders' motives rather than the reasoning. The credited response will identify this flaw.

A. No. The term "all" is too strong: The conclusion explicitly states that legislators should reject "this argument," but this fact does not imply that one should reject all arguments made by union members.

B. No. The term "anyone" is too strong: The argument requires only that union leaders be unreliable sources.

C. Yes. This answer choice describes the flaw of attacking the union leaders' motives rather than their argument.

D. No. The term "only" is too strong: The argument does not imply that the union leaders have no other reasons for opposing multinational control.

E. No. The term "all" is too strong: The argument does not require that union leaders in non-manufacturing sectors argue against increases in multinational control of manufacturing.

20. **E**   Resolve/ Explain

The professor explains that, in the last ten years, significantly fewer people are earning chemistry degrees despite the facts that the number of university students who enter as chemistry majors has not changed in that time and that job prospects for chemistry graduates are better than ever. The credited response will explain why graduates are declining despite the apparently contradictory facts, likely by pointing out some other difference that has emerged in the last ten years.

A. No. This answer choice does not point out a difference that would explain the recent decline in the number of people earning chemistry degrees. Students may always have entered a university without the strong academic background required to major in chemistry.

B. No. The number of students earning chemistry degrees could remain constant or increase even if the number of degrees earned in the natural sciences as a whole declines, so this answer choice does not explain the decline in the number of people earning chemistry degrees.

C. No. This answer choice does not point out a difference that would explain the recent decline in the number of people earning chemistry degrees. Students may always have been unsure of their major upon entering universities.

76

D. No. This answer choice does not point out a difference that would explain the recent decline in the number of people earning chemistry degrees.

E. Yes. This answer choice points out a change over the years that accounts for the decline in the number of people earning chemistry degrees.

21. **B** Parallel Flaw

The argument concludes that human-borne diseases probably did not cause the mass extinction of large land animals and birds. This conclusion is supported by the facts that more than 55 different species disappeared at about the same time and that a single disease could not have wiped out so many different species. The argument fails to consider the possibility that several diseases rather than a single disease wiped out all 55 species. The credited response will match this flaw of assuming that, because a single entity cannot account for a phenomenon, a combination of such entities cannot together account for that phenomenon.

A. No. This answer choice presents a valid argument. High interest rates are neither necessary nor sufficient to cause an economic downturn, so one cannot claim that an economic downturn was caused by high interest rates.

B. Yes. Just because a single person cannot fix both the window and the door does not mean that two people could not work together to fix both.

C. No. This argument presents a flawed argument, but the flaw does not match the argument in the stimulus. The argument in this answer choice assumes that Lena, Jen, and Mark would probably not go to a restaurant outside the immediate vicinity of the theater, that they would probably not go to a restaurant that they did not all like, and that they would go home straight after the movie if they do not go out to dinner.

D. No. This answer choice presents a flawed argument, but the flaw does not match the argument in the stimulus. The painting may be great even if it was painted in a time that produced little great art.

E. No. This answer choice presents a valid argument. It is reasonable to conclude that some people benefit from the influenza vaccine if the vaccine reduces the severity of symptoms.

22. **A** Sufficient Assumption

The argument concludes that the disclaimer a tax preparation company adds to every e-mail it sends out serves no purpose. The premises indicate that the disclaimer's only purpose is to provide legal protection for the company and that the disclaimer provides no legal protection if it is contradicted elsewhere in the e-mail. The argument assumes that if the disclaimer is not contradicted elsewhere in the e-mail, then the company has no need for legal protection. The credited response will prove the conclusion.

A. Yes. This answer choice confirms that the company does not need legal protection if the disclaimer is not contradicted elsewhere in the e-mail.

B. No. Penalties are irrelevant to the argument.

C. No. Whether the disclaimer is ignored has no bearing on whether it serves a legal purpose.

D. No. Whether clients follow advice in the e-mail has no bearing on whether the disclaimer serves a legal purpose.

E. No. Penalties are irrelevant to the argument.

23. **E** `Principle Strengthen`

The argument concludes that attempts to resolve friends' marital problems are usually unjustified. This conclusion is based on the fact that such attempts usually don't work and therefore cause resentment. The argument assumes that actions that are not effective are not justified. The credited response will state a general rule or principle that establishes that only effective actions are justified.

A. No. This answer choice does not discuss whether getting involved is justified.

B. No. This answer choice would support getting involved when it is the right thing to do even if getting involved leads to resentment, so this answer choice would undermine the conclusion.

C. No. This answer choice does not discuss whether getting involved is justified.

D. No. This answer choice denies a connection between the premise and the conclusion.

E. Yes. This answer choice establishes that actions based on good intentions are justified only if they result in success.

24. **D** `Necessary Assumption`

The argument concludes that authors who write to give pleasure can impart truth. The premises claim that if the conclusion were not true, one could simply look at sales figures to determine a book's truthfulness: If a book were popular, one could claim that it gave readers pleasure and therefore that some of the book is untrue. The argument assumes that popularity is sometimes sufficient to prove that a book gives readers pleasure and that if readers derive pleasure from a book, then the author wrote the book in order to give readers pleasure. The credited response will link the ideas of deriving pleasure and writing in order to give pleasure.

A. No. Whether people are aware of a book's like effect on them has no bearing on whether the author wrote the book with a particular effect in mind.

B. No. The argument does not require authors to successfully give readers pleasure whenever they intend to do so.

C. No. Whether readers are concerned with the truth of a book has no bearing on whether the book is in fact truthful.

D. Yes. This answer choice confirms that readers can derive pleasure from a book only if the author intended the book to give pleasure.

E. No. A book that does not give readers pleasure is irrelevant to this argument.

25. **D** `Strengthen`

The argument concludes that most of the new television programs Wilke & Wilke produce for this season will be cancelled. This conclusion is based on the facts that most of the new shows they produced for the previous season were cancelled due to low viewership and that all of their new shows are police

76

dramas, few of which have been popular in recent years. The argument assumes many things, including that Wilke & Wilke's police dramas are representative examples, that viewership from the previous season has some bearing on the current season's viewership, and that the new shows are not, for whatever reason, among those less likely to be cancelled. The credited response will provide new evidence that supports the conclusion or confirms the validity of an assumption.

A. No. The argument concludes that a certain proportion of Wilke & Wilke's shows will be cancelled, so the number of shows is irrelevant.

B. No. A premise states that most of the new shows that Wilke & Wilke produced last year were cancelled, but we do not know if the police dramas referenced in the answer choice were new shows. Furthermore, we do not know if the police dramas in the answer choice were cancelled or not.

C. No. This answer choice leaves open the possibility that Wilke & Wilke did not even produce any police dramas in the previous season—compare with (D).

D. Yes. This answer choice confirms that Wilke & Wilke have produced unsuccessful new police dramas recently, supporting the idea that their next crop of new police dramas will also fail.

E. No. A premise already states that few police dramas have been popular in recent years, so this answer choice is a premise booster.

26. **E**   **Principle Match**

The passage describes a situation: If a corporation obtains funds fraudulently, then the corporation should be penalized for the use of those funds, and this penalty should completely cancel out any profit the corporation made in using the funds. The general rule or principle is that if one benefits from an illicit activity, then the punishment for that illicit activity should completely offset the benefit. The credited response will describe another situation that invokes this general rule or principle.

A. No. The situation does not describe a benefit arising from an illicit activity.

B. No. The situation does not describe a punishment that completely offsets the benefit: "to the satisfaction of the regulators" is a vague statement that could allow the factory's compliance expenditures to be lower than its profit.

C. No. The situation does not describe a benefit arising from an illicit activity.

D. No. The situation does not describe a penalty that completely offsets the benefit: Even if an athlete is banned from future competition, he could still retain the winnings, endorsements, etc. from previous competition. The credited response should describe reparations for past actions rather than a prohibition on future actions.

E. Yes. The criminal would profit from his crime, so all proceeds from the book sales should be donated rather than given to the criminal.

Section 3: Games

Questions 1–6

This is a 1D ordering game with 7 players and 7 spaces. Draw a diagram with the numbers 1 to 7 and the players in this game are P, Q, R, S, T, V, and W.

Clue 1: ~ST & ~TS

Clue 2: Q—R

Clue 3: VW

Clue 4: P = 4

There are several ordering deductions that can be found in this game. Draw clue 4 in the diagram. Then due to clue 2, R cannot be in 1 and Q cannot be in 7. Combine clues 3 and 4 to find that V cannot be in 3 and W cannot be in 5 since V and W must be consecutive and P is in slot 4.

Here's the diagram:

P, Q, R, S, T, V, W	1	2	3	4	5	6	7
	-R		-V	P	-W		-Q

Clue 1: ~~ST~~ ~~TS~~

Clue 2: Q—R

Clue 3: VW

Clue 4: P = 4

---

1. **D** `Grab-a-Rule`

Use the clues and POE to eliminate answer choices that are not possible.

A.   No. This violates clue 1.

B.   No. This violates clue 3.

C.   No. This violates clue 4.

D.   Yes. This works with the clues.

E.   No. This violates clue 2.

2. **C** General

Use previous work and try the remaining answer choices to find the possible list.

A. No. This scenario would cause a violation of either clue 2 or clue 3.

B. No. This scenario violates clue 2.

C. Yes. This scenario is possible in the work done for question 4.

D. No. This would violate clue 1.

E. No. This scenario violates clue 4.

3. **D** Specific

If T is second, then the players must be recruited in one of two scenarios. Either the list is Q, T, R, P, V, W, S or the list is Q, T, R, P, S, V, W. The only answer choice that is possible in either scenario is (D).

4. **B** Specific

If Q is immediately before R, then there are two blocks to place, one on either side of the P and each block will have S or T next to it on that side of P. For example, the list could be QRT, P, VWS or the list could be TVW, P, QRS. Because the blocks must take up two spaces, S cannot be in an even-numbered slot so the credited response is (B).

5. **A** Specific

If W is before R and R is before T then Q, V, and W, must all be before R in slots 1, 2, and 3. Since Q could be in slots 1 or 3, the credited response is (A).

6. **B** Specific

If W is immediately before Q, then the list must be V, W, Q, P, T/S, R, S/T, so R must be sixth and the credited response is (B).

Questions 7–13

This is a variable grouping game with three players, F, G, and H. The diagram should be three groups L, M, and S each with two slots.

Clue 1: Each photographer used at least once and no more than 3 times.

Clue 2: LM

Clue 3: HL = FS

Clue 4: S = ~G

Deductions: The clues in this game do not provide a great deal of deductions, so you'll start the game with a mostly blank canvas. You should write ~G above the S column.

Here's the diagram:

F, G, H

$$L \mid M \mid \overset{\sim G}{S}$$

$$\underline{}\;\underline{} \mid \underline{}\;\underline{} \mid \underline{}\;\underline{}$$

Clue 1: F, G, H = 1–3 uses

Clue 2: ⌐LM⌐

Clue 3: HL = FS

Clue 4: G ≠ S

7. **B** [Grab-a-Rule]

    A. No. This violates clue 4.

    B. Yes.

    C. No. This violates clue 2.

    D. No. This violates clue 3.

    E. No. This violates clue 1.

8. **C** [Specific]

If both Lifestyle photos are Hue, then both Sports photos must be F (clue 4). Since at least one photo must be by Gagnon, there must be a Gagnon photo in Metro. Clue 2 states that the other Metro photo must be Hue. Therefore, (C) is the credited response.

9. **D** [Specific]

If one photo in Lifestyle is Gagnon and the other is Hue, then according to clue 4, there must be exactly one F in Sports. The other sports photo cannot be G, so it must be H. The first photo in Metro must be either G or H to abide by clue 2, and the other photo would be F or G since there is a maximum of three H photos in the paper. This makes (D) the credited response.

10. **A** [General]

Use previous work and clues to eliminate answer choices.

    A. Yes. This can be seen in the work for question 11.

    B. No. This would violate clue 3.

    C. No. This would violate clue 3.

    D. No. This would violate clue 2.

    E. No. This would violate clue 2.

76

11. **C**   Specific

If one Lifestyle photo is F and the other is by H, then according to clue 3, exactly one sports photo must be F. Since G cannot be in the Sports section, the other sports photo must be H. G must have at least one photo in the paper, so there must be one G photo in Metro. Clue 2 states that there must be an overlap between Lifestyle and Metro, so the other Metro photo must be either F or H. The only option that could be true in this scenario is (C).

12. **E**   Specific

If both photos in one section belong to G, then those two photos must be in either Lifestyle or Metro since G cannot be featured in the Sports section. In the first scenario, where G takes up both spaces in Lifestyle, G must also take up one slot in Metro (clue 2). Using clue 3, the Sports section must have zero F photos so H must be in both slots in Sports. F will fill the remaining space in Metro. This scenario aligns with answer choice (E).

13. **C**   Specific

If the photos in the Metro section are one each of F and H, then there must be a G in the Lifestyle section (clue 4). The other lifestyle photo would then have to be either F or H (clue 2). The sports section must have one H and the other could be F or H, depending what happens in the Lifestyle section (clue 3). The only one that could be true is (C).

Questions 14–18

This is a 2D ordering game with a setup that is M, T, W, R (Thursday), F each with two slots. The players are G, H, J, K, and L and each player is used twice.

Clue 1: ~XX same day.

Clue 2: LL = second

Clue 3: G = 1st; ~GG

Clue 4: K = T & F

Clue 5: HJ or JH same day

Clue 6: ~GL same day

Deductions: The repeat players and lack of specific clues defining any slots or sequences limit the deductions that can be found in this game. You will start the game with a blank diagram but should note the interactions involved in clues 2, 3, and 6 as this interaction will drive the game.

Here's the diagram:

G, H, J, K, L

M	T	W	Th	F
— —	— —	— —	— —	— —

Clue 1: ~XX Same day

Clue 2: LL = Second

Clue 3: G = 1st; ~~GG~~

Clue 4: K = T and F

Clue 5: ☐HJ☐ or ☐JH☐

Clue 6: ~~GL~~

---

14. **A** **Grab-a-Rule**

A. Yes.

B. No. This violates clue 3.

C. No. This violates clue 2.

D. No. This violates clue 2.

E. No. This violates clue 3.

15. **C** **General**

Use prior work to eliminate answer choices that do not have to be true.

A. No. This scenario can be found in the work for question 18.

B. No. This scenario can be found in the work for question 16.

C. Yes. This is the only scenario that is not found in the work for other questions. If J is on Tuesday, then K must also be on Tuesday. This prevents J and H from appearing together because either G or L will work in the gallery on the other four days.

D. No. This scenario can be found in the work for question 16.

E. No. This scenario can be found in the work for question 16.

16. **B** **Specific**

Try H in the second slot on Wednesday. In this case, L must work in the second slot of Monday and Tuesday. Then clue 4 requires K to work Tuesday in the first slot. Per clues 3 and 6, G must be in the first slot on Wednesday and Friday, so K must work the second slot on Friday. Since J cannot work both slots on Thursday, it must work the first slot on Monday and either the first or second slot on Thursday along with H. J must work on Monday and Thursday, so (B) is the credited response.

17. **E** Specific

Try G and J on Monday. In this scenario, G is in the first slot and J is in the second. L can then be in the second slots on Tuesday and Wednesday. Clue 4 requires that K be in the first slot Tuesday. Since J and H must be together on one day, put them in both slots on Thursday. That leaves G in the first slot and K in the second slot on Friday and H to fill the first slot on Wednesday. In this scenario, it is possible that J works on Thursday, so (E) is the credited response.

18. **B** Specific

If K works second shift Tuesday, then L must work the second shift on Wednesday and Thursday. Since H and J must work together on one day, place them in the shifts for Monday. G cannot work with L, so G must be the morning shift on Tuesday and Friday. Then clue 4 requires K on Friday in the second shift. H and J will fill the remaining first shifts on Wednesday and Thursday. The only answer choice that could be true in this scenario is (B).

Questions 19–23

This is an In/Out game with a setup that creates two groups: fall and spring. The players are K, L, M, N, O, and P. L is a wildcard.

Clue 1: ~MP

Clue 2: KN

Clue 3: Kf → Of; Os → Ks

Clue 4: Mf → Ns; Nf → Ms

Deductions: Since this is an In/Out game, look for placeholder deductions. Clue 1 indicates that there is a space in fall with M/P and the other is in spring. Clue 4 could also provide a placeholder with M or N in spring but since you already have a placeholder with M, writing this into your diagram can create problems since M in spring would take only one space. Keep in mind that L is completely wild and can always go in either spring or fall.

Here's the diagram:

K, L, M, N, O, P

Fall	Spring
M/P	P/M

Clue 1: [M̶P̶]

Clue 2: [KN]

Clue 3: K$_F$ → O$_F$
         O$_S$ → K$_S$

Clue 4: M$_F$ → N$_S$
         N$_F$ → M$_S$

19. **E** **Grab-a-Rule**

    A. No. This violates clue 2.

    B. No. This violates clue 1.

    C. No. This violates clue 3.

    D. No. This violates clue 4.

    E. Yes.

20. **C** **Specific**

If M is in fall, then clue 1 requires P in spring. Clue 4 requires N in spring and clue 2 would place K in spring as well. The only players not accounted for are L and O and the rules allow them to go in either fall or spring in this scenario. The only pair that could go in the fall with M then is L and O, so the answer is (C).

21. **B** **Specific**

If N is published in the fall, then clue 4 places M in the spring. Clue 1 would place P in fall away from M, and clue 2 places K in fall with N. Clue 3 requires O join K in the fall. L is wild so L could be in either fall or spring. Therefore, (B) is the credited response.

22. **A** **General**

The question task asks which additional piece of information would complete the game, so try each answer choice until you find one that proves the entire game. Since L is wild, the new piece of information must restrict L in some way. If K is in fall and L is in spring, then KNOP must be in fall and LM must be in spring. Choice (A) fully determines this scenario, so it is the credited response.

23. **B** **Complex**

In this question, you are asked to parallel the deductions from clue 4 that create a placeholder for M/N in spring. Diagram each clue and choose the one that makes the same deduction.

    A. No. This clue would restrict L instead of N.

    B. Yes. Since M and P must be in different groups (clue 1), $Nf \rightarrow Pf$ is the same thing as saying $Nf \rightarrow Ms$.

    C. No. This is similar to clue 1 not clue 4.

    D. No. This clue would allow both M and N to be in the fall, which is not allowed in the original clue 4.

    E. No. This is the same as clue 3 not clue 4.

76

Section 4: Arguments 2

1. **C** [Sufficient Assumption]

The argument concludes that Vadim will be laid off. This conclusion is based on the fact that the firm has decided to lay off a programmer and on the firm's policy of laying off the most recently hired programmer when one must be laid off. The argument contains a language shift that assumes that Vadim is the most recently hired programmer. The credited response will explicitly link the premise to the conclusion and force the conclusion to be true.

   A. No. The experience level of a programmer is irrelevant to the enforcement of the policy.

   B. No. Vadim's understanding of the policy is irrelevant to its enforcement.

   C. Yes. This answer choice confirms that Vadim is the most recently hired programmer.

   D. No. Quality of work is irrelevant to the enforcement of the policy.

   E. No. Whether the policy itself is justified is irrelevant to its enforcement.

2. **B** [Principle Match]

Wanda concludes that having many things in her studio is justified. She bases this conclusion on the idea that an artist requires visual stimuli to create art. She bases this idea on a comparison with writers, who require written stimuli to write. She also supports her conclusion by stating that an empty work area would hinder her creativity. Vernon suggests a potential weakness in Wanda's argument: He implies that the visual stimuli must be of a certain level of quality to inspire creativity, just as writers must be surrounded by good writing instead of poor writing such as is found in tabloids. The credited response will describe the principle underlying Vernon's reasoning.

   A. No. Vernon suggests that clutter is fine as long as it is inspiring.

   B. Yes. Vernon indicates that Wanda has to consider the quality of the stimuli in her studio.

   C. No. Neither speaker expresses an opinion on how one should view tabloids.

   D. No. Vernon suggests that messiness can inspire creativeness as long as it is the right kind of messiness.

   E. No. Vernon suggests that clutter is acceptable as long as it is inspiring.

3. **D** [Resolve/Explain]

The passage explains that listing an animal species as endangered causes the enforcement of legal safeguards designed to protect the species. The passage then introduces a paradox: Despite these legal safeguards, in some cases, a species declines more rapidly after being listed as endangered than before. The credited response will provide a reason some species declined more rapidly after being listed as endangered.

   A. No. This answer choice does not explain why the decline intensifies after the listing.

   B. No. This answer choice does not explain why the decline intensifies after the listing.

C. No. The number of species on the list has no impact on the rate at which their populations are declining.

D. Yes. After the animals are listed as endangered, their value to collectors goes up, so they are poached more aggressively.

E. No. This answer choice makes the paradox worse.

4. **B** 　Point at Issue

Annette concludes that Sefu should take the town council to visit other towns that have implemented development plans similar to Sefu's to convince them to implement his plan. Sefu concludes that the council's accepting the trip would give the appearance of undue influence. Sefu bases his conclusion on the fact that he has a vested interest in the council's votes. Annette and Sefu disagree about whether Sefu should take the town council on a trip. The credited response will identify this point of disagreement.

A. No. Presumably Sefu believes that the council should adopt his plan, but Annette, although she offers advice on how to persuade the council, does not actually state whether she believes that the council should adopt the plan.

B. Yes. Annette states that Sefu should take the council on a trip, but Sefu worries that doing so would be misguided.

C. No. Both Annette and Sefu agree that he has an interest in the council's votes.

D. No. Annette states that other towns have successfully implemented such plans, and Sefu tacitly agrees with this statement.

E. No. Sefu implies that the appearance of undue influence should be avoided, but Annette does not address the issue.

5. **C** 　Flaw

The argument concludes that any modernization will cause an increase in worshippers. The conclusion is based on the fact that some recent modernizations of language and ritual have been correlated with increases in attendance at places of worship. The argument assumes that the modernization caused the increased attendance and that there are no other causes or relevant considerations. Note that the question stem contains the phrase "presumes without giving sufficient justification": This phrase indicates that the credited response will state a necessary assumption of the argument.

A. No. The argument does not restrict the possibility of modernization to some religions.

B. No. The argument does not indicate whether modernization alters messages.

C. Yes. The answer choice describes the argument's equating correlation with causation.

D. No. The term "only" is too strong: The argument concludes that modernization is sufficient to increase worshippers but not necessary.

E. No. The argument does not indicate that the increase in worshippers would be irreversible.

6. D `Parallel Flaw`

The argument concludes that Lily does not practice hard. The premises indicate that one must practice hard or be very talented to be in the regional band and that Lily is in the regional band and practices hard. The argument does not, however, state or imply that one cannot both practice hard and be very talented, so the conclusion is not supported. Structurally, the argument presents a conditional relationship with an "or" statement on the right side. It confirms the left-side idea and one of the right-side ideas and therefore concludes that the other right-side idea must not be true. The credited response will match this structure.

  A.   No. The premises do not contain a conditional relationship with an "or" statement on the right side.

  B.   No. The premises do not confirm the left-side idea and one of the right-side ideas.

  C.   No. The premises do not contain a conditional relationship with an "or" statement on the right side.

  D.   Yes. Staying informed requires reading a major newspaper or watching TV news every day. Julie is informed and reads a major newspaper every day, so she does not watch TV news. This answer choice matches the flaw because it fails to consider that Julie can both read a major newspaper and watch TV news every day.

  E.   No. The premises do not confirm the left-side idea and one of the right-side ideas.

7. C `Reasoning`

The argument concludes that eating fish can lower one's cholesterol level. This conclusion is based on a comparative study that showed lower cholesterol levels in the group that ate a balanced diet with two servings of fish per week compared with the group that ate a similar diet without any fish. The argument further supports the conclusion by stating that the groups had similar cholesterol levels prior to entering the study. This statement rules out the possible alternate cause of the first group simply having lower cholesterol levels regardless of their level of fish consumption. The credited response will describe the function of this statement.

  A.   No. The statement supports the conclusion by ruling out a possible alternate cause.

  B.   No. The main conclusion of the argument is that eating fish can lower one's cholesterol level.

  C.   Yes. This answer choice describes the role of the statement as ruling out a possible alternate explanation for the first group's lower cholesterol.

  D.   No. The statement does not clarify why the study was undertaken.

  E.   No. The statement rules out a possible alternate explanation for the conclusion.

8. E `Strengthen`

The argument concludes that satnavs save fuel and promote safety. This conclusion is supported by studies that show that drivers using satnavs make shorter journeys and thus save fuel and that drivers using satnavs drive more carefully because they do not have to take their eyes off the road to look at maps. The argument assumes that there are no other relevant considerations that would indicate that using satnavs is inefficient or dangerous. The credited response will provide new evidence that supports the conclusion or confirms the validity of the assumption.

A. No. The likelihood of a group's using satnavs reveals little about whether doing so saves fuel or promotes safety.

B. No. This fact would give drivers an incentive to use a device that would save fuel, but it does not imply that the satnav is such a device.

C. No. This answer choice suggests that a certain group of drivers would have no need for a satnav, but this fact does not imply that the use of a satnav would not save fuel or promote safety.

D. No. This answer choice suggests that some people who own a satnav would not use it, but this fact does not imply that use of the satnav would not save fuel or promote safety.

E. Yes. The satnavs give directions as they are needed, so using a satnav promotes safety because it allows drivers to drive in a less risky way.

9. **C** **Principle Match**

The passage indicates that managers can extract the best performance from their employees by delegating responsibility to them, especially responsibility that had previously been held by the manager. It also indicates that threats of termination and promises of financial rewards are ineffective motivational strategies because employees must want to do a good job for its own sake. The credited response will describe the principle underlying the idea of delegating one's own responsibility to increase the productiveness of one's employees.

A. No. The situation does not concern one's sense of how power should be used.

B. No. The situation does not compare the desires for prestige and job security.

C. Yes. A manager can enhance his effectiveness by delegating some of his responsibilities to them.

D. No. This answer choice would support a manager's not delegating his responsibilities to his employees.

E. No. The situation does not concern the company as a whole but the performance of individual employees.

10. **E** **Point at Issue**

Richard concludes that abstract art will eventually be seen as an aberration. His conclusion is based on the fact that abstract art is not representational and thus does not meet the fundamental representational requirement of art. Jung-Su concludes that abstract art is part of the artistic mainstream. His conclusion is based on the fact that abstract art is representational, even if it is not literally so, insofar as abstract art represents the purely formal features of everyday objects. Richard and Jung-Su disagree about whether abstract art is representational. The credited response will identify this point of disagreement.

A. No. Jung-Su states that abstract artists reject literal representation, and Richard states that abstract art is not representational, so they agree about this point.

B. No. Richard states that art must represent, but Jung-Su does not state whether representation is a requirement of art.

C. No. Jung-Su states that musicians may reject literal representation, but Richard does not discuss musicians.

D.   No. Richard claims that abstract art will eventually be seen as an aberration, but Jung-Su does not speculate about how abstract art may one day be judged.

E.   Yes. Richard states that abstract art fails to represent, but Jung-Su states that abstract art represents the purely formal features of everyday objects.

11. **B**   ▓ **Principle Match** ▓

The passage presents two principles that can be diagrammed as conditionals. First, if one knowingly brings about misfortune, then one should be blamed for that misfortune. The contrapositive is that if one should not be blamed for a misfortune, then one did not knowingly bring about that misfortune. Second, if one unknowingly brings about misfortune and one could not reasonably have foreseen that misfortune, then one should not be blamed for that misfortune. The contrapositive is that if one should be blamed for a misfortune, then one either knowingly brought about that misfortune or could reasonably have foreseen the misfortune. The credited response will correctly move from the left side to the right side of one of these conditionals or their contrapositives.

A.   No. Riley could reasonably have foreseen the misfortune. This right-side idea does not lead to a conclusion about blameworthiness.

B.   Yes. Oblicek could not have reasonably foreseen the misfortune of the business going bankrupt, so, if such a misfortune does occur, Oblicek should not be blamed.

C.   No. Gougon does not know that serving the hollandaise would bring about misfortune. This right-side idea does not lead to a conclusion about blameworthiness.

D.   No. Dr. Fitzpatrick does not know that the medicine would bring about misfortune. This right-side idea does not lead to a conclusion about blameworthiness.

E.   No. This answer choice does not confirm whether Kapp knowingly dropped the lit cigarette to cause the fire. Without this piece, we cannot conclude that Kapp is to blame.

12. **B**   ▓ **Necessary Assumption** ▓

The researcher concludes that it is likely that the incidence of illness among people who regularly inhale the scent of lavender is reduced by their practice of inhaling the scent of lavender. This conclusion is based on research that shows that inhaling the scent of lavender tends to reduce stress and on the fact that intense stress can impair the immune system and thereby make one more susceptible to illness. The argument contains a language shift that assumes that people who regularly inhale the scent of lavender are stressed enough to have impaired immune systems. The credited response will link the ideas of inhaling the scent of lavender and being stressed enough to have an impaired immune system.

A.   No. The effects of other scents are irrelevant to this argument about lavender.

B.   Yes. This answer choice confirms that some people who inhale the scent lavender are stressed enough to have impaired immune systems.

C.   No. The argument does not require people who inhale the scent of lavender to be representative of people in general.

D.   No. The terms "anyone" and "primarily" are too strong: The argument does not require the inhalation of lavender to be the main mechanism of stress reduction.

E.   No. The term "only" is too strong: The argument does not require that diminished susceptibility to illness be restricted to those with impaired immune systems.

13. **D**   **Flaw**

The argument concludes that the Andersen family's real income must have increased over the last five years. This conclusion is based on government statistics showing that the real average income for families has risen over the last five years and on the fact that the Andersen family's current income is average. The argument assumes that the Andersen family's income was not the same or higher in previous years; it assumes that what applies on average must apply to a particular case. The credited response will identify this flaw.

A.   No. The term "average" is used consistently throughout the argument.

B.   No. The argument corrects the Andersen family's income to account for inflation.

C.   No. The argument concerns a single family only, so it does not require assumptions about the distribution of most families on the income scale.

D.   Yes. This answer choice describes the flaw of failing to consider that the Andersen family's real income did not decrease over the last five years.

E.   No. The term "no" is too strong: The argument does not require the estimates to be accurate.

14. **B**   **Sufficient Assumption**

The argument concludes that preventing the production of high-quality counterfeit banknotes requires making it difficult or impossible to accurately measure images on the banknotes. The premise states that some methods of making high-quality counterfeit banknotes involve making accurate measurements of such images. The argument assumes that no other prevention strategies are required to thwart would-be counterfeiters. The credited response will explicitly link the premise to the conclusion and force the conclusion to be true.

A.   No. This answer choice does not explain the relevance of accurately measuring images to the prevention of counterfeiting.

B.   Yes. This answer choice indicates that the accurate measuring of images is the only hurdle to producing high-quality counterfeit banknotes.

C.   No. This answer choice does not explain the relevance of accurately measuring images to the prevention of counterfeiting.

D.   No. This answer choice indicates that accurately measuring images is generally easy, but it does not explain the relevance of accurately measuring images to the prevention of counterfeiting.

E.   No. This answer choice does not explain the relevance of accurately measuring images to the prevention of counterfeiting.

15. **D**   **Flaw**

Armstrong concludes that we should not use nutritional supplements to treat a particular disease. He supports his conclusion by pointing out that although Dr. Sullivan claims that one should use the supplements, Dr. Sullivan has an ulterior motive to promote them because he is paid to endorse a line of supplements. Armstrong assumes that Dr. Sullivan's self-interest cannot coincide with a valid justification for using the supplements; Armstrong attack's Dr. Sullivan's motives rather than the reasoning. The credited response will identify this flaw.

A. No. The term "supplement" is used consistently throughout the argument.

B. No. The argument attacks Dr. Sullivan's motives.

C. No. The argument attacks Dr. Sullivan's motives.

D. Yes. This answer choice describes the flaw of criticizing Dr. Sullivan's motives rather than his reasoning.

E. No. The argument neither states nor suggests that supplements cannot be used with other treatments. Dr. Sullivan claims that nutritional supplements should be used instead of pharmaceuticals, but these treatment options may not be the only ones available.

16. **B**   **Necessary Assumption**

The economist concludes that a stronger economy is likely to make it harder to find day care. He supports this conclusion by presenting a chain of events: If the economy grows stronger, employment will increase, more parents will need to find day care, and many day-care workers will quit for better-paying jobs in other fields. The argument assumes that the day-care workers who quit will not be replaced by new workers entering the field. The credited response will confirm that those who quit will not be sufficiently replaced.

A. No. The term "most" is too strong: The argument does not require that the majority of new jobs created in a stronger economy pay well.

B. Yes. This answer choice confirms that the day-care workers who quit will not be replaced by new day-care workers.

C. No. The number of day-care workers does not necessarily need to decrease because demand for day care will definitely increase. If the number of day-care workers remained the same, it would still be more difficult to find day care due to increased demand without a corresponding increase in supply.

D. No. The term "unless" is too strong: The argument does not require the situation described in the stimulus to be the only or the most likely cause of day-care shortages.

E. No. If anything, this answer choice might weaken the conclusion by pointing out that a stronger economy will result in less competition for day care services.

17. **A**   **Inference**

The passage presents facts comparing ostrich farming and cattle ranching. Ostrich farms require less acreage than cattle ranching, and ostriches reproduce faster than cattle. Starting an ostrich farm requires four ostriches and one acre of land. Starting a cattle ranch requires a large herd of cows, one bull, and at least two acres of land per cow.

Starting an ostrich farm is more costly than starting a cattle ranch. Ostrich farming can eventually bring in as much as five times as cattle ranching. The credited response will be an answer choice that is supported by a single statement or by a combination of statements from the passage.

A. Yes. Starting up an ostrich farm requires fewer animals and fewer acres of land than does starting up a cattle ranch, yet the start-up costs for an ostrich farm are still higher than those for a cattle ranch, so the ostriches probably cost more than a bull and a herd of cows.

B. No. The passage indicates that ostrich farming is a better source of income than cattle ranching, but this fact does not mean that cattle ranching is not a good source of income: Both ventures could be good sources of income with ostrich farming simply being a better one.

C. No. The passage does not discuss feed consumption.

D. No. The passage indicates that ostrich farming can eventually bring in as much as five times what cattle ranching does, but you cannot use this fact to make a specific comparison between average farms and ranches.

E. No. The passage indicates that the start-up costs for ostrich farming are high, but this fact does not imply that ostrich farmers cannot nevertheless make a profit during their first year.

18. E   **Necessary Assumption**

The argument concludes that hairless dogs must have been transported between western Mexico and coastal Peru by boat, probably during trading expeditions. The argument establishes that such dogs exist in both regions and that hairlessness was very unlikely to have emerged on two separate occasions. The conclusion is supported by the fact that such dogs have never existed in the wild and that overland travel between the regions would have been difficult. The argument assumes that travel by boat was easier or at least more likely than overland travel; it also assumes that there is no other way the dogs could have come to exist in both regions. The credited response will confirm that travel by boat was easier or rule out an alternate explanation for the dogs' existence in both regions.

A. No. The term "never" is too strong: The argument does not require Mexico and Peru to be the only places where hairless dogs have been found.

B. No. Even if most trade goods were transported by boat, hairless dogs could be an exception that was transported overland.

C. No. The terms "no one" and "except" are too strong: The argument does not require trade to be the only reason for travel by boat, and even if it did, this fact would not confirm that hairless dogs were transported by boat.

D. No. This hypothetical answer choice does nothing to confirm that such transportation by boat actually occurred.

E. Yes. This answer choice confirms that travel by boat was easier than overland travel.

19. A   **Inference**

The passage presents facts about the Earth's early crust. Microdiamonds are the oldest fragments of the Earth's crust yet identified. They measure 50 microns across and were formed 4.2 billion years ago. The Earth itself was formed just 300 million years before the formation of the microdiamonds. The passage indicates that the relative dates of these formations are significant. The credited response will be an answer choice that is supported by a single statement or by a combination of statements from the passage.

A. Yes. The microdiamonds, as part of the crust, were formed 300 million years after the formation of the Earth, so even if the microdiamonds were the first part of the crust to form, the crust must have begun its formation no more than 300 million years after the Earth's formation.

B. No. The researchers happen to be working in Western Australia, but nothing in the passage suggests that the Earth's crust began its formation in that region.

C. No. We can ballpark when the crust began its formation, but the passage does not provide any information about how long this formation ultimately took.

D. No. Although the statements indicate that the microdiamonds are the oldest fragments yet discovered, other undiscovered components may have formed earlier.

E. No. The term "all" is too strong.

20. **C** Necessary Assumption

The argument concludes that we must ensure that Internet users have at least as much freedom of expression as did people speaking in the public square in days past. The premises compare the function of the public square and the Internet: Both are important tools of democracy because they are public forums where citizens can discuss important issues. The argument contains a language shift that assumes that we should protect freedom of expression in important tools of democracy. The credited response will link the ideas of freedom of expression and maintaining effectiveness as a tool of democracy.

A. No. The term "complete" is too strong: The argument concludes that Internet users should have at least as much freedom of expression as did citizens in days past, even if that level of freedom of expression was not complete.

B. No. The terms "all" and "same level" are too strong: The argument concludes that Internet users should have at least as much freedom of expression as did citizens in days past, but this conclusion does not imply that all Internet users must have equal access.

C. Yes. This answer choice provides a reason for protecting freedom of expression.

D. No. The topic of Internet discussions is irrelevant to whether we should protect freedom of expression on the Internet.

E. No. The term "no other" is too strong: The argument does not require the Internet to be the only important tool of democracy.

21. **C** Weaken

The argument concludes that the reasoning power and spatial intuition required by chess-playing contributes to achievement in other intellectual areas. The conclusion is based on a study of children who completed a program where they learned to play chess. Many of the children soon showed an increase in achievement levels in all of their schoolwork. The argument assumes that completion of the program was the cause of the increased achievement; it fails to consider other causes or relevant considerations. The credited response will point out another cause for the increased achievement or identify a relevant consideration that would undermine the conclusion.

A. No. Students who did not participate in the program are irrelevant.

B. No. The baseline achievement level is irrelevant because the argument concerns an increase, which would be possible were a student starting at either a low or high level of achievement.

C. Yes. This answer choice points out an alternate cause for the students' increase in intellectual achievement: They were motivated to meet a requirement to play on the chess team.

D. No. The argument does not claim that playing chess is the only way to increase a student's intellectual achievement, so this answer choice can be true without weakening the conclusion.

E. No. Students who did not complete the program are irrelevant.

22. **A** Parallel

The argument concludes that Kate sometimes shops at the local health food store on Wednesdays. The premises indicate that Kate usually buys guava juice on Wednesdays and that the local health food store is the only place she can buy guava juice. Structurally, the argument contains a conditional statement and a "most" statement in the premises and a "some" statement in the conclusion. The credited response will match this structure.

A. Yes. The premises confirm that only teachers may use the kitchen and that most dinners are prepared in the kitchen, so the argument correctly concludes that some dinners are prepared by the teachers.

B. No. This answer choice does not contain a "most" statement in the premises or a "some" statement in the conclusion.

C. No. This argument is flawed: The premises do not indicate that teachers are the only people allowed to use the kitchen, so we cannot conclude that teachers sometimes prepare the dinners that are mostly made in the kitchen.

D. No. This argument is flawed: The premises do not indicate that teachers are the only people allowed to use the kitchen, so we cannot conclude that teachers sometimes prepare the dinners that are produced only in the kitchen.

E. No. This argument is flawed: The premises do not confirm that the kitchen is the only place teachers can prepare dinners, so we cannot conclude that dinners are sometimes prepared in the kitchen.

23. **D** Weaken

The editor concludes that the city will not see an increase in revenue from its new recycling program, disagreeing with the city's claim that they will see an increase. The new program replaces every-other-week pickup with weekly pickup. The city's claim is based on the fact that the more recyclables collected, the more revenue the city gains from selling the recyclables. The editor's conclusion is based on his assertion that there will be no increase in the volume of recyclables; instead, the same volume will be spread out over a greater number of pickups. The editor assumes that there will be no changes once the new program is implemented, including the possibility of an increased volume of recyclables being put out for pickup. The credited response will introduce new evidence that undermines the editor's conclusion or point out a relevant consideration that he missed.

76

A.   No. Trash collection and disposal are irrelevant to the cost-effectiveness of the new recycling program.

B.   No. The editor believes that the program will not be more cost-effective because it will not increase the volume of recyclables collected. This answer choice is hypothetical ("even if") and weak ("might")—compare it to the credited response, which confirms that the volume of recyclables collected will actually increase.

C.   No. This answer choice is consistent with the editor's premise that the amount of recyclables collected will remain the same.

D.   Yes. If the schedule is easier to follow and adhere to, then people will put out more recyclables for collection, undermining the editor's claim that the volume of recyclables collected under the new program will not increase.

E.   No. This answer choice would strengthen the conclusion that the program would not be more cost-effective because the city would pay significantly more for the collection.

24.   **D**   **Necessary Assumption**

The professor concludes that designing introductory science courses as proving grounds has not served the purpose of allowing only those students who are the most committed to being science majors to pass. His conclusion is based on studies that show that some students who are the least enthusiastic about science have passed the courses. The argument contains a language shift that assumes that those who are the least enthusiastic about science are not also the most committed to being science majors. The credited response will link the ideas of being the least enthusiastic and not being the most committed.

A.   No. The argument concludes that the courses have not served their intended purpose, not that the intended design is flawed.

B.   No. The professor would agree with this statement, but it has no bearing on the argument.

C.   No. The argument does not discuss students who are most enthusiastic about science.

D.   Yes. This answer choice confirms that there is no overlap between those least enthusiastic about science and those most committed to being science majors.

E.   No. The argument does not look forward to whether courses should continue to be designed as proving grounds.

25.   **C**   **Resolve/ Explain**

The passage explains that many birds and reptiles hiss to threaten potential predators. This hissing likely arose in a common ancestor. The passage then introduces a paradox: None of the potential predators of the common ancestor would have been able to hear the hissing. The credited response will provide a reason why the common ancestor would have used a threat gesture that was ostensibly ineffective.

A.   No. This answer choice makes the paradox worse.

B.   No. This answer choice does not explain why the common ancestor would retain among its arsenal of threat devices one that seemed to serve to purpose.

C. Yes. The hissing itself is not the threat but the fact that hissing made the common ancestor seem larger and presumably more threatening.

D. No. Even if hissing is energy-efficient, it still needs to be effective as a threat device.

E. No. Even if the common ancestor had few predators, it would still need an effective threat device to use against these predators.

NOTES

NOTES

NOTES

NOTES

NOTES

NOTES